Alyth London
Shabbat Shuva

Dearest Laura –
So great to see
you in your shul.
Thank you —
Much love !
Judith
Edelman-Green

GW00728783

North Western Reform Synagog
Alyth Gardens
NW11 7EN

B
(E-G)

# Immigrant Lessons

North Western Reform Synagogue
Alyth Gardens
NW11 7EN

## Judith Edelman-Green

gefen גפן
publishing house בית הוצאה לאור
JERUSALEM • NEW YORK

Copyright © Gefen Publishing House
Jerusalem 2007/5767

All rights reserved. No part of this publication may be translated, reproduced, stored in a retrieval system or transmitted, in any form or by any means, electronic, mechanical, photo-copying, recording or otherwise, without express written permission from the publishers.

Layout: Marzel A.S. — Jerusalem
Cover Design: S. Kim Glassman

ISBN: 978-965-229-413-5
Edition   1 3 5 7 9 8 6 4 2

Gefen Publishing House Ltd.
6 Hatzvi St.
Jerusalem 94386, Israel
972-2-538-0247
orders@gefenpublishing.com

Gefen Books
600 Broadway
Lynbrook, NY 11563, USA
1-516-593-1234
orders@gefenpublishing.com

www.israelbooks.com

Printed in Israel

*Send for our free catalogue*

*For my father, my teacher, Murray Jacob Edelman
(b. 1919 d. 2001) who made me laugh, and filled me
with my passion for books and learning.*

*and for my mother, my teacher, Bacia Stepner Edelman
(b. 1925) who taught me about perfection and imperfection
and instilled in me the creative impulse.*

And now your ship has come, and you must needs go.

Deep is your longing for the land of your memories and the dwelling-place of your greater desires; and our love would not bind you nor our needs hold you.

Yet this we ask ere you leave us, that you speak to us and give us of your truth.

— *The Prophet*, Kahlil Gibran

All things lovely — are not they
Far away — far away?

— *The Valley of Unrest*, Edgar Allan Poe

---

**A note to the reader**

This book is a memoir, and the events described are real; however, some names and details have been altered to protect privacy. Some of the events that didn't take place are true, and some of the events that did take place are fictionalized. Safta Sarah is very real. The eggplant is real, too (you must try it).

# Contents

# I: Beginnings and Endings

## Aliyah — 1939 and 1984

If caught, they will be sent out to the open sea, headed to Cyprus intern-ment camps. Sarah sees the shoreline; tomorrow when they land it will be her twenty-sixth birthday. There is fear in the air, but she feels determination, excitement, a sense of romance. They will only approach the shore in the dark, so that they cannot be seen. They will climb over the side of the ship, and row to shore. Each will have just a knapsack; no extra belongings can be carried. Sarah's knapsack contains a wooden cutting board and a wooden rolling pin, some underwear and a comb.

A dark curtain covers the boat but leaves glitters of reflected light on the water. Sarah puts one foot over the rail, and her chin nearly touches her chest as she looks down to the rowboat at the other end of the rope ladder. It sways with the weight of each person. There can be no talking or shouting; water carries sound from a great distance.

British soldiers are patrolling the sands near Kibbutz Shefayim, and all along the coastline. The young people on the boat have all left families who will live and then die, under Hitler. The quota of the British Mandate dictates no more Jews in Palestine, but there is nowhere else to go. Europe and Amer-ica, South America are all closed to Jews.

Sarah is now in the rowboat and she checks nervously to see that Morde-cai is by her side, in silence as deep as the sea. The moment that will deter-mine whether the British meet their boats, or if kibbutzniks find them first, is a breath away. Signals are conveyed with Morse code flashes of light. No returning signals are allowed.

The rowboat nears the shore but must turn back to the ships; it is too valuable to be seized. Sarah and Mordecai swim in together. Sarah looks ahead the whole time, using the waves to swim more quickly, feeling a sense of urgency. Sometimes the waves seem to sweep her backwards. Mordecai is worried about his own strength, but sees that Sarah is managing and keeps swimming. Sarah feels her feet touch the sandy bottom; her shoes are in her knapsack.

She runs ashore, and bends down and kisses the sandy ground. "Happy birthday, Sarahleh," says Mordecai, breathing hard and trudging ashore behind her.

As her lips touch the sand, a silver airplane flies overhead, one she cannot see or hear, because it will be forty-five more years before it arrives. It crosses Israel's coastline at the exact spot that she marks with her lips, her fingers spread in the sand, her head bent.

We have left England and are coming to live in Israel. We have shipped our small blue velvet sofa, our new TV (it is actually our first), our tape recorder, radio, pine dining room table. We don't really own a lot else. We have packed suitcases for us and for the baby, and will stay only a few miles from Sarah and Mordecai's tiny house and garden in Ramat Gan, in the urban spread that is Tel Aviv, only a half-hour walk from their daughter Rivka. We have no car. We have the baby carriage, baby clothes and equipment. We arrive at dawn, just as they did.

A volunteer from the British Immigration Society meets us before passport control, and takes us upstairs to an office that issues an identity card for new immigrants. We receive VIP treatment, as he expedites the process.

At the airport we receive two free sets of plastic dishes, one in blue for milk, and one in a hideous orange, for meat, plus a voucher for three free simple beds and mattresses. When we arrive at the absorption center in North Tel Aviv, this same volunteer from the British Immigration Society gives us initial supplies: tea, sugar, coffee, milk, and a box of dry semi-sweet cookies that only have any taste if you soak them in tea. I am most touched by the dry cookies; it is like some unknown mother is here waiting to feed me and care for me.

The British officers are patrolling the beach, but cannot be seen at this moment. Sarah and the hundreds of young immigrants speaking Hungarian, Yiddish, and Polish are herded onto a bus and driven to the kibbutz itself. The windows are covered with newspaper and they are told to be quiet. Sarah is infuriated. "This is our land," she thinks to herself. "Why do we have to hide here more than we did from the Nazis?" The British want to send them to Cyprus, whereas, ironically, the Gestapo had actually accompanied and helped them to leave Hungary; they wanted them to leave.

We have waited for this all of our young lives, to move from England to Israel. Just as we pass the coastline, and the ghost of Sarah's ship, there is a call over the loudspeaker, "If there is a doctor on board, please make yourself known to one of the air hostesses immediately." Danny and I look at each other, as he unbuckles and sways down the aisle to make himself known. A woman has collapsed in her chair. He is out of my view behind the thin dividing wall leading to the cabin behind us.

Beside me our one-year-old son is asleep, and I realize that each of us has missed the moment of our arrival in Israel.

"Is she alright?" I ask.

"Yes, no thanks to me. The airline staff did everything."

A stewardess appears with a gift bottle of champagne. "Thank you so much and welcome to Israel."

We laugh and turn to Danny's sister Sharon, a longtime resident of Jerusalem, who is accompanying us back to Israel after a family reunion in England. Sharon will always be there for festivals and Sabbaths, for birthdays and even for taking in frightened immigrants during the wars. When her children start marrying native Israelis, we will become part of native Israeli families firsthand.

# Immigrant Grandmothers — 1968 and 1984

"I won't see my grandchildren if you live so far away... Israel! It's the end of the world. I don't mind that you married an Englishman and moved to England, somehow that doesn't seem so far from the States, but Israel..."

I fume. "That's irrational. Once you're on the plane across the Atlantic, what difference does it make where you're flying to?" Yet even I know that it is a much more arduous journey to the Middle East, almost beyond endurance.

I remember that we piled into a station wagon once a year and drove for two and a half days from Wisconsin to Massachusetts to visit my Grandma Rose and her sister Sybil. We stayed for about ten days, and then as we pulled out of her drive, my grandmother would stand at the gate of her rented house, sobbing and sobbing. My mother would send my older brother out to give her one more hug. She wouldn't see us again for a whole year. She was inconsolable.

My mother also does not like to see her first and only grandchild move away. "How can you take Raphi to live so far away? You'll never be able to afford to visit. I don't know if we'll send for you every year, and it is too far for us to visit very often. I won't see him." I picture Grandma Rose's desolate face at the gate.

Grandchildren are indeed the compensation for old age. I am depriving my mother of her compensation. She doesn't say anything about wanting to help take care of Raphi, and I don't think of it either. All around me Israeli grandmothers and grandfathers pick up babies during the early afternoon hours between the end of nursery school at twelve thirty, and at four o'clock when mothers and fathers can get off work. Or perhaps those with a handy bubbie and zaidie can work later. I watch as grandfathers drive or wheel children home from day care or school. We use bicycles and do it all ourselves; sometimes we ferry two children and the groceries on one bicycle.

I don't know who helped my mother when she was a young mother, living halfway across America from her mother and doting aunts. But I do know that her mother was also an immigrant mother. Why can't she understand that I have chosen to be an immigrant mother, and that it involves extra stresses, extra work? I think she and my father helped each other, although he was out at work until early evening, like men of his generation.

My mother does visit when my second child is born. I ask her about her immigrant mother. I have a mental picture of Grandma Rose as beautiful, old, and wrinkled; the sum total of love. She laughed with delight at everything I did and said and exclaimed, "Gotteniu." She called me diminutive names like "darling doll face" and showered me with truly delightful gifts; I remember a wooden doll set with petticoats and a sunbonnet. She cut up her wedding dress to make doll clothes. Once my brother called me a pig. Or did I call him that? "Oh, call him a bluebird!" cried Grandma. My brother and I collapsed with laughter, hiding our giggles behind a big sofa.

My mother and I take a long drive in the desert on a winding road down to the Dead Sea. At first glance one sees only yellow, but if you look with my mother's artist's view, there are many shades of browns, and greens, sand colors or all hues, and then the shocking Monet blues of the Dead Sea. We talk about her immigrant mother.

"Oh, my parents were so ignorant, they didn't know anything," my mother says rather bitterly.

I am shocked; I had Rose on a pedestal of knowing about life, if not book learning. I knew that she spoke perfect English; her only accent was Bostonian, and a rather snobby accent at that. She spoke Yiddish with her sisters, and knew a number of European languages. She read poetry. Only her writing was rather primitive, but I knew that she had never been to school in America. And there were packages of candies and doll clothes which accompanied her scrawled letters, so what did I care?

"What were they ignorant about?" I ask my mother.

"Everything," she says with venom. "When my sister was run over by a truck when she was six years old, my mother went into mourning for the rest of her life. The dead child, Beatrice, was an angel, perfect. She got better as the years went by and she remained dead."

I grab the steering wheel and slow down. The harder the story becomes, the more purposefully I drive because automatic pilot is extinguished. A heavy feeling of my mother's burden keeps me from turning the steering wheel without an effort. Her sadness freezes the sunny biblical landscape of a winding path down a desert road. Lot's wife turned into a pillar of salt here. There is an impulse to water, fertilize and plant my mother.

"I was the bad child. I could never be as good as the angel Beatrice. She was perfect and I couldn't compete with her, I couldn't fight with her, yell at her for being so perfect. She wore a pristine white dress in the photographs. She never got dirty by playing with me in the yard. Dead people don't dirty their clothes."

Bacia sculpts an image in my mind of a father who punished with his hands, and a mother who lived with heartbreak and grief, who loved her children but could only speak kindly to her dead, perfect daughter. No one else lived up. There were fierce fights about money, never enough. There were also fights about Rose's sister Sybil who lived with them. Sybil could afford to buy the children treats; she was the only one with any money. Rose and Sybil were more of a couple in the sense that they shared life and all its troubles, they read poetry to each other, and Maurice was left out completely. He was bereaved and broke, and alone. When he took my mother out for lunch when she was putting herself through art school, he would "forget" his wallet and she would have to pay.

"He would pretend that he had just forgotten it, and I had to fork out, while I was paying my own rent and tuition."

The abandonment is like the dry desert hills facing us in Jordan. No one lives on them, nothing can be planted there. They remain perfect, and barren, untended. Pangs of leaving her alone visit me.

My mother was molded by immigrant mothering. Her immigrant mother wasn't at hand to help her raise her children. Her immigrant daughter did not give her compensation for all that she endured in childhood.

My father also had an immigrant mother and grandmother. His household was always saving money to take in the latest cousin from Europe, before the war. His immigrant mother, Sadie, was widowed in the 1920s when she had a thirteen-year-old and nine-year-old twins. She and her husband Kalman had set up a variety store so that she could support her family when he died of heart disease. She cried at night because the neighbors could not afford to pay their bills during the Depression, and if they could not pay, she could not pay her bills. The riches in the house were mainly books and learning, but also food cooked by his immigrant grandmother, a rich Jewish life, and love of music, like the opera singer Enrico Caruso. Dad said that even scratchy records of him moved them to another world of harmony.

She died soon after I was born and I would only hear about Grandma Sadie again and really get to know her when I was in Israel, and met our relatives.

# The Meeting That Almost Wasn't — 1978

I almost sailed through life without knowing about or meeting my Israeli relatives. I was a middle-class Jewish American. I came to Hebrew

University to study, to enjoy student life, not nessesarily to look into my roots. The silver plane and the illegal immigrant ship almost didn't cross.

A new Israeli friend, Iris, from Hebrew University in Jerusalem, encouraged me to telephone my relatives, my father's first cousin and his wife. They had lost a son in the Six-Day War. I knew it was Remembrance Day for the Israeli soldiers who had died in all the wars. I asked her, naively, "What do I do, send flowers?"

"Oh, no, not in Israel."

"Well, what do I do?" I asked my guide.

"You go there. Be with them. Share the experience."

"I don't know what to say, I am afraid. I can't speak enough Hebrew. I won't understand them. I don't know them and they don't know me. They don't even know I exist."

I dial and a voice answers that must sound like my grandfather's, only speaking Hebrew instead of broken English.

"Allo. Yes?"

"Shalom."

"Yes?"

"Uh, this is…Murray Edelman's daughter, Yehudit. How are you?"

"From America? Murray's daughter? What's your name? Yehudit? Sarahleh, come, its Moshe's daughter, just arrived in Israel. She speaks Hebrew."

"I am in Tel Aviv and thought it would be nice to come meet you and your family."

"Where are you? How come you speak Hebrew?"

"I am a student at Hebrew University this year."

"And you already speak Hebrew? That means you have been here a while, and you haven't called your relatives? It is April — have you been here since the school year started?"

I am uncomfortably aware that I have transgressed some cultural expectation that is still invisible to me. I haven't known about these relatives during my whole twenty years. I have never seen pictures of them nor corresponded with them. I have only just learned about them from my older cousin Laney, who lived in Israel for two years and who speaks fluent Hebrew.

It reminds me of the time in England when I was late for a work meeting and someone commented, "Oh, the Yanks are always late for everything."

Someone explained to me that he was referring to WWII; the Yanks were late in coming in and I was being held accountable.

My dormitory mate Lizy, a native Israeli, is disparaging. "He sounds like a country bumpkin. You will have nothing in common with them. Don't waste your time." Yet for some reason, I am not nervous and I am determined to go through with the meeting.

Mordecai explains which bus to take and where to get off. It is only one bus; he says he will meet me at the other end. He doesn't tell me what he looks like. I am worried during the bus ride that we won't recognize each other.

As I step down from the bus, I don't hesitate for a moment as to who is my relative. Mordecai looks like my father's twin brother Milt, only shorter and stockier. His freckled face is framed by a straw gentleman's hat, like one that Milt wears to protect his bald head; later when Mordecai takes off his hat, I see that he is bald! He doesn't hesitate either: I look like an American student in Israel, wearing a long, striped peasant dress from the Arab market, green Jansport knapsack on my shoulder. He doesn't smile, and I look searchingly for warmth in his eyes. He kisses me formally. He is brusque but seems familiar or familial.

I smile to myself. Mordecai walks with his elbows almost touching behind his back. My father and uncle walk the same way, only I never noticed until I saw Mordecai. He is slightly formal and speaks in grunting questions; it is clear that he is kind, but of another age, another culture. Very direct, he recounts for me the visits from my uncle and from my cousin who lived in Israel for two years. My own father and mother came to visit a year before for the first time. I follow him in my fledgling Hebrew.

Before I can absorb an impression of the two-story apartment building, there I stand face to face with a brown door with the name E-D-E-L-M-A-N written in ceramic tile on the door. I see myself in the mirror of Hebrew letters.

The door opens suddenly, and I catch a glimpse of a short woman with streaked grey and brown hair, and I am being covered with kisses. Hugs and exclamations fly at my stunned cocoon. She is energetic in her hugging and kissing. I feel that someone who lost something precious to her has found me, and that I have found something, which I didn't know was missing because I haven't experienced it.

"Ooh, I have to phone Rivka!" She runs to telephone her daughter, but keeps smiling at me.

This woman, I know, must be Sarah. She beams immediate and permanent acceptance. I am not surprised to be welcomed so enthusiastically by the older generation, who are somewhere in between my parents' and grandparents' age. However, I am certain that this kind of greeting would not be forthcoming from my generation. Israelis are not known to be soft or polite, but straightforward and rather unsentimental.

Sarah seems to be wearing a partial brown wig, with strips of real gray hair brushed back over them. She has the figure of Golda Meir and the same plain dress that must have been in fashion twenty years ago, thick opaque stockings and sensible black shoes. It is hard to guage her age. Early seventies? She certainly does not look like American women who age in their sports clothes, dyed hair and makeup. Sarah has many liver spots and wrinkles; she looks like she has been aged in a dryer, with her smile left intact.

Conversation doesn't seem to be what is important here. Not like my house of origin. It is all atmosphere and comfort, pleasing all the senses. Hot lemon tea and homemade sugar cookies, which smell and taste of butter, appear before visitors. The sugar feels gravelly on my tongue as the cookie melts away.

The door is flung open and I am being hugged and exclaimed over by a blonde beauty. Dimples, olive-shaped Middle Eastern eyes lined in black kohl, big gold loops in her ears and perfect skin. A little curly blonde girl, about age seven, is bouncing with excitement.

This beauty, who looks a lot like my cousin Laney, is their youngest daughter Rivka. She looks about thirty. Their second youngest was Rafi, who died in the Six-Day War. That is his photo on the wall, with his unit's insignia. Squinting in the bright light, he looks beautiful too, turned partially away from the camera. There are two more living siblings, Yuval the oldest, and Ilana, their second child.

Rivka grasps immediately that I want to speak only Hebrew to them so that the parents will understand; she will not try to practice her English like all the other young Israelis. Jolly and fun, she seems aware that I have just landed on a foreign planet. We will play the game of throwing the Hebrew ball back and forth as many times as we can before it goes splat on the floor. Then we laugh, pick it up and try again. As he reads the newspaper incessantly, Mordecai is the hardest to understand, and seems to have a vocabulary that I haven't learned yet. Like my father's very rich English.

The new relatives are intrigued that my father is a twin.

Murray and Milt were once forbidden to be in the same room because Murray had the measles. So they put a chess board in the doorway of the room and played chess. Milt got the measles. Apparently they had their own twin language; they read the *Book of Knowledge* (a child's encyclopedia) together: they lost their father together at age nine, sneaking into the hospital to visit him one last time; they played the trombone equally badly in order to get into football games for free. They walked to Hebrew school, *cheder*, together, and every time the story was recounted, the railroad tracks grew longer; eventually the walk to school became so long that they got up before they went to bed! They would both wiggle their ears later to entertain children and grandchildren.

Mordecai has a yellowed letter from the twins' mother, his aunt Sadie, my grandmother, who I never knew. She sent them a package during the war. They had no money for clothes, and received a sailor suit and ballet costume from Tanta Sadie. I make a mental note to feel love for my grandmother whom I was too young to know. I knew that she was a widow who ran a variety store during the Depression and lived hand to mouth herself. Her letter is dated 1960. She apologizes for not having written sooner, but she had been ill. Since she has last written she is delighted to tell them about a new granddaughter born some time before. I think of all my female cousins' ages; by process of elimination I work out that she is writing about me. This is the most direct contact that I have ever had with my grandmother. And I had to go several thousand miles from home to feel it.

Mordecai's father and my grandfather, Sadie's husband, were brothers. A distant memory returns to Mordecai of his father sobbing when my grandfather, Kalman, died. I never could have known this if I hadn't stumbled into this kitchen. We are distant relatives, yet closer than we had imagined. We each only know our part of the story and have a lot to share with each other.

He fills in some details about Kalman that no one in America remembers or passes on. My grandfather, whom I never met, had wanted to be a lawyer. Poetic justice, I smile; he worked in a cigar factory, but three of his granddaughters became lawyers.

Grapefruit trees and an orange tree line Mordecai's urban garden. I exclaim over the beauty of the trees, I don't know if I have seen citrus trees in a garden before, ripe with fruit. Lettuce and spinach are growing in the garden. Apparently Mordecai, who just retired, babysits for Rivka's baby Yael, and tends his garden. At first I don't understand the word for "retire" in Hebrew; it is literally "to go out on a pension."

At the end of the session, Rivka's daughter Smadar, the curly blonde, hands me a picture she has drawn while listening to the conversation. She has drawn twin brothers climbing up trees picking oranges and grapefruits.

She has written on it, "from your cousin Smadar, age seven, with lots of love and welcome to the family."

# Uncle in Hebrew Means Beloved — 1944

"What are you doing?" Mordecai asks his younger cousin visiting from America.

"My grandmother asked me to bring her some earth from the Holy Land," Milt, my father's twin brother, replies as he fills a brown paper bag with earth from Mordecai's garden.

"To be buried with? We had that custom too."

"Yes, I think it will include her in those buried in Israel, if she has a pillow of earth from here."

They smile at each other, both knowledgeable about traditions and customs, but not bound by them.

Mordecai leads the way from the small garden into a tiny ramshackle house. He opens the refrigerator — a box with a huge ice cube inside, delivered by horse-drawn cart a few times a week — and takes out some cold beer.

Sarah is nursing her baby daughter. Yuval is playing with some tin cans, building a tower with them.

Mordecai inspects his American cousin wearing a uniform. He has just come from Egypt on his leave, to meet his only cousins to survive the war. Mordecai has never met his American cousins.

Milt hesitates about asking after the fate of Mordecai's large group of brothers and sisters in Europe. Auschwitz is already in the newspapers.

The two feel very close.

Milt tells of his twin brother Murray, my father, who is serving in intelligence in Labrador, Canada, his knowledge of German helping him to decode German messages.

Milt's older brother Seymour is in the navy.

Milt himself is in the air force. He was sent to Casablanca where the Air Transport Command flies passengers and cargo all over the world, which is more challenging in wartime. On days off Milt can write his own orders for travel and so he flies all over the Mediterranean. He writes himself an order to fly to Palestine to see his cousins.

Except that eight first cousins, Mordecai's siblings, are behind enemy lines in Europe.

# Graveyards — 1978

The evening of my first visit to my relatives, we all gather at a public ceremony in Ramat Gan, a large suburb of Tel Aviv. The name of every soldier who fell in all four wars is read alphabetically. Edelman, in Hebrew, is at the very beginning of the alphabet. As the name "Edelman, Rafael" is read, Mordecai lights a large yellow candle. It does not drip, but what looks like hot wax drips down his cheek in the yellow glow.

A ten-year-old boy, with a fresh, outdoor face introduces himself to me. He is the son of Sarah and Mordecai's older daughter Ilana, who is there with all four of her children. "Do you know why they call me Dror?" he asks me solemnly but kindly. "I have two r's in my name, for Rafi. He died for freedom, that's what Dror means."

His cousin Dafni, roughly his age, chimes in: "I have a middle name, I am named for Rafi. My middle name is Rafaela." She is the middle of the three daughters of Yuval, Rafi's older brother.

Ilana adds, "I couldn't say the name Rafi, couldn't hear it every day, but I gave all my children names with the letter *r* in them: Dror, Nir, Ronit and Shirley."

At that moment I decide what I will name my first child.

I am single at the time and have no concrete plans for building a family. I didn't know Rafi, and I haven't known death personally. However, I am impressed by these young people who can look at death, feel it, and put it somewhere useful. They enjoy the family atmosphere, each other, are curious about the new cousin from America. I feel that I have a lot to learn from them; at age twenty, I have never really dealt with death.

The next day we all meet again at the graveside. Each grave is like a bed, with the names and dates written where the pillow would be. The sides of the bed are rough blond stone, and the "mattress" is a bed of plants that parents and relatives can tend to, allowing them something to continue to nurture.

I look at the stone pillow. There is the name, Rafael Joseph Edelman. He died when he was twenty years and three months old. For the first time looking at the mirror image of my age on the grave, I realize I am exactly Rafi's permanent age.

My associations with graveyards are slightly different. When I was ten years old I was playing hide and seek with my friend Amy and her sisters and brother in a graveyard of immigrants to New Glarus, Wisconsin, dating back to the seventeenth century. Amy was hiding behind a massive salmon-colored hewn stone. The ground was damp and spongy from the spring thaw, and the graves, even the towering ones, were unstable. As I ran forward to tag Amy, the stone fell and trapped my foot. I screamed and Amy's mother came running. Her father tried to pull me out from under the stone, but I was trapped. My foot burned, ached, and then went terribly numb, with occasional sharp, shooting pains. Amy's father, frantic, ran across the highway to get help. Amy's mother cradled me on the damp ground. Amy's eyes reflected the fear that they all felt. I heard the word "amputation." I didn't know what it meant but did know that it was drastic. With an entire football team in tow, Amy's father and the young men inched their fingers under the giant stone. Heaving and grunting, eventually they lifted it enough to drag me out from under it. Then the pain seared into me.

I was carried to the car and driven to a local country doctor. He felt the foot, which had turned impressive colors and was puffed out like a large melon.

"How old are you?" The doctor asked sternly.

"Ten," I sniffed, feeling very bruised and frightened.

"Then why are you crying? It isn't broken," the doctor pronounced. However, he hadn't x-rayed it.

I ended up later in a cast for six weeks; every toe bone was broken in two places.

My father carried me to the bathroom for the weekend until I could walk on it. He fed me chicken and orange juice. My mother was away visiting her mother, Grandma Rose, in Boston. This was the late sixties; unlike television families, mine was not necessarily gifted when it came to emotional communication. So no one actually told my mother that she was coming home to a child in a leg cast. We surprised her at the airport. While my father went in to meet the plane, I posed outside the car. As they came out of the airport I stood there grinning, proud of my crutches and leg cast.

Being extremely accident prone, I was always showing up at school with casts, bandages, crutches and stitches. It satisfied my need to be "special" and to get attention. No one believed my story of the graveyard, assuming it was one of my attention-grabbing tall tales.

The day after soldier's Remembrance Day, and meeting my relatives for the first time, I am sent back to Jerusalem with a bag of homemade sugar cookies and some of Mordecai's oranges. They are homegrown, and they seem to glow against the light brown paper bag.

# Gefilte Fish — 1978 and 1930s

Rivka is dressed in a turquoise bikini and sunglasses and has a towel around her waist.

"Come, Yehudit, let's go to the beach."

"I think I'll stay here and learn how to make gefilte fish from your mother," I reply. "Is that OK, Sarah?"

Rivka can't believe it and Sarah seems bemused as well. A young person, a twenty-year-old who would rather watch an old lady in the kitchen than go to the beach for a swim and a tan and the fun of being out with other young people. Later I learn that to lie on the beach is called "frying breaded cutlets"; you get browned on both sides like a Wiener schnitzel.

The narrow kitchen circa 1950 is Sarah's laboratory, or her office, or her sanctuary.

"I used to skin the fish myself, chop it by hand. Now Mordecai buys it for me ready chopped."

My own tendency is to use a store-bought frozen chopped fish mix, but I keep that to myself.

"You get the fishmonger to slice a whole carp in slices, and you ask him to grind up a second fish for the filling." A fishmonger? I am not sure that there is one in Madison, Wisconsin. Isn't that what supermarkets are for?

An accordion of carp slices is neatly lined up on the counter, Sarah's knife flying across the body of the fish.

The room has the fragrance of a bowl of broth simmering on the stove. It has in it slices of carrot, celery, onion, bay leaves, whole pepper corns and a fish head.

I feel a pronounced sense of calm as I watch her, listen, and inhale.

In a simple red bowl, she breaks in two eggs, some finely minced onion, a tablespoon of sugar, a pinch of salt, and some matzo meal. Her hands mix rhythmically, telling their own story; they have done this since she was my age or younger. It sort of puts my university studies in context — they don't smell this good, they aren't this defined.

She forms balls and deftly applies them to the slices of carp, which have a natural hole in the center, if they have been scaled and cleaned. She gently lays each stuffed slice into the broth until it is just covered with liquid. She covers the scuffed, ancient pot and smiles at me.

Sarah learned to make this fish from her mother.

Sarah apparently was the daughter most like her mother, a *balabusta* — she knew how to cook and clean and take care of everything. She sewed from the age of six, weaving fence wire together on two sticks she found in the barnyard.

She baked breads and rolls, cut homemade fresh noodles, milked the cows and made cottage cheese and butter. She made jams, cakes, fish and meat dishes, and vegetables, fresh or cooked, sugared carrots, stuffed zucchini and tomatoes.

Her mother was very proud of her handiwork, very proud of her cooking, and loved to have her help. Sarah was tireless; by seven in the morning she was often sitting down to sew after a full morning's work. Her father sometimes woke her and her sister Dvorah up at three in the morning to help with the crops. Then she baked fresh bread for breakfast.

Sarah's mother's handiwork was so renowned that it hung even in some of the local churches. She loved it that Sarah could sew and knit so competently.

With Sarah being such a help to both her father and mother, it was an extra hard blow when Sarah left home. First when she became involved with the youth movement and then when she left for the He-Halutz training farm, her mother punished her by silence.

As Sarah tells me about her youthful rebellion, she is chopping fresh vegetables into an Israeli salad. It is clear that she could literally do this with her eyes closed, and that her focus is on the story she is telling.

# The Dream, Yasina, Hungary — 1933

*For seven nights the dream had been like an urgent prophecy. Sarah had never seen a machine driven on wheels, except for a train. She had never seen such a machine. Yet Sarah watched as it moved on its treaded tires and a scoop, the size of a big water trough, but with teeth. It scooped up bodies that were wasted to skeletons. Heaps and piles of them. They were in the church graveyard of the village. Thin bodies with their bones showing through the skin were tossed in the air. The machine was burying them under the earth. The rows of skeletal bones were like heaps of matches, a countless number, enough to set fire to the universe. Sarahfeigie shook herself to stay awake. Any defiance, confrontation was preferable to the terror of the soul, facing that dream. It confronted her with an insistence of its realness.*

Sarah is locked out of the house and is pushing on the door handle. She has gone to a Zionist youth group that puts the hope for a Jewish homeland above religion. This is unacceptable to Sarah's parents and her mother has locked her out. Sarahfeigie wills the door to give so that she can go into the lamp-lit room. She can feel the pressure of her father's hand on the knob on the inside. Determined to match him, she leans on the handle. It budges but doesn't turn. He won't answer her pleas. Mama's muffled but agitated voice is directing Papa not to answer, not to open the door. There is a warm wetness on her arm, a splinter from the heavy wooden door. Sarah licks the blood off, kicks the door, spits into the dark and stomps off, lifting her long skirt. "That will teach her," she hears her mother say.

He-Halutz is so exciting. For three nights she has had no fear. No waking up shuddering from dreams of bones. They like her at the branch headquarters. There they talk of living in a land where no one can pass laws forbidding Jewish business to sell to Gentiles. Sarah thinks to herself, "Mama forbids me to go. Mama forbids...young men and women together in one room. I will go again."

It is an amulet — as long as she goes to He-Halutz, she is protected from the terror of the dream.

Sarah plucks an apple from a tree in the farmyard, and defiantly sits down on a pile of hay to wait until her parents have gone to bed. The goats are bleating, horses swishing their tails. A damp wind tickles the hay. Sarah eats her apple determinedly. The only uncertainty gnawing at her is whether the dream will return tonight. She sees her parents' agitated figures through the window; they too are determined. Looking out the window, they cannot see her in the dark shadows of the farmyard. She sees them and bites into the apple, then throws away the core.

Preva is exasperated with Sarah who is vegetarian out of defiance. Sarah will only eat dairy-based meals, steaming milk straight from the cow, homemade cottage cheese. Thick black bread spread with homemade berry preserves. She won't touch the chicken on Shabbat, or the rare beef that is served when a cow is butchered. She tends the cows on the farm and they have become friends, not food. A good worker, much more than her lazy older sister Klari who prays over the Psalms and sits and reads. Sarah has milked the cows, baked bread and mended a pile of the family clothes before the sun is very high in the sky. Her seams are invisible. She can use odd bits of colored thread, and have nothing show on the other side. Just from her head, she can create patterns out of wool.

Klari doesn't dream and her hands are idle. She brushes her light brown curls, and reads Ethics of the Fathers. She is about to get married; this is the proper thing to do. Sarah monograms sheets, towels and pillowcases for her. They are green cloth with a darker green thread; when they are done they look ready to adorn Cleopatra's own bed. Sarah isn't praised for her work.

When Klari marries, she shaves her head; no more soft brown curls, and she covers her head with a tichel, a full head scarf. She runs a religious home, even more so than Mama's. She is pregnant with her fourth child when she goes to live Sarah's nightmare.

Perhaps Sarah will stop talking about this youth movement nonsense if she is employed. One afternoon, after the midday meal of potatoes creamed with farmer's cheese, Preva takes Sarah to town to Anya the dressmaker. It is a shop that Preva would like to frequent with her daughters; here young brides are fitted for their white wedding dresses. Sarahfeigie looks around the shop, at the pearls in boxes used to adorn the dresses, skeins of lace borders, white on white on white. She thinks of the sunshine in Palestine, of the white sands, and turns her back on her mother, and on the shop of luxury and slavery. She will go to work with her friends from He-Halutz.

There is a new kind of freedom living in a village of young people working like her. Sarah has been assigned to the kitchen. She is proud that she is so skilled. She doesn't mind eating meat that she has tended to, and that she herself has cooked. Here she doesn't have to rebel against her mother. There are fifty of them on a training farm, preparing them for the precarious life in Palestine. It is not exactly a kosher kitchen, but Sarah, as she is now called, never mixes milk and meat.

*The dream stopped coming when I found my place at the He-Halutz movement branch meetings. We were young pioneers and were going off to rural Hungary to learn how to work the land. I was in the kitchen. Oh, how they loved my cooking. I had been brought up to bake fresh bread, to bone and skin fish and make gefilte fish, to milk cows. I rolled out noodles on a wooden board by hand. I cut each noodle with a knife. Before I left home, for some reason meat turned my stomach. I preferred dairy meals. I milked the cow and drank her milk warm. They raved about my cooking at Hachshara, at the training farm. Young people who'd made a daring step to leave home were nurtured by my food. It comforted and pleased them. I was very popular and I loved the attention. Sarah, make us your stuffed zucchinis, stuffed peppers, and stuffed eggplant, cabbage. Sweet and sour fish for Shabbat? They licked their plates. Kneidlach, Sarah, for me. Eventually, I begged to work somewhere else, in the fields, in a factory. I am strong as an ox. They said no, when you find someone else who can cook as well as you can, you can work wherever you want. This took two years. They finally found someone whose cooking was not bad and I got to work in a chocolate factory.*

Safta (Grandmother) Sarah's gefilte fish is done. Rivka has come back from the beach. Her tan has deepened and she smells of suntan lotion, sea salt and mild perspiration.

"Is lunch ready, Ema, we're starving! Nu, Yehudit, did you learn how to be a *balabusta* yet?"

I assumed that the gefilte fish was the complete lunch. But no, first comes the clear chicken broth with clear circles of fat swimming in it. Then we are served the gefilte fish, together with sweet magenta-colored horseradish. The carp on the outside is light and flaky, the inside fish mix is solid and textured, sweet and savory at the same time, with only a hint of a fish taste. I eat three pieces, and am unnerved to discover that there is then a *main course* served. It is fried breaded chicken breasts that they call "schnitzel." There is cucumber and tomato salad cut into miniscule pieces, and seasoned only with lemon and salt. There are honeyed carrots and tiny potato cubes. I find room to eat a mound of that. I refuse the fruit compote for dessert. But I have fallen in love with Sarah and her food.

# Rebellion — 1934

Sarah tells her mother and father that she is going to leave home, at age twenty-two, and go to a training farm to learn how to be a pioneer in Palestine.

"There are three stages, mama," Sarah explains. "First we organize, as we have been doing in our local branch. That means that we vote on collective decisions, we have officers, and we plan for the next two stages which are going to a training farm in Europe, and finally, making *aliyah*, which means going up to the Land of Israel."

"Listen to the language that she's using," Preva says to Yosef.

He listens silently. Respectful but with a severe presence.

Preva feels fear that this daughter, the one who takes after her, who has been such a "good girl," who cooks so well, sews, works so hard, will now choose to leave her. And for what? She feels desperate. She will have to punish her.

"If you leave this house and go live with boys and girls together in a place that is not God-fearing, I will not let you visit, I will not write, this will not be your home any longer."

It is not easy to leave this home. Leaving means that she will not be the favorite anymore. Leaving means giving up her home.

Sarah loved the horses at the farm. Especially Susiya, a black mare with a trim frame. Sarah marveled at her; she always looked to her like a naked woman parading around her stall. She was so friendly, poking her pinkish white nose over the bars, asking for an apple or a carrot, or a sugar lump. She drank water out an enormous tin tub that Sarah filled herself. She ate straw that Sarah pitchforked into her trough. She pranced an impatience dance while Sarah milked the cows. Sarah leaned her head against their warm, soft sides, listening to the barnyard cacophony of chickens being fed. Cows lowed and the horses let out their breath. The contrasting smells of manure and fresh milk, fresh fruit and flowers filled the air. The apples grew rose-colored on the trees dotted behind the barn. One could always pick an apple to spoil Susiya on the way to milk the cows. And Mama was always waiting for the fresh milk.

"I would wash my hands with homemade soap, and then begin kneading dough. There was a hot breakfast waiting for the farm workers by five a.m. with fresh-baked rolls, new milk, fried eggs, farm vegetables and apple, peach and plum jam. Then there was apple pie or peach cobbler for dessert.

"But I could not read my father's eyes, did he feel the same way as my mother about my leaving home? Could he see the special nature of moving to Israel when Europe was affected by Hitler's rise to power?" Sarah recalls to me decades later.

Later in private her father said to her: "You believe in this 'He-Halutz' the way I believe in the Holy One praised be He. God, May His Name be praised, will go with you on your journey. It will not be an easy journey. Your mother and I will miss your cheerful presence. Always be cheerful and helpful as you are at home, my Sarahfeigeleh."

Sarah's mother did not change her stance that Sarah should stay at home, not mix with boys at the youth movement, and live a religious way of life reflecting her own. Sarah was very angry with her mother. She never let her see her own doubt about leaving home, only her determination.

Sarah's mother kept her word. For three years, she did not write a word, nor visit.

# Rebellion — 1969

When I was about eleven years old, I was drawn to a neighborhood house with a turret as if by a magnet. Ilona and her artist mother lived there. Recently divorced, she reached out to nurture her thirteen-year-old daughter's friends. They had garden vegetables for dinner and then smoked marijuana for dessert. I wanted to try some.

Ilona calls out, "Mommy, can I turn Jude on (to marijuana?)" "After supper," replies Teresa responsibly.

It is the sixties in America, a university town. I cough a lot, but when I finally manage to inhale some, I feel light and floaty. Laughter and voices come from outside our bodies. This seems hilarious to us, but we are forced into serious reverence by the stillness of shadows that change on the wood floors. Ilona and I climb up the stairs to the turret room and look out. Ilona shows me a unicorn that she has calligraphed on the wall.

"It is a symbol of my virginity," says Ilona.

"What's that?" I ask, intrigued.

"Brother, you don't know anything. I will teach you."

However, I know a few things that Ilona doesn't. One evening I am being yelled at, at home down the block. I have spoken back to my mother and feel like scum. The yelling hammers into my head. I scream out BITCH at the top of my voice. The hammers become hands pummeling at me from all sides. I remember running down the back hall steps so quickly that the metal on the end of each stair clicks as I fly down to avoid the hands following me. They do not hurt so much as shock. I run blindly up the back alley, away from the voice yelling COME BACK HERE RIGHT NOW!

My legs take me to Ilona's house. The turrets make it look like a castle. But instead of approaching the front door, I walk around to the back, to the garage that is never used, as Teresa has no car. I enter, shut the door and lie down on the filthy oil-stained floor and cry face down. It has become black and quiet outside. I decide never to go home again, but I lack a plan. Eventually, I knock on Ilona's front door. Teresa sees the disturbed and hysterical state that I am in. I cannot say anything.

"Your boyfriend break up with you, Jude?" I have never had a boyfriend and shake my head "no." Teresa, whom everyone calls Tree, pulls me inside, tells me Ilona is not home, introduces me to her ex. Then she puts her arms around me and I sob.

I cannot speak for a long time, having no tools for expressing the hurt. Much later I scribble on a piece of paper to answer Teresa's inquiries.

"My mother doesn't love me."

Tree repeats this. I experience an odd sensation; I have been heard, not judged. The phone rings. It is my father.

"He sounds scared," says Teresa. "It's after eleven o'clock and they didn't know where you are. You'd better go home." I am too young to refuse, to come up with an alternative solution, a way of getting so far away that I never have to deal with the hurt.

The door opens for me, but there is no talking. I click up the back hall stairs, which will now always hold a reminder. I wash the oil off my face and go to bed.

No one deals with my pain. No one talks to me, tells me the story of their childhood, or what it means to grow up.

# Flying — 1984

It is very hard for me to fly. Every shake of the plane convinces me that I am about to plummet in slow motion to my death, but only after experiencing impossibly horrific bodily sensations. The plane dips sharply, rolls, tilts to the left. I will it to be on an even keel, to avoid air pockets. What is a stable course when the dips don't have a secure middle ground?

The plane takes off and I have left adult independence. I will not have car keys in America; I will have to ask permission to borrow the car from my parents like a teenager, and will have a deadline to get it back. I will have very little cash, almost no spending money. On an Israeli salary there is no extra to spend, even at K-Mart. I am bringing presents, because I will not be able to treat anyone to anything there. Especially the first few years, I hope that my parents will offer me some cash for spending money, or I will go without. But then I hope that they won't offer, so that I can retain some shred of my adult facade. At my age, my parents weren't taking handouts from their parents.

After I have left America, the prices there seem alluring. A good pair of pants goes for only $19.99. The latest Marge Piercy novel: I have read everything else she has every written — will I sacrifice one of my greatest loves? I remember drooling at the Fisher-Price farm when my children were young. Or a pogo stick. Or borrowing money and then buying my children large and expensive gifts and wondering where to hide them. I literally hid them in the trunk of the car once, but they got found. I was judged for borrowing money and then buying "extravagant" gifts.

The plane lands back in Israel and I am confused. My childhood roots are now an ocean away, my connections to the past, people who know my story. No one on the Middle East side of the ocean has ever heard me play the cello, seen braces on my teeth, and met my grandparents, uncles or aunts. Except Safta Sarah, who has met some of my close relatives, and besides, she knows everything she needs to know about me.

In Israel, where I have car keys, my own job and apartment, where I vaguely manage to function as an adult mother, no one cares about my children the way my parents care about my children. Danny is working late. There is a party at Raphi's nursery school for Chanukah. It is the peak celebration of nursery school. However, his younger sister Shira's toddler school party is scheduled for the same day, the same hour. I end up explaining to Esther, the nursery teacher, that I cannot be in two places at once.

"Esther, I won't be coming to Raphi's party; I have to go to Shira's, and their father is at the clinic until late."

"That's unheard of and unacceptable! You can't miss your son's party —

he's singing and dancing…" Esther was adamant. "Send a grandma or a grandfather. Someone from the family has to be there to see him."

I choke up and try to explain that there aren't any. Trampling on my sorest place, where I choose not to walk. There are no grandparents for most immigrant parents.

"Preposterous," says Esther, "you must have some relatives."

I ask my friend Linda to go as a surrogate "aunty"; she has done without herself and has never asked a similar favor from me. Why am I always needier?

I invite Sarah and Mordecai, but as they don't drive, they can only make it after the party. They join us for a cozy dinner with Linda. Safta Sarah looks around my apartment. I see her nod the silent language that exists between longtime partners. She is nodding at the cobwebs hanging from the ceiling that I didn't notice between work and two little children. I don't really mind; I know that cleanliness means more in her world, playing with children means more in mine.

# Love — 1938 and 2003

Mordecai appears to be strong when Sarah watches him approaching. His shoulders are broad, his waist is slim, but he has meat on his bones. He has an exceptionally kind face. He is not exceptionally tall. However, he has a cough and when he comes back from work in the fields, Sarah has some chicken broth waiting for him.

She chatters and smiles and does everything except spoon it into his mouth. He is silent. He notices that her soup is a brighter yellow than Hedva's soup, the other kitchen girl. The noodles are handmade, each one a different shape. The carrots are clean, peeled and cut very evenly, in chunks exactly half the size of the tablespoon. There are hints of other vegetables that have been strained out, to make a clearer soup. It is so hot that the steam goes up his nose. Like the touch of a woman's hand, warmth spreads throughout his chest, the steam on his face, sweetness and the lovely texture of lightly cooked noodles sliding over his tongue. He closes his eyes and slurps. Opens his eyes and nods quietly to Sarah. Their eyes lock.

It turns out that hard physical labor does not sit well with Mordecai, even though he is willing to work all the hours of the day — he is never lazy. He has a penchant for reading the newspaper, almost religiously, the way he used to pore over a page of Talmud.

In yeshiva, it was customary to study with a partner. They would share a desk, sit closely together, read the text and then discuss it. They would decipher the meanings of words, of phrases, and of whole texts. If a person dies in Babylon and the family wants to bury him in the Land of Israel, when do they observe the week of mourning rites in Babylon? When the body is removed (presumably by camel), or when the body arrives and is interred in the Holy Land? This point is discussed from every angle. But Mordecai has left that world and objects to religious practice to prove that he has indeed left.

Mordecai does not read the paper to Sarah, nor necessarily share his reactions to it with her. It is never many words that they share. Not many affectionate words. It is almost completely a relationship of actions. She cooks, he eats and enjoys. Later when they live in Israel, he shops and brings her groceries to the kitchen. He earns money, she fills in the gaps by babysitting and taking in laundry. While he is looking for a job, she earns money.

Sarah and Mordecai go walking at night around Brunn, something that all the lovers do, but which is seen as somewhat anti-social by the rest of the collective. He takes her hand. His hand is large and soft; it is the hand of a yeshiva student, and not of a farmer. They speak about the present, a little about the past, their families of origin, and mostly about the future in the Land.

They speak about marriage but never about their current relationship. Except that Sarah doesn't believe in sharing a room until they are married, as Shimon and Lena do. Mordecai finds it harder to wait. They are not so very young and they are away from home. They spend some time behind closed doors, but Sarah always goes back to her room to sleep.

Mordecai is gaining weight on the extra bits of food that he receives.

A letter arrives from Yasina, in her mother's handwriting. Yitzhak Moshe, Sarah's brother, was married last month. The wedding dress from Preva's favorite seamstress, with silk and pearls, and a wedding feast that Preva and her daughters prepared all with produce from the farm. How Preva would have enjoyed Sarah there, as her right hand, to cook and sew and bake, to decorate and to make presents for her brother. They didn't tell her ahead of time because she has chosen a new life, where boys and girls live together and eat forbidden foods and talk about Palestine. She obviously doesn't care what changes occur in her family of origin anyway, so there was no need to invite her to the wedding.

On the bed in her room, Sarah is restless. She runs outside, and crashes into a group of visiting dignitaries from the central headquarters of He-Halutz. One of them, Felix, recognizes her. Crying is not particularly acceptable at Hachshara, and she fights to remain in control.

Felix excuses himself from his comrades and asks Sarah to come with him to speak in private in the kitchen. They find a quiet corner just outside the kitchen. He picks up an ear of corn on the cob and throws her one.

"I will help you shuck the corn, Sarah, but tell me, why are you so troubled? Can I help?"

Sarah cannot yet speak, but her hands automatically shuck the corn. He must know her fairly well to know she can cope if her hands are flying.

"Sarahleh, you know that you are a valued worker, no one has ever run a kitchen as you have…"

She warms to his compliment.

"I had a letter from home. My older brother got married. They didn't invite me or even tell me about it. They haven't written in over three years. My mother doesn't approve. I cannot go on with Hachshara. I am part of the family too. My cooking was needed more at home, my sewing skills… They think that I don't care about them. I have to go."

"And remain in Europe when the end comes? Be left out of building a home for the Jewish people?" Felix smirks at her. "You think they can build the Jewish state without you?"

"I was always such a good girl, did what my mother wanted, and now she punishes me by not even telling me."

Felix sees that Sarah can't really hear him. This is not a time to speak to her of ideology.

"Sarahleh, we will not give up on you. We are your family now."

Sarah wipes away tears. "I have blood relatives. My brother got married. My mother is wrong not to invite me. I think I will leave the Hachshara and go home. I will perish with all of them when Hitler invades Hungary. I…"

Felix takes a new tack. "I believe you have a boyfriend? When the war comes and sweeps through Europe many people will die. Whole families, parts of families. You and your boyfriend can build a good life in Eretz Yisrael, create a family of your own. Create some pioneer babies," he winks at Sarah.

Sarah smiles shyly.

"Thank you, Felix, come get some sweet biscuits. I am afraid to go visit, and I am afraid not to go. You have made me feel as though I do have a family here. I will tell Mordecai."

"And Sarah," Felix adds, "we need your skills here. You are a beloved sister to all of us."

She has seen the comfort her soups and stews and stuffed vegetables can bring to people. She feels an unarticulated sense of what she may do in the future. Something about being strong for other people when they are having trouble coping.

Sarah wipes away a few tears and tells Mordecai about her mother's letter. He becomes enraged at her mother, but also understands. He calms down and holds her close. He kisses her on the mouth, kisses her hair, she kisses his eyes.

Mordecai is never a sensitive type like Felix; he tends to make final statements without listening. Yet he is hers, solid.

She writes back to her mother, and tells her that she too will be getting married as soon as she and Mordecai can set up a home in Palestine. She will be coming home just before they depart from Europe to say goodbye to everyone.

Alone on the bed of her retirement home, last night Sarah didn't feel well, and there was no one to pat her hand, to listen, to sit with her. She is telling me about the loss of Mordecai, the empty nights, and days that are empty in their fullness. She talks about sex — it is rampant in the retirement home but not for her. "Mordecai was my first, and he was my last. He was my only one."

"Do you feel that loving someone else in that way would be betraying Mordecai?"

"He would not be my first and my last if I did that," replies Sarah simply.

She tells me about the attentions of the men with whom she plays cards; they adore her, they spoil her, but they are loosely knitted friends, not woven of the same thread.

# The Immigrant Lesson of the Floating Ship

*A liyah* is the term used for immigrating to Israel. It means to "go up," in the spiritual sense, to ascend. It is thought of as climbing the rung of a spiritual ladder to arrive at heavenly Jerusalem. In my experience, it is more like the forced and incessant rocking of an ocean liner. In the early sixties I took ocean liners across the sea to Europe, and was seasick the entire way. The lack of control was overpowering, sickening, disheartening.

A joy at first, then a shock, then panic, then my aliyah was a series of calamities. There were mini-disasters like a fire in our apartment building, and our car getting stolen. Then the pace increased, my husband being drafted and having to either to be separated, which felt very scary and lonely after leaving family, or to uproot and leave our community and go with him to become an army wife. As a feminist who protested the Vietnam War, being an army wife would involve being an appendage, to aid and abet the war machine. And I was supposed to bring up two small children there?! Then when we survived the year and a half in the middle of nowhere, with our marriage flagging and panting, the Gulf War came and we spent nights awake in a sealed room, trying to comfort children who might be gassed at any minute. These are the problems that I chose?

Yet, knowing Sarah Edelman taught me that the illegal immigrant ship of my aliyah was in fact…afloat. I left parents of my own free will. Her parents didn't survive Hitler. I could go back to visit. She could not, and if she did, there would only be a reminder that there was no one left. She came with a wooden cutting board and a rolling pin in her knapsack. I shipped a small lift with furniture, dishes, electrical appliances, and clothes. She had no formal education. I had a BA and later in Israel got an MA, but who was the wise one? She had no one to greet her. I had her, to be delighted with us. Her story and mine are not of equal weight; hers put mine in perspective. Yes, it was hard, but not impossible.

State security checked on us with our closest relatives when we arrived in Israel. A security agent went to Sarah and Mordecai's house and asked if we were known to them. Sarah almost chased him out of her gate with her broom, "They are good people, don't you go asking about them." Then, she served him a full meal beginning with chicken soup and ending with fruit compote. Our security status was never questioned again.

I don't know when I started feeling good here, but I do know that when I was in Safta Sarah's small apartment in Ramat Gan, or sitting with her at the retirement home, I felt more secure, more full of meaning than ever. The gnawing loneliness left me at the door.

The reasons why I made aliyah only unfolded with time.

# Lessons about Love in America in the 1970s

More unknowns at Ilona's. A twenty-seven-year-old man with black skin moves in with Ilona; she is thirteen. The unicorn looks down on their shared bed in the turret. His name is Pop. He holds Ilona on his lap and tells her to get good grades in school. Teresa also takes a boyfriend about the same age, a friend of Pop's.

"To stay part of her life," she explains reluctantly to me. As if I as an inexperienced eleven-year-old can judge her.

One day Ilona asks to take a bath at our house. But she locks the door. When she comes out she says, "Your asthma medicine is speed, right?"

I don't know, but have a feeling that something is not right. Ilona asks me if I have ever kissed a man properly. I say no. Ilona takes it upon herself to provide me with a friend of Pop who has been instructed to only go as far as I allow. I like it very much, but know that I am out of my league and am confused. I stop him and run home after some heavy French kissing.

Since then, looking at the life I chose, full of meaning, which came into being by marrying Danny and moving to Israel, I am aware how easily I could have become a mother as a young teenager and ended up living on welfare estranged from my family and middle-class life. What if I had gotten involved with him? What if I had left school and traveled with him? What if I was away from my family, had no money and became pregnant? How different my life would have been.

One day Pop took Ilona and me to the lagoon by the vast green lawn park in our neighborhood. He lit up a joint and spoke to us teasingly.

"Now I will blow this smoke into your mouths and I will give you a little lesson about life. You girls, you gotta go out and GET your man. You gotta shine your tails and CHASE them boys. You are PRET-TEE, but you gonna get a whole lot prettier, Jude, when you get yourself a figure."

Pop was enjoying our naiveté, our youth, the summer morning, reflections of the grass in the water.

When Tree and Ilona leave town to escape their lives, they buy an old yellow school bus and fill it with scatter rugs and big cushions. Tree is trying to keep her daughter young; they leave Pop behind. Ilona gives me a carpeted beanbag chair, black and about seven feet in diameter. It takes us forty-five minutes to roll it down the two blocks from the turret house to my house.

"You are an innocent," she says not unkindly. "You will marry your first boyfriend and he will be the love of your life." She sighs. She makes fun of Tree and me who hug and cry together bitterly. Tree cries because her daughter is unreachable; I cry because my mother is unreachable and I have known great warmth at the house with the turret.

"I have to follow her so as not to lose her," Tree explains. I feel Tree's pain and her own loss, and some degree of relief.

Six years later when I am in college, a roommate reports that there is an Ilona on the line on the public phone in the hall. I am thrilled to hear from her. She is trying to run up a long-distance phone bill as retribution to an abusive ex-live-in boyfriend. She has had brain cancer, but may be OK. A few months later she shows up in town, not on drugs anymore, but is having chemotherapy and her lovely blonde curls have fallen out.

I babysit for a funky family from San Francisco. One day the baby's hair smells like marijuana when I bring her back from the zoo. Jackie gently asks that I refrain from smoking while babysitting. Jackie and David encourage me in my collage-making and music. David teaches me new ways to pick on the guitar, new chords, and lots of folk songs about freedom and peace. They give me attention, listen carefully. I have never felt valued by an adult in this way.

On long evenings when Jackie and David have gone out, and I have put the children to bed, I cut out photographs from magazines. They are a study of the sixties, women in flowing dresses, curly disheveled hair. There is one woman I cut out three times. She has dark blonde hair in ringlets around her head, and languid green eyes, made up with brown eyeliner. She is thin and a simple cotton print dress hangs around her. Her pose is saying, I refuse to play the game, I am who I am, a daughter of the sixties. When I have gathered a pile of cuttings about a foot high, I make a collage on my bedroom wall of the photographs with wallpaper paste. There are women in fun hats, wearing peace signs and making them with their fingers. Men with long ponytails and John Lennon glasses. The Eiffel Tower with a peace sign perched on top of it. The wall is a splash of color, and seems to move with the gesticulating, dancing, and smiling young people.

I play my cello while looking at my wall collage. I never know if the deep, rich sounds that emanate from my instrument make me a musician or not. On one hand I have auditioned and been accepted to the state youth orchestra. On the other hand, my audition was not really very good; I left it in tears. My older brother is concertmaster and first violin. He tunes the other instruments. I am second to the last cellist; maybe they just took me because they needed a partner for the worst cellist in the orchestra. Sometimes I love the sounds that come from my cello, and am driven to practice for long hours. Self-competition takes over; a perfectionist, I work on scales and smooth position changes and different bowings until they sound rich and dark, like chocolate. The best moments of cello playing are when my cello blends with a piano accompanist, or the quartet that I play with in school.

The other three cellists in the quartet are boys. Playing in a quartet with them is a way of being with that other species, and yet really interacting comfortably with them. The boys like me because I am myself with them. I wear jean overalls, and a peasant blouse with ethnic embroidery on it, my hair in long braids that are brown with blonde and ginger highlights. I am always capable, but not outstanding, so they feel fine with my playing first cello in the quartet, leading off "Rosemunde" with a nod of my head. Sometimes cello playing brings me despair. If I cannot do it profoundly, why do it at all? Better not to try. But drawing the bow across the strings and hearing the honey rich sound resonates deeply inside me.

At age twelve, I discover books about the Holocaust. I read everything that has been written and live the dramas. I cannot be at meals when called to come down, or take a shower, or clean up the clothes cluttering my floor. I am too busy escaping from the Warsaw ghetto, fighting with the partisans in the forests of Poland, being led to the gas chambers at Auschwitz and planning an escape for my children. I also read classics, poetry, and nonfiction. My family is not religious, but history is a melody that is understood. I am going to read the shelves of the library dry, and become a famous cellist, and do well in school, and have lots of friends, and...

I don't really know that this happened to my immediate family until much later, when I see my name written in Hebrew letters on a wooden door and on a stone gravestone.

# Dry Bones — 1938

Sarah and Mordecai walk around the training farm. It is dark, there are crickets singing, and a crescent moon. Mordecai takes Sarah's hand. Fantasizing about life in the Land of Israel: this is the main topic of conversation here. Very few of the trainees dwell on the past.

Sarah wants Mordecai to know that a stronger force propelled her here. She wants him to know about her dream. She tells him about the skeletons, the tractor with teeth, the churchyard, and the nagging sense that she had to flee, quickly.

She peeks at his face to see if he took her seriously, and notices a complete absence of their usual sense of joking together. He is silent for a long time. Crickets speak for them as they pace towards the woods at the outlying boundaries of the training farm.

Mordecai keeps walking and looks straight ahead but he finally speaks.

"Your dream sounds like the story of the prophet Ezekiel's dry bones."

Sarah smiles inside, thinking about how Mordecai always denounces religion. Yet here he is sounding like the traditional yeshiva student that he was. She understands that learning is part of him; his way of analyzing current events is often related to Jewish history, even ancient biblical history.

"However," Mordecai continues, "there are a number of differences."

"The prophet Ezekiel insisted on justice, and felt that the people deserved the tragedies that befell them because they had sinned. It is clear that if your vision of skeletons were to come true in Germany, that the Jewish people do not deserve this. Ezekiel wants to change the people by calling them to repent. You, we, want to change the course of our history by leaving this land that is so evil to our people. We see that the only answer for us is to have our own land.

"Ezekiel can fight his fight for the souls of our people. By contrast we will work in factories and farms in our land, and rebuild a future for them; we will make an attempt at survival."

Sarah is very touched that Mordecai has listened to her, taken her seriously. She has always taken her own dream very seriously.

Mordecai continues. "There are two other differences." He pauses.

"One is that Ezekiel's dry bones got up and danced, and I don't think yours will..."

Sarah searches his eyes.

..".and he was a *meshugeneh* who saw wheels and chariots, and you aren't nearly as crazy as he was."

They laugh and Sarah caresses Mordecai's face. He kisses her very tenderly.

Tomorrow there is to be a visit of one of Mordecai's family members. Someone he loves very much. It is important for Sarah to meet this person.

Who is it? He won't tell her, she'll have to see.

# The Other Brother — 1938

The straw crunches under Sarah's feet as Mordecai leads her to the gate of the Hachshara training farm.

"What is my surprise? When will you show me?"

Mordecai smiles. "You must meet someone very important to me."

A man can be seen approaching on foot in the distance. He bounces with youth. They watch him as he becomes clearer. Sarah can see that he looks very much like Mordecai, but is thinner and about ten years younger. He has blonde hair and is dressed immaculately.

"Sarah," he reaches out his hand and kisses her on the cheek. "So you are Mordecai's Sarah. I am delighted. Oh, this is for you. Some chocolates. I have some work tutoring a young boy; I saved up so that I could buy these for you." His smile is piercing and so genuine.

The two brothers embrace. Mordecai clearly loves his little brother very much. Mordecai left home when he was just thirteen years old. It left a hole in him yearning for this little brother.

She is enchanted. This young man is her only taste of Mordecai's family of origin. She will not taste his mother's food, nor hear his father's stories; she will not meet his sisters nor his older brothers. This teenage boy is so kind and warm, and speaks in such a thoughtful manner. She is reassured that she is joining a family that speaks to her heart. Most of all, Kalman is very human. Sarah decides right then, without her father, without her mother, she has found a family.

Kalman looks at Sarah. He thinks, human beings are not so simple. Here is a woman who seems so open to others. If you are open to others, you become protective of them and can be very hurt and lost at sea when they leave you.

We will not see each other much during our lifetimes.

Kalman saw himself as a little protected and sheltered, unlike some of the other brothers. He was never aggressive; he helped his mother at home. His mother was a gentle woman, and his father also was very gentle, twenty years her senior. He had a sort of sorrow about him. The townspeople, with only two Jewish families in their midst, said, "Don't buy at Edelmann's, he is so sorrowful." He did not ask his children about their schooling but kept a distance, except when he was giving them their Hebrew lessons. He did not play with his children. On Friday nights they walked the dusty or muddy road to Bresovica.

"Father had two bookshelves. Talmud, not so much. *Shulchan Aruch. Machzorim, Midrash, Chumash*." Every Friday they also went to the *mikvah* to purify themselves, even as young boys.

Kalman's closest connection was with his mother, who was mild mannered and polite. Ten children did not succeed in making her lose her temper. There were seldom conflicts with Sandor, the father; the few were solved by giving a flick or a *potch* in the *tuchus*. When the older brothers and sisters came to visit, it was a great celebration. Normally only four or five children were home.

Even at Passover it was rare for all of the family to be together. Simon was away studying medicine. Rachel went to Circe to visit relatives. So did Esther sometimes. Rachel's wedding was an exception when all were home.

All this Kalman told Sarah at the Hachshara farm, and told me in Prague sixty years later.

# Mothers and Perfection — 1939

Sarah does not cry as she says goodbye to her mother Preva.

"Please take me with you," Preva pleads.

Sarah feels hard inside. Her mother did not want her to go to Hachshara, did not write to her, she was not invited to Moshe Yitzhak's wedding. No news passed between them. Mama has not seen her become a venerated cook. And now Mama is begging Sarah to take her with her. It is called a youth transport; it is impossible to take an older woman. Mama was so against the youth movement that is now saving Sarah.

"No, Mama, you cannot come with me," Sarah says firmly, not unkindly.

"At least let me give you some money. I have some saved and put away."

"No," says Sarah, "you cannot give me anything to take with me. We are allowed to take one knapsack, no money is allowed." Sarah can feel the hurt of refusing to take something. She has always been very correct, done the right thing. It is not possible to take anything. Later she will know what it is to give to one's children and to have little to give.

"I have embroidered sheets for your wedding one day, towels, pillowcases, with your initials, done with care. I will not survive Hitler. You will *never* come home again. Please take something to remember me and your home with you. Something to ease your way."

Sarah will not take and will not give. Tears will not soften her when she hugs mama, a permanent goodbye. In some ways she is proud of insisting on leaving, on having worked so hard to leave Europe, on having acted on her dream against her mother's wishes. Yet, she is not unfeeling towards her mother. What will become of her now?

Sarah's religious sister Klari has a daughter who slept with Sarah in her bed when she came to stay at her grandparents' farmhouse. Sarah missed her the most when she was in Hachshara, and the girl she left at two is now five. They reestablished their bond with the first chocolate cake that Sarah made for her.

Klari's daughter Feigele comes running over to Sarah and holds onto her waist, buries her face in Sarah's soft chest. "My mimeleh, my auntie, I want only you, Sarahleh."

After the train pulls away, Sarah cries for two days. She knows what Feigele's end will be.

She will not know Preva's until much later.

The Nazis invaded Hungary and marched the Jews to the camps. Preva and Yosef did not want to fall into the hands of the Nazis. (It was for Sarah's father that the name Yosef — Joseph — was etched on Rafi's gravestone.) The Gentile neighbors who bought their milk wanted to hide them. Yosef refused; how could a religious Jew live in the house of a Gentile, and live off his food and favors? This was not a life. He had no choice but to go with the Nazis, to go to his death as a religious Jew.

Preva took another path. She went up to the roof of the farmhouse. There was a post overhanging, under a false decorative top roof. She watched the Nazis approaching with their forced march of deported Jews. Yosef would soon join them with the three youngest girls who remained at home. She would not. She took some rope used to lead the cows to pasture, tied it around her neck and around the post, and jumped off the roof. Sarah heard that her mother had hung herself many years later when she was already an immigrant mother. Two sisters had survived and immigrated to Canada; they had seen the body before they were marched off with their father towards the waiting cattle cars.

"Please take me with you. Please take me with you. Please take me with you." These words echo in Sarah for the rest of her life.

When Sarah had severe dementia decades later and was having an operation, and didn't know where she was, a nurse asked her for her father's name for a form. "Yosef," Sarah said without hesitation.

# Early Days before Children — 1939

Ironically the Gestapo helped the group of Youth Aliyah cross the Hungarian border. They wanted the Jews to leave. They protected them and expedited their exodus.

Sarah cried until they changed trains to get across the border. Keep busy, keep busy. Yarn came out and she began knitting a gray sweater for Mordecai. He had broad shoulders; he was round, but not muscular. He was not tall, but to her, most men looked tall. No pattern was needed; she could measure his shape with her eyes. Especially since she had been in his arms.

"Wake up, Sarahleh, there is a birthday present waiting for you."

Sarah had been very nauseated with the sea crossing. Five days on the ship, the *Colorado*. Passengers slept anywhere that they could on the decks, in the crowded public spaces below, two to a bunk. Ironically there was a cow on board, meant to be a bribe for the crew members. Sarah was expected to care for it, as she was an experienced farm girl. It was comforting to hear the mooing of the cow, in the middle of the ocean, although along with the sounds and smells of home, the cow brought the ache of leaving her former life.

There was no toilet on board. Sarah went to urinate over the side of the ship, holding onto the rail; her girlfriends held a blanket out for her, and she for them. She washed her face in a bucket, combed her hair, rinsed out her mouth. She smoothed down her disheveled hair. Mordecai was waiting. She felt the excitement of his attention.

He took her elbow and guided and led her up the two flights of stairs to the deck. From the stairwell she could see that it was still dark, although the stars were disappearing. She could not spot the moon.

At the top of the stairs she immediately saw the rosy horizon, hinted shapes of...land. Home. This was her birthday gift. The date was April 21, 1939.

The group was too agitated to eat. Everyone was gathered now at the rail. They had brought up their small knapsacks, put their shoes inside as they were told to do. Blankets were left behind. Heavy coats were left behind. Extra food and water would be left behind as well.

Little boats came out to meet them. They were told that they would later have to jump into the water, swim to the lifeboats, and then keep silent. The kibbutz was their destination.

Sarah was afraid to jump, afraid to swim, afraid to be separated from Mordecai, afraid of what might meet them. There were so many stories of the British returning illegal immigrants to Europe. In the eyes of the British they were lawbreakers, these immigrants who felt that they were coming to the only home left after Europe was looking to dispose of them.

Sarah looked at the horizon and thought about her birthday. She knew that she was being given a new chance that wasn't offered to her mother, or sisters, or to Feigele. "Hitler gave me a birthday present," she joked many times.

I found out very recently that Sarah's knapsack was lost when she swam in. She never had a photograph of her parents. Mordecai did. He also had correspondence with Europe until no more letters could come. Sarah did not.

The cutting board and the rolling pins that I thought she had brought from Europe were in fact purchases from her wages in Israel. Preva was left in Europe to hang herself after trying to offer Sarah her worldly goods. There was nothing that she could equip her daughter with, except a spirit that would not give up in the face of adversity.

It became clear in the first discussion that there was only work for the men on the kibbutz. The men could stay if they would do field labor. The women could make more money in the city.

Sarah and Mordecai were left to feel that they had no choice but to live separately for a time.

"I will just have to make enough money so that you can move to the city too, Mordecai, so that we can get married." The onus was on Sarah.

He reluctantly agreed. He would earn his room and board and a few *grush* a month.

Sarah would earn ten *grush* a month as a housemaid. She was lucky; she found work almost immediately as the housemaid to an American woman who was bedridden with her third pregnancy. Joan needed someone to cook and clean, to take care of the children and to wait on her as well. The husband, Boris, was a Russian immigrant. The language in the house was a beginner's

Hebrew for all of them. So needed and busy, Sarah was happy and didn't have too much time to pine for Mordecai. She did worry about him, though.

He took buses from the kibbutz and arrived late on a Wednesday evening. He had worked all day picking field crops, and then shifting boxes in the warehouse. Sarah could tell that he had bathed, changed his clothes, and combed his hair before setting off to see her. She was touched, even though now he had a faint line of fresh perspiration under his arms, and dust all over his shoes, which he was trailing onto her immaculate floors.

She was thrilled to see him, and he ran his fingers over her hips when they hugged. Yet she was shy about how to entertain him in her place of employment. She led him into the kitchen. They didn't light the lamp, but sat in reflected light from the living room across the hall. She gave him a glass of water but was nervous about feeding him as it was not her home.

Mordecai seemed hungrier for company and to look at her than for food. She knew he wanted to kiss her and hold her, but that would have to wait until she walked him back to the bus stop.

Mordecai told her about his work schedule, that he wasn't so strong, and wanted to come to the city, to be near her, to marry her, and to work in a factory or an office. Farm work didn't suit him. She told him about the children whom she watched, speaking in Hungarian so that the household wouldn't overhear. She told about Joan, a new immigrant from America who never got out of bed, and how much she appreciated Sarah's efficiency. Money was always a topic of conversation; she was saving up so that they could rent somewhere in town. When she had enough they could marry.

Boris was suddenly standing next to them in the kitchen and he looked concerned. "You do not offer your young man a meal, a hot drink, some beer? Is this not your house, too? I am offended that you do not feel at home here. There is a goulash left from dinner, I believe."

Then he warmly held out his hand to Mordecai and introduced himself.

Sarah smiled gratefully and opened the icebox. She took out several pots and containers, and soon the kitchen was filled with the familiar aroma of her cooking. She sliced some bread for Mordecai and sat down to watch him eat. Goulash with meat and potatoes and carrots, cabbage salad, and large slices of bread, with homemade pickles.

They walked hand in hand to the bus stop. There was a dark grove of fruit trees in a private garden near the stop. Mordecai leaned against a carob tree, next to a pomegranate tree and several orange and lemon trees. He looked into her eyes and smiled. "Come to the kibbutz and stay with me in my room over Shabbat."

Mordecai is an old man, sitting in the tiny room off the kitchen in the house he has owned for thirty-five years. Sarah has demonstrated how to make homemade noodles to the young cousin who has emigrated from America. A worn wooden cutting board, a tarnished rolling pin and dough that smells like Italy, the work of her hands. Mordecai is telling about the kibbutz and the months that they lived apart just before they were married.

Sarah, who rarely stops cooking or working, sits down next to him with an amused look on her face. Some memory amuses Mordecai, off in a reverie.

He elbows her in the ribs, pinches her arm, and quips, "She used to sleep over at the kibbutz before we were married."

Sarah laughs and tries to shush him.

"No," he laughs, "she is interviewing us; she wants to know about that." He winks at me.

We have a meal together of golden chicken broth with homemade noodles, stuffed peppers with meat and rice, Israeli salad, homemade olives, and fresh fruit salad.

Sarah doesn't like the food in the retirement home where she moved after Mordecai's death.

# Marriage — 1940 and 1990

Sarah has saved up thirty *grush* and can now provide a wedding for herself and Mordecai. She has rent for about six months, but they will both need to work hard.

She arranges everything. She bakes biscuits covered with sugar and raisins. There is Kiddush wine furnished by the kibbutz.

There will be no white bridal dress, no monogrammed sheets. No one can afford a ring of any kind. Although she is not sure that she completely subscribes to socialist ideals, Mordecai does, and their reality is such that this will not be a wedding that Preva would feel comfortable participating in.

It is not religious in nature. There are no family members present at the wedding. Not a one. Sarah is not a shy young bride. She is a hard-working young woman who has experienced more of life than her sisters had when they married. She knows what she wants. A home with Mordecai.

She takes it in hand to make it happen.

Fifty years later in 1990, the three remaining children invite the extended family and close friends, and hold another wedding ceremony for their parents. The relatives fill up a small meat restaurant in Tel Aviv. We are among the guests, driving up from the air force base where Danny is doing his army service as an immigrant doctor.

Their daughter Ilana acts as the rabbi, reading from a scroll that she has written, a poem about her parents. With a fancy puffy hairdo piled on top of her head, Sarah is holding flowers and is laughing and laughing. She loves playing the part in her elegant black dress. The grandchildren, in their mid-teens mostly now, hold the marriage canopy and the others hold a long candle. Rivka and Yuval walk their parents up the aisle. When they assemble under the *chuppah*, Ilana hands her father a diamond ring to give to Sarah, who never had a proper wedding ring. He cries softly remembering the simple wedding that they had fifty years before, wiping tears from his red face. Sarah's eyes sparkle and she can't stop giggling. She holds out her finger, ready for the diamond ring. They kiss and everyone claps and hugs them; dancing breaks out. Sarah throws her bouquet to her oldest granddaughter, Lital.

Sarah wishes that her parents were here. They, victims of the Nazis, all but two of her sisters as well, and all her nieces, nephews, siblings-in-law, dead. All of Mordecai's but for two were also heaped in mass graves in Eastern Europe.

She and Mordecai had four children. Three survived the wars in Israel. They had nine grandchildren. Their grandchildren were the main fruit remaining in the Sobol and Edelman lines.

Celebrate fifty years of marriage? Absolutely.

# Spending Money — 1955

The other children in the neighborhood seem to be able to buy popsicles in the summer heat, or a bag of sweets. This is less of a problem, because Mordecai works for the Elite chocolate factory and at least on Shabbat there are chocolates to go around.

Sarah works as a laundress, a babysitter during the day, and often goes out babysitting at night. She saves small piles of change and puts them behind some unused dishes in the pantry. She tells the children that it is there for them to take, to offer the other children in the neighborhood treats as well.

One night Mordecai comes home at 9:30, late from the early shift. He is tired, too tired to speak. He sees some popsicle wrappers in the wastebasket. "Where did the children get the money for these?" he demands.

"I have been out slaving to put food on the table, to pay taxes, to pay rent, and you melt it away with popsicles?" He glares threateningly at Sarah. She is silent and tense. Going behind his back, Sarah works in ways he doesn't know about, saving money, giving a few *grushim* to the children. She wants them to have everything that other children have. She wants them to be happy as well as clean and well dressed. She has a vision of her mother trying to offer her money, of her refusing to take anything of her mother's with her to Palestine. The giving is so genuine and she is so much closer with her children. Yet she doesn't like to be caught or to be thought of as a "bad girl," not by Mordecai, and not with her children watching.

Mordecai grabs Ilana's arm; she always wants pretty things, expensive things. "Where did you get the money?"

Ilana cowers. Sarah is silent. Rivka yells at her father: "Leave her alone. Ema puts a few coins for us here in the pantry to buy a few things like the other children. It's not a crime. We don't take a lot, just a few *grush* here and there. Leave her alone now."

Mordecai seems frozen by Rivka's words and by Sarah's deception, but he feels more helpless than ever. His grip releases Ilana. Sarah shoos them off to bed.

She is left with Mordecai and a cold silence between them.

There is more money than the spending money for the children. Holding out her hand, she gives him a wad of scrunched up bills, saying quietly that she will work even harder. She does not plead her cause. The object is to work harder, so as to forget, to forget Preva offering her money, forget her children's lack of spending money, forget Mordecai's tiredness and overwork.

She goes outside to hang the laundry in the dark.

Rivka just told me that as the youngest she never lacked spending money.

She earned money the easy way, without getting a job; she was a paid slave to her siblings. Ilana was a waitress, the brothers sold flowers, and they bribed Rivka to do their menial tasks for them. She was wealthy.

# Middle-Class Necessities in the 1970s

When I got home from my Puppetry making class at the Center for the Arts, I saw that my new black, Triumph bicycle had been stolen. I was crushed. It had been a birthday present and had been the best, and fastest bike that I had ever had.

Replacing it was up to me. My parents were happy to buy me one bicycle, but not to replace it when I had left it unlocked in the yard.

I got a job as a book shelver at the local library. I earned fifty dollars a month. I wanted to buy a bicycle and a guitar and some new clothes eventually. My parents gave me twenty dollars a month, but did not buy me clothes except underwear. I was supposed to work to earn such things. Working as a shelver in a library gave me a chance to read every book on the shelves about the Holocaust, never knowing how close the story was to me.

We lived in a four-story house, it was old and looked like a barn. However, there was beautiful art decorating the walls. We had a station wagon car. Four bikes for five people. A canoe. A sailboat. Skis and sleds. We were not frivolous, we didn't have an electric lawn mower, we had one black and white TV. Almost primitive by the standards of my wealthier friends who had four cars for five people. Other people had closets full of jeans alone. I was "deprived" in my perception, or at any rate, certainly not spoiled.

When I came home from guitar lessons, I ran out to the library to shelve books. I needed a bike to get around, so I bought a cheaper one than the Triumph and was never satisfied with it. But I bought it with my own money, and only this cheap bike was possible. In an extravaganza of middle class necessities, I got to take extra curricular lessons of twenty varieties before I was eighteen. Figure skating, weaving, stitchery, skiing, horse back riding, sculpture, swimming, field biology, gymnastics, cello, recorder, piano, guitar, Hebrew, orchestra, archery. I was outstandingly mediocre at all of these non-skills.

Also we traveled a great deal. There were trips to Boston, a trip by myself to San Francisco when I was fourteen. A year in Italy. A year in England. Excursions to the theater in Milwaukee or Chicago. Visits to museums. Cross-country skiing in the winter, boating in the summer.

We didn't eat a lot of McDonald's or fast food. Never ordered pizza. We did go out to Italian restaurants sometimes, and my parents would order in Italian if the waiter was a real native. At home we had meat about five times a week. Meatloaf, hamburgers, stew, or our favorite, roast beef.

We babysat. We washed cars and mowed lawns. I did all of those at various times.

Why did I leave these comforts, luxuries, delights? I don't know. I know that some of my immigrant friends feel a tremendous urge to visit the comfort of "home" long after their parents have aged and moved out of their childhood homes, and have new family configurations. When you go back you can no longer find the spending money to go out for coffee, to the theater or to buy books on Amazon.

My best friend Martha calls my parents' home when I am taking care of my father in his dementia, three weeks before he dies.

"Judith isn't home. She's out buying books with my credit card," Dad quips.

"Nothing ever changes," Martha and my father laugh.

# Ironies of Immigration

You leave home in order to come home.
You leave home and when you go back to visit, it is no longer home.

You lose your fluency in your mother tongue as you learn fluency in another language.

Whenever you speak publicly in one language you can only think of the other language or absurdly, high school French pops into mind when you're struggling for a word.

You can't help a second-grader with her homework.

Your children have a bigger vocabulary than you do.

You may not be able to read signs, maps or menus.

You show up for parties at the wrong time.

You wear the wrong thing.

You give the wrong gift. I gave all my cousins' children meaningful Jewish objects for their weddings; they preferred cash, which I saw as impersonal.

Your parents may rebel against you for leaving them.

Your parents age faster, because every time you see them, they have aged.

You cannot read or write when you are in your forties.

Your collective memories — the events represented by Jewish and national holidays — are the same as everyone else's.

Your private memories are different than everyone else's and culturally incomprehensible to the natives of your adopted country.

The news happens at lightning speed in the Middle East; you limit yourself to hearing it once a day — that is more than enough.

All roads lead to the Land of Israel; just stay off the roads.

You move to Israel, and a synonym for a perfectly heavenly society in Hebrew is "America!"

# Chicken Soup and Stray Cats — 1955

Rafi answers the door and Shmuelik from across the road shuffles in the doorway.

"Can you send your Ema; my mother is not well and is asking for her," Shmuelik asks conversationally.

In the 1950s in Israel, there aren't a lot of luxuries, nor a necessity for them. Neighbors feel more like family if the niceties are left aside.

Rafi calls out, "Ema, come quick, Dora across the street isn't well. She sent Shmuelik."

"What? What?" This is a rhetorical question, knowing that she won't get a straight answer from a teenage boy. With a pat on Rafi's shoulder, she crosses the street, confident that he will have the good sense to offer the younger boy a sugar cookie and some juice while she is gone.

She goes straight to Dora. Dora is wincing in pain; it is her stomach. The men in her family are unable to help her. Sarah speaks soothingly to her. Some herbal tea from lemon grass and mint growing by the pavement should help. A wet washcloth on Dora's head, reassurances soothe her to sleep.

Just as important as the patient is her pride, and Sarah will cover for her, make her house presentable in case a doctor comes by, or another neighbor with a pot of soup. All the neighbors in this simple complex have very little, but it is a matter of pride to present a clean and efficiently run home to each other. Cookies appear as if by magic, there is always food for company, everything is always in its place, with little to clutter the two-room apartments.

Raisa, a neighbor who also works at the Elite chocolate factory, comes by with some chicken soup and the two women chat.

Sarah tells Raisa how her mother, Preva, was the neighborhood medicine woman. She was called for births, and sick babies, fevers, coughs, colds, flu and worse. She had remedies, usually soups and care and the secret of touch. Preva knew the magic of just listening to a woman's troubles, and seeing into her eyes, seeing her beauty under her head scarf and bowed shoulders. Healing took place when she held their hands, or rubbed their foreheads or shoulders, to wash them down gently, to pat them, to allow them some space to cry quietly when no one else could hear. The tears helped the most, falling on her linen busom.

Hungry children were a magnet to Preva; she used to visit widows who were adjusting to a new reality, and she would adopt travelers, students, even the homeless. Taking after his mother and grandmother, Rafi's kindness extends to sick cats and dogs roaming the neighborhood. New immigrants, family, no matter how distant, are all fostered by Sarah's kitchen and with Rafi's attention. Mordecai complains if she spends too much money on food for company, but he is pacified by Sarah's kindness when his family appears.

His brother Tuvye and sister-in-law Sarenka arrive nine years after he did. Tuvye's Sarah shows signs of her ordeal, having survived Auschwitz, and then the camps in Cyprus. Their older son Alexander suffers from asthma. Sarenka gets a job immediately at a dress shop. There is a department for fitting brassieres and Sarenka finds that she has a talent for this. Many have tattooed numbers from the camps on their arms just as she does. They want to look elegant but feel branded, disgraced. She treats them like royalty, even when she bosses them or bullies them. They are beautiful to her; their tattoos are a badge of courage. Caressing them and pandering to them, she sells them black bras to make them feel extra special, when she can read that their souls are extra injured.

Tuvye works as a tailor.

Alexander has a terrible cough that won't go away. The mud of Cyprus internment camps has been his playground. He turns blue when he coughs, and wheezes even on the sunny, warm winter days in Tel Aviv. He gets fresh air, good food, and sunshine, and yet he is too tired to roughhouse with Rafi or to accompany his cousin Yuval on his errands. Ilana likes having cousins, but Alex is always coughing and tires easily.

Sarah has her housework, she is pregnant again, and takes in four neighborhood children as well as bits of laundry. Every night she has a hot meal for Mordecai when he comes home from the factory. They have Sarenka and Tuvye and the two boys living with them.

Sarah takes Alex in with her other infant charges. He grows weaker and seems to have trouble breathing.

Inquiries are made and she finds out that there is a doctor for breathing troubles in Tel Aviv. Leaving her charges with Dora, who also looks after children, she wraps Alex up warmly and takes him across town to the doctor. She takes a number. Hugging him and singing, she plays with him until he falls asleep on her chest. Finally the doctor calls her in. Alex has severe asthma; he will have to come twice a week for inhalations and checkups.

On the third visit, the doctor notices that Alex and Sarah don't have the same surname. "Who are you to this child?" he asks.

"The aunt."

"How do you get here from the Elite neighborhood?"

"Buses."

"And you are just the aunt?"

"When we came here, there was not even an aunt for my children. I would take six buses if I had to. You will make him well, I'm sure."

The women in the neighborhood also remark on Sarah's devotion to Alex. They criticize her sister-in-law for being more interested in her work than in her sick child. They criticize her "lady" appearance, but Sarah defends her to them.

"She has been in the camps, we can't even know what she suffered there. We all have sisters and brothers who went through the same thing."

Sarah has recently received notice that Nelly and one other sister, she isn't sure which one, have survived the camps and are living in Canada. She doesn't know who has survived and who has perished.

There is a sense of superiority of the *vatikim* ("veterans") who have been in the country for ten or more years, compared with the *olim chadashim* ("new immigrants") who are just arriving after the war. It is a mixed emotion, of fear, sadness, and jealousy of those who settle in quickly and get jobs, after the veterans have lived in relative poverty for ten years.

One day when Sarah has taken Alex for his inhalations and shots and is particularly tired, Sarenka comes home from the shop with a package.

"You have been very good to me. I know that you don't want any thank-yous, but you have been better to me than any sister would ever be. Here..."

Inside the package is a bra and girdle set of the finest quality. Sarah blushes with pleasure. In one fluid motion she embraces her sister-in-law and hands her Alex to hold.

When I came to Israel many years later, I was not even told about Tuvye's existence; I only met him for the first time at Mordecai's funeral. He was my father's cousin and I did not know about him, or very little. There was so little family, and yet Mordecai and his only brother in Israel were not in touch. Countless people lost a lot of family members in the Holocaust. Mordecai's brother's and mother's names are etched on his gravestone, as they have no marker in their mass grave, and Tuvye comes to visit him only after he is laid to rest.

What had they fought about? Everything. But there was a secret source of tension gnawing at their bond.

Trying to make peace between the brothers — this was the only thing that Sarah demanded. *Sholem* ("peace") was her motto. Peace, after her rift with her mother. Peace after Hitler had torn up Europe. Peace after the War of Independence in 1948 when five armies attacked fledgling Israel. Peace between brothers. Internal peace. Eternal peace in the City of Peace.

# The Brother

"My parents had an accent, but so did everyone's parents," says Rivka, her dimples showing:

Having immigrant parents was the norm. Ephraim Kishon said that Hebrew is the mother tongue that parents learn from the children. And that is true. I corrected my mother's Hebrew, but she never pronounced things any differently than she had before.

My brother Rafi was my idol. He was a 'Gingy,' had red hair and freckles and the personality to go with it. We shared the living room as our bedroom, and we stayed up late at night talking.

He was a rascal, always pulling practical jokes. He stole fruit from the neighbors' trees. He made everyone laugh.

But he had a serious side. During the Six-Day War, he was a soldier. His brigade was not called up for action. He was sitting out the war and feeling frustrated. Everyone heard that Jerusalem and the Wall of the Temple were now in our hands. He was so thrilled and touched. He volunteered for duty. He did not have to go to the Sinai. An older member of his unit was supposed to go. This man had a wife and a child. Rafi said, "I am a bachelor, I am young, I will go." Twenty years old he remained.

"Was he afraid?" I ask.

She looks dreamy.

He was a redhead; are they afraid of anything? He was also very young. I don't know if young people ever believe that they can be killed.

He was climbing out of a helicopter in the Sinai desert, which had just been captured from Egypt after they attacked us. A sniper's bullet shot him as he put one foot down. Apparently he was not killed immediately. We were told after his death that when he arrived in the hospital he was still alive. But we were only informed of the tragedy two days after he was shot, and had already died. The war ended and we heard nothing from him and began to worry. The country was in an emergency situation and communication was bad.

Every year at the graveside I meet the family — Sarah, Rivka, Ilana, Yuval, their spouses and children. If a photographer took a picture at the grave every year, the photos would show the children growing and changing every year. The lens that I see them through is like that yearly graveside photographer's. I also get to look through the lens at every wedding and at the birth of every great-grandchild.

Rivka always says, "Rafi would laugh at me so much to see me as a mother. He always taunted me that I was too ugly to ever get married." It is frustrating to her that she never got to show her brother that she does indeed have a husband and children.

Her children and grandchildren are interesting to look at: blonde, curly-headed, dark skin. Rafi probably knew that she was beautiful, too, and that is why he called her ugly. Like any good brother.

Rivka became a grandmother at age forty-five. None of the grandchildren were redheads.


# Mysteries


Sculptures that form a bridge between imagination and reality are my mother's most beautiful pottery. As she ages, her work gets freer and more colorful. She does whimsical teapots with backgrounds of castles. I have one in my living room.

What is the secret libation inside her teapots? What is the secret of choosing to live life away from the background of the castles and turrets of my youth? Why did I come to live in Israel? Home was not defined first and foremost as Jewish. Perhaps before that came art, music, literature, nature. Why would I go so very far away?

The most profound loss caused by living here is that my brothers have never seen and shared my life, and I see very little of theirs. Even with all the tensions in Safta Sarah's family, I feel true envy that they are a family.

There are mysteries, though.

There was something that Mordecai was holding on to in Europe. But everyone was dead, weren't they, and I couldn't ask too much; it was picking at a sore spot. What did the two brothers who survived the war, Mordecai and Tuvye, fight about? If they were the only two left, how could they not seek each other out? I remember that there was a relative in Europe to whom Milt and my father Murray sent checks. Who was it?

If someone were to question me too closely about how I could possibly abandon my family in America, I would become breathless. I did not know this callous side of myself. How *did* I do it?

There are mysteries in everyone's lives. What tipped Sarah's mind about marrying Mordecai, when he was a yeshiva student and not very communicative or romantic? And what am I supposed to do if there is ever a war or a terrorist attack? What can you tell me about that, Mordecai?

If you were alive now, I would ask you how to cope.

# June 1967

Sarah runs out of the house, barely stopping to close the door. She runs after Rivka on her way to school. Rivka averts her eyes and doesn't speak to her mother; how can she follow her to school when she is in the twelfth grade? She eyes her mother's bedroom slippers and dowdy housecoat. She stops. "Go home, Ema. You can't follow me."

"Rivkeleh, we haven't had a word from Rafi. I am afraid. I can't be alone. They may come knock on our door with bad news..." She cries, but doesn't sob. The Six-Day War ended two whole days ago. Not a word. It was a brief, dramatic and fierce war.

Rivka turns to go to school, turns back and looks longingly at her mother. She would like to give in to fear, too. Her mother has always been so careful of her children's safety. She watched them cross the dirt road outside their home, she warned them about falling. Especially Rafi who climbed trees, rode a motorcycle too fast, and stayed out late at night.

Rivka hugs her mother and turns into the schoolyard. "Go home, Ema," she says firmly.

Sarah hesitates, and then reluctantly turns to go home.

There are soldiers waiting at the entrance to the apartment building. They have solemn looks on their faces and they are looking at her.

"Palestine," she remembers herself saying, dreaming. Pleading with her parents. The land of freedom, where Jews can hold their heads up high.

"My son is dead." Abyss, emptiness, falling off a cliff. "Come in the house," she says to the soldiers, sparing them the task of having to say the words.

Sarah spends the next twenty-five years working without stopping until she can't work anymore.

# II: Limping and Flying

## Immigrant Mothers — 1983

When I was pregnant with my first child, I was expecting a girl, and even though new machines with ultrasound can tell which sex the fetus is, we had chosen not to be told. So why was I expecting a girl? Because I was a girl among brothers, because I was a feminist. She had to be a girl.

Such a modern mother — when told that the labor will be long, I go out to the garden and folkdance to bring on heavy labor. The next-door neighbor in Manchester, England, taught me the Highland Fling. Waves of pain come with the high feeling of dancing, barefoot on the grass, of taking control of the uncontrollable. Then walking, up and down the garden, leaning heavily on Danny when the pains come.

I labor like a pioneer facing the hardships of a new land.

The baby is put into my arms. I look down at the baby and see a penis. "It can't be; aren't all babies girls?" I think with the foggy, otherworldly thoughts of a new mother. It is a boy: we will name him Raphael after Rafi. I expected a girl and got a Raphael.

Ten days are filled with the irregular rhythm of bodily needs. Sore and dripping everywhere, even from the eyes. Slowly taking on care for the baby's body, before my body is even in a rhythm. Breast-feeding is painful at first, but Raphael is very good at it, and my mothering instincts come gushing in with the milk with ferociousness. I air my sore nipples in the back garden in the hot July sun. My breasts are engorged to the size of watermelons. I send a picture to the relatives in Israel showing me, bloated and double-chinned, breast-feeding the baby when he is less than a day old. There is no vanity about how I appear to them. My baby is like an offering at the ancient Temple.

The baby won't be named until the circumcision ceremony, which is postponed because the baby is mildly jaundiced. This is normal. Three weeks go by before the breast-milk jaundice disappears.

I telephone Sarah in Israel. I haven't spoken to her in more than a year and I know that my phone call is out of the blue. I want to express my pride and delight in this baby. I feel so powerful, so in touch with the flow of life. I want this to be a healing gift to Sarah and I want to say that to her, but I know that my Hebrew isn't up to it. Yet there is no other language that we have in common.

"This is Yehudit calling from England, Sarah."

"Yehuditkeleh??"

"Yes, how are you?"

"Fine, fine. How's the baby?" They have received the picture.

"He is wonderful. Eats very well." I know that this is the most important thing to her, and it is to me as well. "Sarah...we want to name him Raphael, Raphi, after your Rafi."

"Yes, yes, of course you do. You are a good girl."

"It's alright with you?"

"Yes, of course." The deep understanding is unspoken. It is clear, it had to be. That is his name.

We later receive a letter from Ilana, Sarah's daughter. Each letter of her brother's name, my son's name, is written in a different color.

# Immigrant Mother — 1984

The movers in Manchester, England, are cheerful and experienced men with grimy work overalls. Our ancient falling-apart armchair is plunked out on the grass; they give me a radio from their car, and tell me to make a "cup of tea."

"Set here, Love, and when we are done, we'll chuck out the chair fer ya."

The radio reports that there is hyperinflation in Israel, that the Peres government is failing or falling or both.

I flag down the moving men, who are not Jewish.

"Stop! Put it all back, we're not going!" I yell towards the movers.

"Don't worry, Love, they *all* say that when they move to Israel. Now sit back and switch to a nice music station and stop listening to that rubbish!"

Raphael, who has just taken his first steps, Danny and I make the move to Israel, despite the latest politics. The first six weeks are spent in an absorption center, in limbo. It is the done thing to complain about these basic accommodations. We call it the "Hilton," and believe it is, but are eager to set up more permanent housing, to get jobs, to find friends. Danny has sorted out work almost immediately; he just has to figure out which city to live in. I spend most of the days in the park, playing with Raphael. The first month is euphoria.

This euphoria doesn't seem to see that we can't afford paper diapers, and wash the cloth ones by hand in the bathtub, that we don't have a car and go everywhere with baby, carriage and shopping baskets, on buses. The heat pulsates off the pavement. In the absorption center there is no phone, and the public one is usually broken. Messages don't get delivered efficiently, if at all. I prefer to play in the park than to think about looking for work. Raphi has a delightful sense of fun and of humor. He hides under the slide, pretends to eat flowers, chases pigeons pretending he is a lion roaring. Later, when he is a soldier in Israel, I keep thinking of his babyhood in England and the early days in Israel.

Danny is out interviewing for work and getting his reaccredidation as a doctor. I am left with my toddler, who is beginning to get bored with just my company, and have errands at various government offices. One morning, I feed Raphi cereal and put him in the stroller to take the first of three buses to get an Israeli driver's license, although it will be a year before we buy a car, and then it is a gift from my parents. The bus stops but the driver is impatient while I struggle to close the stroller. I am wearing my purple flowered sundress and my long hair in a ponytail. The driver asks if I want a youth discount ticket.

"Be serious," I say, "this baby is mine. I'll take an adult ticket."

On the third bus, I am feeling dizzy from traveling and the baby is crying. He vomits his morning cereal all over my purple dress, the stroller, my hair and himself. People on the bus complain. I go into automatic pilot, stunned heroic mode.

The driver's registration office is not far from the bus stop. I ask for a bathroom. A ten-minute walk on the other side of the lot. I wash down Raphi, calm him and change him. He is fresh and clean, ready to sleep in the stroller that is washed but wet. I didn't bring a change of clothes for myself. I dab at the stains on my dress with warm water; the smell won't wash out. So I march ahead into the office. Perhaps this will make the clerk deal with me faster.

Another bus, another day, another office. A woman on the bus compliments me that the baby is so fat. As I do not have a lot of grandparents or aunts and uncles crooning around my baby, this stranger's interest makes me smile and I brag that it is all breast milk. The woman says she doesn't think that it is possible to get so fat on breast milk and turns to a man standing next to her, announcing, "This baby is fat on breast milk."

The man eyes my figure. I am in my mid-twenties, have large breasts and am taller than average. I have a large frame but am well proportioned for my size. He looks displeased. "I don't think it's good for the woman's figure to breast-feed," replies the man.

Soon the *entire* bus is discussing the baby's size, my breast size, and the pros and cons of breast-feeding.

"It is best for the baby, period!"

"But is it best for the woman's figure?"

"What does that have to do with it?"

"Well, look at her, she has a healthy-looking chest, I'd say."

Adamant and opinionated, the discussion goes on with yelling and gesticulations even as I get off the bus.

A stranger stops me and touches my arm. "Put a hat on that baby, the sun is beating down on his head."

I do so ambivalently, and walk about thirty yards. An elderly woman points at the baby, "Take that hat off, he needs some sunshine!"

Well, I guess I don't need to miss family here, I think to myself. They all think they are my family.

Once at the office, the line is interminable. Heat and exhaustion overpower me and I can see hours of waiting ahead. I pull Raphi's thumb out of his mouth and he screams. "Excuse me," I say boldly to the next fifteen people in line. I move ahead and they let me for the most part. Gently, I ease Raphi's thumb into his mouth and rub his cheek. "Thanks," I whisper, "I owe you one."

# Job Interviews — 1984 and 2004

I am a professional woman. I keep telling myself that so that I will believe it. My main occupation seems to be to push the stroller around Kfar Sava. There isn't a sidewalk on our street and I have to push Raphi, who is the size of a baby elephant, uphill on our street, in the middle of the road.

Twice I have job interviews with Raphi in tow. It is a good thing that he is there, because my self-confidence has been left at Heathrow airport. At least one of my tangible achievements is present. Yet, having a baby with me makes me doubt my ability to work. Friends encourage me to go see the mayor of Kfar Sava. I have never heard of such a thing, but am getting desperate for a job, if not for the money, although that is a central issue as well. If I don't work, then I am a fraud, not really making it in Israel. I'm not even really here. So somehow I make an appointment and go to see the mayor. I splurge on a small bag of pretzels to keep Raphi happy. He is reasonable if I am.

The mayor asks me what work I do. What I did was Jewish education, but that seems like impossibility in Israel. Another irony. I tell him that I am a community worker. He makes a phone call to an English-speaking social worker and asks her to show me the social service department. He arranges a time and a day. He warmly welcomes me to Kfar Sava, coos to the baby.

Years later we became warm friends, when I was directing a national program for children with special needs, giving them a Jewish education and a bar or bat mitzvah ceremony. He was the local dignitary at the ceremony. Sometimes Raphi would come to help, or to read Torah. I think I forgot to remember my humble beginning with the stroller and the pretzels.

I telephone a school that emphasizes Jewish identity in education, Tali in Hod HaSharon, the town next to Kfar Sava. I tell the principal on the phone that I am an experienced youth worker in informal Jewish education. He asks me if I can make pedagogical games on the holidays. I say that I ran a resource library for four years in England. He asks me to come for an interview. I say yes, but there are the obstacles of the child care and no transportation. He says, "I'll be right over to pick you up; wait outside with the baby."

Ten minutes later he drives up in a dusty blue car. He gets out and folds the stroller into his car. This is a principal of a school? I ask myself which planet I am on.

We arrive at the school. He holds the baby on his lap, and takes an orange from a bowl. He peels the orange and feeds sections to Raphi, expertly, keeping everyone happy. He barely asks me any questions, he is enjoying holding the baby too much — what a good eater! "How's your written Hebrew?" and "Can you start tomorrow?" He never does find me a paid job, but he gives me three months of having a reason to get up in the morning. He applies to the Ministry of Immigration to get payment for my small salary. We wait for a reply. Before I can make a resource library, which really excites me, they keep asking me to fill in for English teachers. This is not of any interest to me and seems like such an immigrant profession: teach your native language. I am not trained as an English teacher.

I put Raphi into day care and show up at work every morning. I hate teaching English. The children are unruly and jump out the windows and conk each other over the head with large knapsacks. My informal methods don't work. Formal methods don't work. I wanted to make educational games. I wait three months in vain for a salary, but I feel so grateful to the principal for the interview, for the orange and holding the baby, and the welcome to the world of the useful that I volunteer during this time.

Immigration is like a game of chutes and ladders except the rule is that no one must tell you the rules.

Twenty years later I am again in the mayor's office. This time I speak Hebrew well and I am explaining to the mayor that I want to build a village for adults with special needs. He has seen my work with those with special needs, and agrees to be a partner in this endeavor and to help to designate municipal land for the project. I am still playing chutes and ladders, but now am learning the changing rules.

# Acclimatization — 1984

We move into our new apartment in a suburb of Tel Aviv. It is rented but large for three people. It is part of a concrete mass of apartment buildings, six to eight floors high, with four families on each floor. It is a three-bedroom apartment, with a large kitchen, by Israeli standards. The rent is a quarter of Danny's monthly salary. There is no phone, and we still have no car.

Mordecai gives us a check for the first month's rent. "There was no one to receive us when we arrived in Israel," he says. He is very moved to give the check, and I am to receive it. I feel that this makes us more of a family; we still have some polite distance. I invite the entire family to a meal, with vegetable pies and lasagna. They are surprised to be served a dairy meal. It is Raphi's second birthday; I am five months pregnant. They all sing and dance and Raphi works his toy tape recorder by himself. All the adults play musical chairs. Ilana and Rivka have a talking contest to see who can outtalk whom. Rivka wins hands down.

Ilana buys Raphi his first tricycle. "I want it to be from me," she says with feeling. Gaggles of them crowd around me and coo over my newly budding stomach.

A few months later, they all gather together again in the apartment after Raphi's little sister Shira is born. About eighty people are in the little living room. Everyone brings a cake, a plate of hummus; many people bring whole cooked meals to put in the refrigerator for later. I have sold my girlhood cello to be able to afford a refrigerator. The handle reminds me of the bridge of the cello. The spiritual has become the material in Israel. And vice versa.

My parents help us to buy a car. We would desperately like to buy an apartment, but don't have the funds. The car is small, but shiny and new. It smells good and feels safe to transport the children in. It makes life much easier.

One day Danny returns home immediately after setting out for work. I am lying in bed, feeding the baby. "The car is not in its place. It has been stolen." I am shocked and begin to cry. "Don't cry, it's only a car," Danny says kindly. "No one was hurt."

"But how will you get to work? How will we get anywhere? On buses with two children who cannot walk far?" I think of the trip to the drivers' registration center. I think of my parents' generous gift.

Raphi is in day care. It costs an eighth of Danny's salary, and I am not working steadily yet, but can't even think of going out to work if Raphi isn't in childcare. Catch-22, it seems that I can't work until he is in childcare, but he can't be in childcare until I have the income of steady work. All two-year-olds seem to go to nursery school (*gan*) in Israel; there is no stigma, and I enjoy that. One day I go to pick him up and am informed that the price has nearly doubled. I tell the childcare worker that I will have to withdraw him from nursery school. The prospect of working seems to be dangling above my head, now completely out of my grasp. I have learned that I am not a stay-at-home mother, that working is essential for me. I burst into tears, grab the baby in one arm, Raphi in the other and run down the street fuming. There must have been a trail of smoke.

Soon the day care teacher and another mother, named Shlomit, appear at my door. "We know you are a new immigrant, we will pay the difference." They really mean it. I feel touched, angry, confused and ashamed. "No, no, we can take care of it." We'll stop buying meat and fruit, no newspapers. Forget the dream of disposable diapers, chickens for Shabbat and gas to run the car. I'll figure it out, maybe I'll work full-time to pay for day care for two children.

There are many phone calls to look for work. There is a public payphone outside the building. It takes about five minutes to get down to place a phone call. Stroller in the elevator, toddler holding on. Toys and bottles falling. Often the phone is out of order, or there is a long line. Mostly new immigrants like me. I have made a telephone friend, whose last name is "Frankenstein." I know all of Frankenstein's intimate details. She has made a gynecologist appointment for Thursday. She had an argument with her mother-in-law yesterday. She can't pay certain bills. Her parents are very upset that she has come to live in Israel and doesn't even have a phone at home for them to call her on.

It is my turn to use the phone. The line has disappeared, the phone seems to be in working order today, and I have enough telephone tokens. I dial, the person I need to set up an interview with is *in* and has answered the phone. "This is too good to be true," I say to myself triumphantly. I am proud how well I cope without a phone.

"Hello, yes, I can meet you at ..." Just then the toddler runs into the street.

I slam the phone and catch him just before he gets away from the curb. I turn around, and someone else has taken the phone and is dialing. I put up a fight and teach Raphi some colorful vocabulary, but it is no use.

I will call later when Danny is home. Of course, when he is home, the people I have to make appointments with may also have left work.

I can't afford to get a babysitter to make phone calls to look for work, because I don't have a job…

Challenges seem to crop up together, a whole field of them. Within weeks of the birth, the car being stolen, the price war at the *gan*, Danny's father takes ill and needs a gallbladder operation. Danny leaves the next day; he doesn't want his family in England to feel he has abandoned them. My parents arrive from the States to see the baby. This is a great joy, but a great strain for me as a new mother of two. My mother is making dinner and she can't find anything in my kitchen. We have to hurry because we are invited out for coffee and the babysitter is coming. Some friends from my home state of Wisconsin, who have also immigrated to Israel, have just moved to Kfar Sava like us. I forget that I told them to come to eat when they have unpacked. That was before Danny was called away. My mother is yelling to me to hurry and dress.

I am pulling my tights on, and trying to find a shirt that is not stained with breast milk. My skirt doesn't fit, but I don't allow myself to take time to care.

The doorbell rings. My friends have arrived, with their baby, and announce they are hungry after a day of unpacking. There are four small pieces of fish and four small potatoes. I am in my bedroom, and think that no one can hear me. I mutter to myself, "I can't take any more." I see that Raphi has opened my bedroom door; everyone is crowding in the doorway looking to me for guidance. I pull up my tights and try to welcome my friends. But they feel unwelcome and leave swiftly.

After a night of little sleep, coping on my own and struggling to wake up to feed the baby three times, the same childcare worker who raised the price and then offered to pay decides that she has had enough, and quits. Danny is still in England. My parents are leaving Sunday and I have a freelance job at a museum (work which I so desparately want!) on Monday. The parents of the playgroup decide to remove their children immediately to another setting. I don't know how I'll take Raphi to the new playgroup on Monday and make it to work at the museum on time.

I have found a part-time babysitter for the baby, who is now three months old. Iris is a beautiful young Yemenite mother of a three-year-old. She is a religious woman who wears a headscarf, and a very caring person. I remember the babysitter in England who was anti-Semitic. Already I feel at home.

The night before my parents leave I admit to them that Raphi got lice at his playgroup, a fact of life in Israel. My parents are frantic and want me to check their hair for lice. Our precious last minutes together are spent with me going through their hair with a lice comb. "All clear," I smile at them. They leave and I am left alone. Danny is out of the country still. "All clear," I sigh to myself.

The next day, having left the children with a neighbor, I arrive, by bus, fifteen minutes late. My boss, who is single and always impeccably dressed, is frantic. "We had to show them a movie to keep them busy while we were waiting for you. You look a mess — didn't you have time to put on makeup this morning?"

I smile to the group and begin to guide them around the museum, willing my automatic pilot to take over. But it doesn't. I keep thinking, do I own any makeup? Can I afford makeup? I am not very good at putting it on. I have always preferred the natural look. But I also need time to look in the mirror. I hope that milk doesn't leak and make a telling spot on my bust, which is one and a half times its normal watermelon size. This is not a time when being attractive is a great concern. I think of my boss, the tourists, the children, my parents, Danny and the whole world and wish that they'd do the opposite of being attracted to my attention, and just LEAVE ME ALONE.

A fire breaks out on the second floor of the apartment building when Shira is five months old. The intercom buzzes and I answer it. There is some incomprehensible yelling, by schoolgirls. The frantic and urgent Hebrew doesn't click and I decide it's a prank. They ring again and again, until I finally make out the word "fire." We are on the sixth floor. When the door is opened it is clear that the stairwell is filled with smoke. Hand-calligraphed marriage contract in hand, I grab the baby, and start running down the stairs. The smoke gets thicker and I have trouble breathing.

"I am twenty-eight years old, and I am going to die," I think to myself. I have to throw the marriage contract into the smoke so that I can maneuver the baby under my shirt to protect her. While walking down the stairs, I become overcome by smoke. I change direction and begin climbing the stairs. The smoke hasn't reached the eighth floor yet. The building has mostly emptied out, but I knock on a neighbor's door, still two floors above the smoke, and she lets me in. We run to the window, and see massive crowds have congregated below. There are several fire trucks. I yell down to send up a ladder. The fire workers signal that it will be OK. However, they do not send up a ladder. I see that Danny is below with Raphi. He leaves Raphi and approaches the building, but comes out a few minutes later choking. He signals to me that he must stay with Raphi.

"So that one parent will survive," is what he explains later.

I sit down to breast-feed Shira, so that she will have some comfort before we die. So that she will not suffer. I contemplate tying sheets together and lowering the baby down. Later I am terrified by what could have happened if I had attempted this. We are saved by a lone firefighter, who is covered with sweat and is black from soot. "Follow me," he says and leads us down the smoky stairs. He doesn't communicate that the fire is out and doesn't think about protecting the baby from smoke inhalation. Again I tuck her instinctively under my shirt.

We are taken to the hospital for smoke inhalation, and then released. But they've told me that I have toxins in in my milk, and that I can't breast-feed the baby for two days. I wipe the black streaks from my nose and from the baby's. A friend of mine, Gingy, breast-feeds her baby and mine for two days. She is the friend who moved to Kfar Sava when Danny was out of the country and my life was unraveling. Here she is nurturing us back to life when we have been burnt…

A week later I am guiding another group around the museum. I get to the section on Poland and smell smoke. I ask one of the visitors if there is an unusual smell. "Something burning," he says. With outward calm I guide them to the basement, for an early coffee break, but I don't use the elevator. Clandestinely I alert my boss that the museum may be on fire. It turns out to be a lightbulb and they all laugh, "You thought there was a pogrom in Poland, and Poland's burning." I catch hell for the early coffee break and for breaking museum routine.

The insurance money for the car brings in a few extra thousand dollars. We buy an old car, and can use the extra towards an apartment. This together with the immigrant loans available to us from the government are enough. We find a cheap second-hand apartment in the building next door. We can't afford to hire movers, but we also don't own very much. A few friends come over. We move the oven first, plug it in and put a pizza in to cook. By the time the baby's crib has been set up, and the sofa hauled in, the pizza is ready, and everybody sits in the new apartment to eat. There is a phone in the new apartment. I rarely see Frankenstein anymore.

Danny sees private patients in the evenings at the new apartment. I am working every day at the museum now — I have been hired full-time. I commute to Tel Aviv, a forty-five minute drive in traffic in the morning. Danny works a split day. He is home to take the children from day care at lunchtime, and to feed them and put them down to nap. This saves on childcare bills, and on parental guilt.

The children are just waking up when I walk in the door at four o'clock, and Danny walks out for the afternoon shift. The playground is our destination every afternoon. I am too tired to talk to the other fathers and mothers, but not too tired to give the children attention. If they gave out PhDs for swinging two-year-olds on the swing, or playing kickball, I would have a higher degree. Just so that no one, including myself, will think that I am neglecting them.

At seven p.m., I am ready for bed, but Danny's private patients come then. "What did you make for dinner?" they ask. "Why are your kids in pajamas already?" "Why aren't your kids in pajamas already?" The baby takes her potty and clunks it down next to a patient and proceeds to pee in the pot. I like her sense of humor.

# Resettling — 1989

Just as soon as we really get settled, Danny is called up to the army. That means leaving all that has sprouted roots. Most over-the-hill immigrants over the age of twenty-one serve for three months. Yet, as a doctor, at age thirty-four he is called up for a year and a half. His monthly army pay will be enough to feed one person. I am working very part-time as a youth worker, having left the museum; my salary is enough to buy falafel once a week. We soon realize that if we are to survive the army period both financially and as a family unit — which is key to our survival — we will all have to move to army housing on the air force base in the Negev desert. The Negev is literally a desert, brown plains with desert brush surrounded by sandy mountains.

We will have to leave our new friends, my job, and our synagogue and become an army family. We will have to uproot our seedling roots. I grew up during the time of the Vietnam War. All I know is that anything military is abhorrent to me, and now I will be a military wife. Danny leaves first. Two months later, I have to move the household and the children down to the desert.

The movers arrive. They claim that they don't pack glass or dishes. I call Linda, SOS, "help!" She is at work.

Baby Shira and I watch the movers load the last of our cartons onto the army moving van. A rare photo from 1920 of my grandmother and her sisters falls off the truck and breaks on the pavement. One of the workmen sneers, "Oh, look, Grandma fell on the floor." They laugh.

I sweep the floor, kiss the mezuzah, take the children to the toilet. Just then Linda runs up to kiss us goodbye. She is wearing her work clothes and has two little children on her bicycle. We hug and I cry. I cannot fathom why I am living in Israel. I am leaving my best friends, my community, and my job and going to live a military life in a desert. A friendless, jobless desert without a family.

Linda waves bravely as, armed with sandwiches and bottles and drinks and lots of tissues for their noses and my eyes, we pile into the car. Shira's guinea pig is in a cage between the children. The guinea pig squeaks and scatters sawdust all over the car. It is a beastly hot day. We do not have air-conditioning in the car. The children sing, then fight, then fall asleep.

Four hours later we arrive at the end of what was supposed to be a two-hour drive. There is a security check at the gate. My documents are investigated and recorded. "Are you Green's woman?" they ask. *No, I have my own name and I am my own woman.* But I do want them to let me in. This security check is standard procedure for the next year and a half. I am never waved through. Every day we are woken up to the siren and at nightfall it sounds as well. The children remain asleep. "Welcome home to the military," a siren wails.

During this year and a half in isolation, I will have very little contact with Sarah and her family; if I were to see them more, it might save me from spiraling downward.

# Chinuch Means Making Anew

Education is *chinuch* in Hebrew, making anew, like the word for Chanukah, rededicating. It is a different sort of education that my children receive in Israel. Raphi does not learn how to be polite like he would have in England. He does not learn to be politically correct as he would have in the liberal Midwest of America where I grew up. We have a mythological family story that before a trip to England we practiced Politeness. "Please pass the salt": we repeated it over and over. In England, at Grandma's and Grandpa's, Raphi performs beautifully: "Please pass the salt," he says. We all beam. "Oh, *shit*, I dropped it." Eyes are on me: who else would have taught him that?

Raphi's first grade is in the desert town of Arad; he is bused there from the army base where we live temporarily. On the first day there is a ceremony to which parents are invited. Children all wear blue and white. He has a new bookbag on his back, a slight potbelly, a big boy haircut and a big grin with new teeth. Each first-grader is paired up with a Big Child from sixth grade. A boy with blonde hair takes Raphi gently by the hand and leads him in a parade through a shiny archway, into the halls of learning.

I notice as they sing "My Israel Is Beautiful and Blossoming" and "Land of Torah" that Raphi knows every single word to every song in Hebrew. He has received something from his *gan yeladim* (nursery school) years in Israel, which I never had. I sob. The other Israeli-born parents stare at me in amazement. They smile at the children singing, but it does not bring tears to their eyes. "I'm an immigrant. My son wasn't born here; I can't believe he knows the words to songs in Hebrew," I explain, laughing and blowing my nose.

Safta Sarah was a babysitter in her small home in Ramat Gan. She raised half a neighborhood. Ilana, her daughter, ran a series of kindergartens in her backyard in Tivon, which had as many children as the scarlet pomegranates on her trees. Smadar, Sarah's granddaughter who first welcomed me to Israel with her drawing, studied and became a qualified nursery school teacher.

Raphi's nursery school planted pomegranate trees in the winter, and baked matzot at Passover. They danced with white crowns on their heads at

Shavuot, and ate apples and honey in the autumn. Some of the stories were about Jewish history or taken from the Bible.

Smadar took her class to a Bedouin tent to bake *pittot* and to ride on donkeys. When guests arrive at the *gan*, she teaches the children that it is a good deed to receive guests kindly. Ilana took care of all six of her grandchildren in her various kindergartens, and saw each of them every day. She grew lemons and grapefruits and grandchildren, all in the backyard. She was an expert at making wholesome, delicious meals for them. Another of Safta Sarah's granddaughters is a nursery school teacher; Ronit now runs an afterschool program for the grandchildren and some neighbors, as Ilana has retired.

Some of the songs that the children sing in *gan* are the same songs that I sang in youth groups in America and England. "*Sisu et Yirushalayim*," the joy of Jerusalem… "On her walls I have placed guards, all day and all night." I think of Raphi and Rafi, who received the same education but never knew each other. Or did they?

# Survival — 1941 and 1992

Mordecai sends a telegram to Europe that reads, "It is a boy, healthy, name Yuval, Sarah is well." If it had been sent a year later, there would have been no one left to read it. Yuval was born on October 19, 1941. Mordecai's brothers and sisters become names etched on his gravestone. At the time of the birth of their first baby, all of his sisters and brothers were still alive.

Mordecai pours the sweet Kiddush wine and tells me, his cousin's daughter, "My father had a good death, before the war. He was buried in a graveyard and mourned for properly. The others have no marker for their mass graves." A good death, what a concept.

One day I rush in from work. Danny waits until I run to the bathroom to pee, take a long drink of water, and come into the kitchen to look for food. I notice that he is more solicitous than usual. "Yael Sharon called." This name doesn't click at first because it is Mordecai's daughter Rivka's daughter; I am not used to hearing Yael's last name.

"She said that your cousin Mordecai passed away last night."

I am stricken, frozen, thinking *no no no no no* to myself. *But I can't be without him; he is my only blood relative in Israel. I will be alone. OK*, I bargain, *he was eighty-two, his time had come. He was here to welcome us to Israel and to bless my baby daughter at her baby naming. But for Safta Sarah, her time with him is cut short.*

I have never been to the shivah of a close relative. I take the children and show up at the apartment which is overflowing with grandchildren of all ages. Astonishing to me that the atmosphere is not tragic. Sad, but it is mostly a family get-together. My children are BORED, so I get out some cards for them. Mordecai's older grandchildren are amused by the competition, the "it's not fair," as reactions to winning and losing. Apple strudel and cinnamon cakes are served. Someone jokes that they wish Abba were here, he liked a good party.

I steal a look at Safta Sarah. She doesn't seem to have taken in what has happened, although she repeats the story over and over in order to absorb it. Nir, Ilana's son, and his girlfriend Ronit were sleeping over. They got up early and peeked into their grandparents' room to say goodbye. He later laughs, "I waved goodbye to a dead man."

There is a man at Mordecai's funeral and shivah who looks like family. "Have you not met Tuvye ever?" Rivka asks me.

"No, you mean the brother that survived the war?"

"Yes, the one who came to Israel… There was another one."

"Another one what?" I ask. What did she mean?

"This is the other brother who came to live in Israel."

Before I can ask any more, Tuvye approaches us and shakes my hand. He is quite formal. He looks sad, distracted.

We chat tentatively, quietly. It is awkward that I know these relatives so well, and am meeting him for the first time at his brother's funeral. Why had they fought? I have nothing against him; I just have never been introduced to him. Yet he is also my father's first cousin.

Sarah stands by the dining room cupboard which is filled with glasses and dishes. It is ornamented with wedding photographs in black and white, first art projects of grandchildren who are now in their twenties, glass dishes which have lasted for years and have been acquired slowly, medallions from the army. She speaks slowly and thoughtfully:

> We came here together, to Israel. I was never without family, I had Mordecai. Everyone else was killed by Hitler. We made a life, children. These children have children now. You work. You eat. You celebrate. My Rafi died, and I worked so hard so that I wouldn't have time to cry anymore.
>
> Life goes on anyway. We are still here, look, we are together.

It is a non-recipe recipe. Survival is survival, just do it.

Who else has survived? There is another one? I have lost my close relative, my father's cousin, and have met his brother at long last. Who else has survived?

# Feeling Alone — 1987

Just three years after coming to live in Israel, at low moments I feel jealous of the closeness of Safta Sarah's gang. I am in it, but am outside of it too. We, like all immigrants, have found surrogate family; friends in our small town become family after years of helping each other with the children, inviting each other for Friday night. They are our age, have the same sense of humor, know all the same songs. Our friends play the guitar and they go on outings around Israel together. Their children are our adopted, local nieces and nephews.

I am very lucky. I have two sets of friends from my high school days in America, one set from camp, Linda and Zvi, and one set from home, Gingy and David. David and I know each other from the same neighborhood in America. We all lived together in college. We had babies together. We packed them when they set off for Israel while we were visiting, and then had a welcome to Israel party when they moved here.

They are unhappy here, are having money problems, miss their families. Gingy's parents are Holocaust survivors and she feels that she cannot live apart from them permanently. They are leaving. They don't want their children to fight in wars here, to be exposed to terrorism, violence. I feel that they are right and my new, thin foundation is being shaken. I feel that I have built a home of paper on an earthquake fault under a volcano. I am jealous and sad, and hurt and abandoned. Danny is stubborn in his faith about staying in Israel.

Of course, he did not come to Israel to find stability, but maybe to find a more exciting and meaningful life. He always knew that his parents adored him and approved of him. He has such a comforting and solid base that he could…leave it. Danny always jokes that the reason that he came to Israel is "so I could wear shorts and sandals, and throw my suits and ties in the rubbish!"

I go with Danny to visit Safta Sarah. Danny holds me in the elevator going up to the ninth floor of the retirement home. I lean on his soft shirt. No family, no friends. He never asks if he is not enough. Just believes that my motives are good for loving my friends so much.

Safta Sarah is excited to see us, although she cannot hear today. Her hearing aid is being repaired, and the conversation has to consist of her talking. I exclaim over the knitting, an amazing and intricate green and white pattern. She holds it up to Danny and says, "This is my cure and treatment." She pauses and smiles. The TV, which is never turned off, is blah-blahing about the elections in the background. "It keeps my mind from thinking about…you know." She nods her head in the direction of the photographs. They are all clustered together, the dead and the living, smiling in their frames. Rafi's photo stands out as the only black and white photograph. "It keeps me busy all day."

Sarah peeks at the Purim package that I have brought her, and then looks wistful. "I wish I could invite you to stay for dinner," she says. I look around. Even the electric toaster oven is gone now; Safta Sarah no longer has a way of pampering her guests with cooking. I silently make a vow that I will make Sarah's stuffed eggplant for her so that she will be able to serve it to her next guest.

"I have everything," says Sarah. "I have enough money to give to the children. Every birthday, every baby that is born, every new apartment. Owwww have I told you about the modern kitchen in Shirley's new apartment? My leg gives me pain, but even with my health I cannot complain. I had the flu, but I am strong again. I have friends here in the retirement home."

When I make ready to leave, Sarah says, "I tell them all that I have four children — you are my fourth, Yehudit. You are like my daughter." This is followed by her parting blessing, "Enjoy the children, Yehuditi."

Danny plays with my hair in the elevator, "You are looking perkier, like you always do after a dose of Safta Sarah. She sees the positive, Jude."

I look sadly in the mirror: OK, keep your hands busy, count your blessings, and enjoy the children.

# Not Wanted Here — 1983

It is a year before we make aliyah to Israel. I have no older friends who have babies, no models for going back to work. I have already moved countries once, from America to England, and then moved to the unchartered country of parenthood. No landmarks. It is a cold autumn in Manchester, England. The baby has to be dressed in all his homemade sweaters and hats when taken out in the cold. His American snowsuit is layered on top, making him a neatly packaged but heavy bundle.

I decide that at three months, like Israeli mothers I have heard of, I will go back to work. Work will be in the afternoons only, after giving baby Raphi my full attention all morning. I sneak in a nap when he does, though. I will make up the work Sundays and evenings when Danny is home and can take care of the baby. As I juggle work with breast-feeding, my pump becomes my best friend.

I am delighted to find a babysitter across the street. This will rule out having to drive the baby in the cold and rainy weather. A week before I am supposed to return to work, I meet the designated babysitter, by chance, in the street.

"Some of the neighbors were talking about your baby's circumcision, and I didn't know he was a *Jewish* baby," says the neighbor. " I won't have a Jewish baby in my house."

I cannot think. I cannot think to answer. My jaw hangs open.

"It's the food, you know. They eat different food."

I monotone, "Breast milk. He only has breast milk, I would leave a few bottles."

She is not negotiating and the truth is that I am not either, just pointing out that her reason isn't applicable.

My pure baby, who is all love and breast milk, laughs and cuddles, *is not to be admitted to someone's house.*

Danny is livid. I am numb, and when I am able to feel anything, it is depression. Anger turned inward.

That is not the only time that my son is the target of hatred against the Jews. In 1989, we spend the summer with my mother and father in Madison, Wisconsin, with its beautiful shady trees, pastoral parks, islanded lagoons, tolerance, liberalism, love and peace still hanging in the air from the 1960s. Since our visit is extended, always out of thirst and guilt from living so far away, my mother arranges for Raphi to go to a summer day camp, Camp Shalom. An anti-Semite dabs the synagogue with a swastika and cuts the brakes on the camp bus, hoping to kill fifty Jewish children. The vigilant bus driver checks the bus before she drives off to collect the children and finds that the brakes have been cut, right in front of the synagogue with the fresh dabbing of hate.

# Family — 1999

My Raphi's youngest sister Ilana is now seven. It is the first time that she is aware of her visit to the grave on Remembrance Day for soldiers. She is in the first grade and has just learned to read. She reads the name slowly, and exclaims, "Oh, look, it's Raphi's name. And here it says Rafael Yosef and also Rafi. Oh, look, it says that he is Safta Sarah's son. And it says the Six-Day War, I heard about that one. And it says that he was twenty years old. Is that old, Ema?"

I am busy hugging Safta Sarah and petting her hair. After thirty-two years it is easier for people to think of this as a tragedy that doesn't hurt acutely anymore. Safta Sarah is crying; some years she doesn't cry noticeably.

The family, from all around the country, enjoys being together, all four generations. No one is busy with Safta. I am standing next to Sarah's portable chair and patting her gray hair. The distance in terms of family relations allows me to be close enough to caress her. I think about how little touch Sarah must be getting these days.

"You are my fourth child," Sarah says sincerely. There is no doubting her tone, although I want it so much that I am not sure that I can have it.

"You are my mother," I say equally sincerely, knowing that my own is so far away and that Sarah's mother died tragically.

# Hospitals (But Really about Love) — 1990

Mordecai has just come out of the hospital. He buttons his white shirt over his rounded tummy, dresses meticulously, and combs his thin white hair. His cheeks are red from effort and from his heart pumping hard to support his stout body.

"Sarah, is there anything you need at the corner store? Make me a little list and I will get you what you need."

She is worried about his health, schlepping groceries in the heat. But when he goes to the corner store for her, or to the pharmacy to fill a prescription, she feels that he is courting her. It brings a flirtatious smile to his face, although he would never express his feelings in words.

"We need 5 percent white cheese, some apples for strudel, a small bag of cake flour, some raisins, a little oil. Maybe some milk, one bag is fine. That's all. Don't schlep too much."

Sarah loves to tell guests that Mordecai takes care of her. I am such a guest. Mordecai, who has returned from the grocery, tells me about his hospital stay. "They are such good Jews there. They brought me a Purim basket." He has tears in his eyes remembering the thoughtfulness of some religious youth who came to visit.

Whenever I have lunch with Sarah and Mordecai, he makes a ceremony out of pouring me some of his homemade syrupy sweet wine.

"L'chaim, Yehudit, to your good life."

# Hospitals (But Really about Love) — 1993

Weak hearts must run in the family just like the name Kalman does. Mordecai told me a story repeatedly about how his father Sandor sobbed when he heard of the death of his younger brother Kalman, my grandfather, from heart disease. If there had been penicillin at the time, he could have lived past his twin sons' ninth birthday. One of the twin boys was my father. Mordecai's children and I have the same great-grandparents; I wish I could tell our common ancestor that we have found each other from across the world.

I stand by my father's bed when he is unconscious. His head is swollen to twice its normal size, features distorted. He wakes up calling my mother's name three days later. The jetlag makes the days like walking through mud and I can't sleep sharing a room in a cheap motel with my mother. There are sleepless days, worrisome nights. Scenes in the hospital with my brothers, who have also not slept. In the hospital cafeteria I end up throwing my tray at my brother who is unsympathetic about how tired I am.

I pine for my baby who is three years old; my other two children are nine and eleven. I tell my mother. "Well, go to her, then," she snaps, angry that I have other priorities. I stomp out of the room, my mother screaming after me to come back.

To ease the tension, I go for a walk along the beach with my mother every day. When I can't sleep, I go to the five-star hotel across the street and read the paper by the light of a log fire at five in the morning, and help myself to free hot apple cider in the lobby. I write faxes to send to my children via a kind neighbor, Nahum, who has a fax machine. I reread a fax, mostly drawings, which they have sent me.

My brothers are fighting with each other; no one is getting along. I feel lonely and do not want to be here. I want to go back to Israel, and am worried that I have left a new job that I am not established in yet.

I cannot picture life without my father. I have made a life without my father.

# How to Maintain Positive Thoughts — 1986

I have been in Israel for two years. I have a baby and a toddler. A rented apartment, a car, a loving husband, and a community, even a job. I also have some old friends who will soon be ex-friends. And some new friends who may become old friends. My parents blame me for living so far away, for keeping their grandchildren so far away. My brothers won't write regularly for another twelve years, until e-mail becomes available, although the letters they do send are beautiful. Ah, how I miss my family. They won't visit for another twenty-five years, until the baby who is now sucking on my breast is ready to be married. (That hasn't happened yet.) I feel guilty and I feel that I am missing out. A great sadness creates a dark, empty hole, which needs to be fed, to be touched, to have a sweater knit around it.

I go to see Safta Sarah. It is Holocaust Remembrance Day, and I often observe historic moments with invented private rituals. This is my ritual: I go to see her on this day.

"Sarahleh, I came to see how you are, on this sad day."

"Yes, too many died."

"Tell me about your mother."

Sarah clicks into the past at the speed of light. Any question will send her there.

"She didn't want me to go on Hachshara. She didn't want me to train to be a pioneer in Eretz Yisrael and to move far away. She knew that the pioneers didn't keep religious observances. They worked on the Sabbath. Didn't pray every day, but worked in the fields, dressed without modesty, mixed with the opposite sex. I still do that," she says with a twinkle in her eye. "There aren't many men left, but they come to play cards. They used to like my cookies and cakes; before that they used to like my cooked meals. Before that they used to like my beautiful white skin." She holds up her arm and laughs at her age spots. "Elderly people should only live as long as they can help themselves with their own hands, you know, not a moment past that." She is adamant.

"Anyway, my mother, poor thing, begged me to take her with me on aliyah to Israel in the end. But it was too late."

"What do you mean it was too late?"

"She couldn't come. It was youth aliyah. She was an older married woman, nothing could save her. She took control when Hitler invaded Hungary. She jumped off the roof."

Silence.

"Do you knit?' she asks me. "It keeps the mind occupied. Always do something with the hands. Train yourself to bring positive thoughts when you are knitting."

"I write."

"Then teach yourself to have positive thoughts when you write, Mumeleh."

# Friends — 1990s

Many times when I visit Sarah at the retirement home, she says something like this:

Only have friends who are genuine, who love you like I love you. You can lie to people about how you feel about them, but real feeling comes to the surface, it is known and felt with or without words. You really know how close you are to a person and how real the feeling is.

Take my neighbor. She starves herself. She is flat chested, and skinny and looks malnourished — it really puts me off. She starves herself and also allows no joy, no *nachas* from her life.

Take you and me. I loved you from the first moment. You came bouncing into our home with your arms stretched wide open, with your love of life.

You loved my food, you loved each member of the family you met, loved Israel.

Only look to friends who are positive about you, and positive about life. Otherwise you make yourself miserable.

# Help (Timeless)

"When we came to Israel, we didn't have any help. My greatest joy comes when the family gets together, like here on my birthday." She points to a photograph of all her remaining children, all her grandchildren, and her great-grandchildren. It is gratifying to see that I am there, with Danny and the kids, an integral part of Safta Sarah's eighty-sixth birthday celebration. In the picture my hands are on Safta's shoulders, my children are mixed in with the massive crowd of offspring, and they fill in a gap age-wise; they are teenagers, and everyone else is a young adult or under-fives. They were babies at a time when there were no babies; Rivka had commented how nicely they filled Sarah and Mordecai's house with baby sounds at a time when it was devoid of them, and when her children and their cousins were teenagers.

"This gives me a reason to live, to carry on," Sarah says. It is not something she takes for granted. It is clear that when she doesn't feel reason to carry on, she will decide not to. This will come when the pains in her legs take over her thoughts more than the offspring who now fill a fair-size banqueting hall, frequently.

The day before we left England, Danny's extended family gathered at a banqueting hall to celebrate Grandma Googy's eightieth birthday. This is what we left. This is what we miss and what we later created, what Safta Sarah and Mordecai created out of... only themselves.

Sarah looks proud, calm, settled deep within. "Mordecai and I decided that we would help each grandchild when they got married, thirty thousand shekels towards an apartment. No one could help us; there was no one here to do so. When each great-grandchild is born, we gave each one a thousand shekels to start out with.

"An oven here and a bookshelf there," Safta Sarah laughs. "They delivered a bookshelf that I ordered for one of them here," she points to her tiny retirement home room with a bed, a small fridge and a table for playing cards. "We had nothing," she says, obviously feeling blessed in all things of importance now. "We were illegal immigrants; we came with a knapsack each. No one helped us." Her income now is from her husband's pension. The Ministry of Defense pays her rent, and the gifts to the children…they come from the government of Germany, which is paying reparations. This is the way that history has paved for her to make a living.

She shuffles to the refrigerator and takes out a bar of fancy chocolate from a cardboard box. "It's from the Ministry of Defense; they take care of us at holiday times." It is almost Rosh Hashanah, the Jewish New Year. Sarah is so pleased with the chocolate. I cannot help thinking that in Safta's place I would feel bitter. A box of chocolate and a note from the State, to whom she has given her younger son. "Take this home to the children." She also receives a small amount of reparations from Germany for living under Hitler for three weeks. Not for losing her entire family, only for the three weeks.

What a way to make an income, from a dead son and from the Nazis' reparations. There is also a pension from Mordecai's work.

Sarah and Mordecai created a scholarship to the university in their son's name because they did not want to use the money from the Ministry of Defense. When their grandchildren went to university, their Uncle Rafi paid their tuition. The State also made a double grave for Mordecai, with space for Sarah, just across the wall from Rafi.

"We had no one to help us when we came."

## Purim in Israel throughout the Decades

I am a twenty-year-old student with long hair and an Arab dress. I get on a bus and a cowboy is driving it. A woman is standing holding her black cat, which has whiskers painted on a baby's face.

I am a mother in labor with my third child. My two young children are making Purim baskets. We have baked Hamantaschen, and they are filling lines of paper plates with dried fruit, our baked goods, fresh fruit and candy. Every year we give them to our friends in the community, and receive them in turn. The kids need help tying the ribbons on the cellophane, but I am having more and more trouble bending with labor pains.

Nine years later, I am a daughter in mourning, and cannot take the jolly atmosphere while the Scroll of Esther is read in synagogue. I sit at the back, ambivalent about my costume; it does hide me from prying eyes, but it is too festive for me. Wild noisemakers and confetti fill the air. Laughter and boos for the villain of the story. This year I will connect more to the nearly tragic elements of Purim.

I am a middle-aged woman. I have invited Safta Sarah's granddaughter Lital to our synagogue for Purim. She comes with her boys dressed up as a black belt in karate and a spirit of some kind. Yuval comes to help with the kids.

The holidays in Israel are for me a celebration that I am not out of synch with my environment, that my history and culture is similar to others.'

On Purim I can take off my mask of differentness and be who I am.


# Europe — 1989


My little son Raphi, age six, draws a picture. He is breathing heavily, with total concentration. His long eyelashes are focused on the blues and greens of his felt tip markers, filling the page with a battle scene. There is a discernible tank, guns in many forms, all lethal, with their carnage spread over the page.

Danny and I have just returned from a trip to Europe, a gift from my parents. While there we were immersed in art, both ancient and modern, and I am still appraising the world with this perspective. I look at Raphi's picture. Yes, he seems to have captured all the major themes.

There seem to be three themes embodied in art: glory of the human body, glory of religion, and glory of war. Quite awestruck by the nudes, especially when emotion is involved, I find glory of the body is clear to me. Danny and I laughed about whether or not the statues were circumcised. They were not. Except when the tips broke off, either with time or enforced modesty.

Glory of religion is a human attempt at finding a balance on the tightrope between fear and gratitude. Both of these are huge, towering emotions that cause human beings to build great cathedrals and to decorate them with an artist's soul.

However, what is this glory of war? Why are there so many scenes of death in battle? The death scenes are reflected in the Christian art, portraying every emotion and stage in the death and dying of Jesus. Fear. Fear of death, of the enemy, of lack of sovereignty, of losing everything and of being alone. Even without yourself.

For Sarah, Europe is not a study in art.

# Immigrant Father — 1955

The Elite chocolate factory in Ramat Gan is Mordecai's workplace. He walks to work every day for shift work. Voted head of the worker's committee, he is known by all his comrades at work, and respected, and maybe feared.

My memories of Mordecai are very positive. He would tell me off if I didn't call often enough. Or was that just a feeling that I had? That I didn't call enough, that I didn't know how to intertwine their lives with my own. But he treated me like his flesh and blood in a land where I didn't have any flesh and blood except for those who came out of my own body. It was like having a window into my European family, one generation before my father, those who survived and those who didn't. We came from somewhere; we didn't just appear in America. And I didn't just appear in Israel; we came from some-where, somewhere where it made sense to end up in Israel. The bridge between my immediate past and my chosen present was Mordecai. And he was a benevolent bridge.

However, it turns out that he himself was under terrible strain as an immigrant. But am I making excuses for him? Maybe it was just his personality. Maybe it was his upbringing. Maybe it was the loss he experienced in his lifetime. Maybe it was poverty.

Mordecai works two shifts at the factory. When he comes home the children are in bed. In fact the children have limited contact with him. But he leaves his mark on their development.

Yuval, the oldest, carries a sack of grain for the chickens on his bike, and keeps the few *grush* coins given to him for bus fare as his only spending money.

Mordecai notes what a good boy Yuval is. He expects no less from all his children. So he is not at all prepared for Ilana wishing that she could have nice clothes and not being satisfied with hand-me-downs. She has hand-knit first-hand sweaters and vests, scarves and hair bands. However, in the fifties she is an elegant dresser, she dresses like a "lady." She wears tailored suits with slim skirts and tucks at the waist, which she has earned waitressing, and high heels, nylon stockings. She can't afford many ornaments, but she wears makeup well.

Mordecai doesn't recognize Ilana until he hears her speak to her friends, unaware that he is trudging home from the late shift at the factory. He is shocked at how ladylike and adult Ilana looks. He pulls her home against her will, by the arm. She feels that she will die from the embarrassment of being manhandled away from the crowd. Inside the door he removes his belt and lets loose his full wrath, not knowing when to stop. Her outfit shocks him, how different from his sisters who could not dress so elegantly and fashionably, or from the austere "do without" fashions of the He-Halutz girls. How foreign to him. Beating it out of her will reach her, he thinks; he is unable to accept the independent nature and style of a teenager. Sarah is afraid to intervene, but finally she, the peacemaker, convinces him to come have something to eat.

Yuval's grades are exemplary. Mordecai expects nothing less. He does not praise him, but he is silently proud. But Ilana... It is so hard for parents to change their parenting style when their children grow beyond being a reflection of them. The world has gone crazy with Hitler and camps and wars and starvation; as an immigrant father, he does not understand Ilana. What place is there in the world for beauty? That is a luxury.

The principal calls Sarah and Mordecai to school. Mordecai is so furious that he takes a shift off work, and comes to the school. The principal suggests that Ilana be sent off to a kibbutz to learn some work ethic. Mordecai remembers his days on kibbutz when he lived apart from Sarah. He was miserable. Suddenly he can see the sense in sending Ilana to a kibbutz boarding school. She will be away from her mother and brothers and sister; she will learn a little respect. It will make her more like him. The principle gives them the name of a school in Kfar Sava.

He pulls Ilana out of class and takes her home with them. She protests the whole way.

"We will teach you the meaning of money; you won't have any at the kibbutz." He flashes on his little brother Kalman who had to be sent away to board because there wasn't enough food in the house, on his mother remaking clothes herself from parcels received from abroad. The girls became seamstresses because they were so practiced at remaking hand-me-down clothes. There were potatoes from the neighbor to eat.

"I won't leave my school, my friends, my home. You can't make me."

"The school principal wants you to go. She doesn't want you disrupting her school anymore."

"Why didn't you stand up to her? Why didn't you tell her that I am as smart as Yuval, that I can work as hard as Ema if I want to, that I am a good girl?"

Ilana cries. Mordecai slaps her face for talking back, for not knowing that she is not a good girl. He slaps her for having to miss a shift at work, for the embarrassment of having to go to the school. Mordecai is angry that Ilana has made him so angry. He picks up the cooled iron from the ironing board and holds it threateningly above her head.

"I could kill you for making me so angry. You help your mother and be a good girl. Not much time left at home before you go to the kibbutz. You WILL behave there."

He slams the door and goes off to work at the chocolate factory. Uprootedness, different values can make you irrationally angry, helpless even if you are the head of the worker's committee.

# Repairs — 2000

"**I** can fix anything," says Safta Sarah as I walk her to Rosh Hashana services. "People bring me buttons to sew on, and tears to mend."

"You fix a lot of things," I tell her, with a gentle smile. If she only knew how much she crochets my frayed heart. I try to explain to her honestly. "It is the Jewish New Year today. Jews all over the world are trying to make themselves better people, to look honestly at the parts of them that are ragged and torn, and to mend them. You are good at repairing, Sarah."

She makes a dismissive motion with her hand, but is clearly pleased; she giggles as she does every time I visit her.

I come that morning at nine-thirty. The congregation that I am taking her to starts praying at nine o'clock, but no one gets there on time, ever. When I knock and let myself in, she looks very pretty. Her eyes are just beautiful — never a trace of makeup, although there are eighty-seven-year-olds who might wear some.

She is wearing a blue dress with white polka dots and a lace collar, a cameo pin and earrings, and a white glass necklace together with the gold chain that she always wears. Her white hair is neatly piled and lacquered on her head, with a little flair on one side. She also has on sport socks with a stripe...and high heels. "Did we miss the prayers? You're late!" she rebukes me as I walk in. I reassure her, and we set out on the difficult task of getting her to synagogue without her walker.

We take the elevator down to the basement; from there it is only half a room's walk to the door. It is only four or five blocks to a local small congregation with mixed seating for men and women, and with equal roles for both. Sarah is thrilled; it reminds her of the Reform synagogue to which she belonged for thirty years.

Someone notices her, perhaps her joy, and gives her an honor: she will be the one who dresses the Torah. The logistics of this are even harder than getting her to synagogue. She can't walk or stand without her cane, and she is stooped over, and yet she has to reach above her head and put a velvet coat over the scroll of the Torah. I help her. I hear people whisper, "Must be her daughter."

The rabbi is young and dynamic. I see Sarah nod her head as the rabbi speaks about Abraham who had to face sacrificing his son Isaac. "I used to know this by heart," she says. Does she relate to sacrificing one's son? One can know God by studying old texts made new with relevant explanations about the history and beliefs of the Jewish people, by prayer, and by good deeds, the rabbi says, and Sarah exclaims in approval. However, the example given for prayer is when Abraham Joshua Heschel marched with Martin Luther King, and said that marches for civil rights were "praying with one's feet." Sarah stands up and shuffles to the door. "Time to go," she says, her feet echoing the prayers as she shuffles with her cane out the door.

# Meeting Other Mothers — 1993

Sarah has limped for years. Her bones are crumbling.
"I feel like an eighteen-year-old inside," she says. I only ever see her eyes; I don't see her age spots, her wrinkled skin, and her bent body. A hip replacement brings her to be hospitalized in our little town, Kfar Sava. I am torn, as usual, between small children, work, household duties, communal commitments, and friends, whose lives I take on too readily. So I am grateful that she is in Kfar Sava, so that I can manage to visit her.

There is a nurse's strike. There is no one to serve meals, change bedpans, make bed, give meds, moral support. To listen.

Sarah is comfortable and non-complaining after her operation. I see that her bed pan is full. It has been left in full sight.

In a stage whisper, Sarah intimates that the woman in the bed next to her is from an Arab town. At the moment the room and the whole ward seem silent. There are no other visitors, and the other patients are sleeping. We have it to ourselves.

"We are both grandmothers," she tells me. "Both mothers of sons and of daughters."

"You know I have nothing against Arabs," she says. "We are cousins. Really the same. All I want is peace, so that no mothers have to lose their children anymore. Sholem. That's all I want for you and your family here."

It occurs to me that not everyone in her position would be devoid of any hate. I think she is past making generalizations until she shares her next thought.

"You know who I resent?" she adds. "Our own Jews who are so religious that they don't serve in the army; they take government money for education, but don't give anything to the country. But the Arabs, I believe that they have suffered and want peace just like we do."

I listen for a while. Sarah takes the apple juice from my hand as I make sure that she has enough food. Her children have provided her with everything.

Before I leave I empty her bedpan and wash it out. I kiss her goodbye and promise to bring Danny and the children to visit, although how I will orchestrate it, I don't know.

I work in a museum. There is a woman from an Arab village who cleans the offices. Trying to beat the commuter traffic, I have arrived just at sunup. We have a cup of coffee together. Wafiya is wearing a long traditional dress with a hand-embroidered design on the bust. She speaks no English and little Hebrew. I speak almost no Arabic. We sign to each other.

"It is hard to be a mother of sons in this country."

"How many children do you have?" Ten fingers. Six boys, four girls.

"How many do you have?" Two fingers. One boy, one girl. I feel almost apologetic that it is so few, seeing myself through her cultural eyes.

"You are still young, you can have many more," Wafiya signs. Somehow it is as if we are speaking the same language.

We manage to convey to each other that we are afraid and want our children to grow up in peace. I know the Arab word for peace, she knows the Hebrew word.

We hug, and she goes to clean the floor, I to teach the museum visitors about Jewish history.

# Hebrew Twenty and Sixty Years
## after Immigration

H. N. Bialik said that reading in translation is like kissing through a handkerchief. If you don't understand the words you are about to read, then you will experience the left-out feeling of being an immigrant!

Danny receives a note from the nursery school: "Please send a *tapuach*," for the bonfire holiday, called Lag Ba'omer. He gives Raphi a red apple to take to school. Raphi comes home crying. "Everyone else brought a potato! It's not fair, I had the wrong thing."

Danny looks at the note. Indeed, it says *tapuach adama*, which translates as "apple of the earth," or... a potato. Like *pomme de terre*. Our Israeli friends can't stop laughing. "You don't know about roasting potatoes in the fire?" Nope, never heard of it.

When I was studying at Hebrew University for my BA, in 1977–78, I was on the one-year program in Jerusalem. Ironically, by playing with children from deprived social backgrounds as my fieldwork placement, I learned some degree of fluency in Hebrew. Or so I thought, huh! I wanted to take a course in interviewing skills, done in a practicum in the community. One had to have a high degree of fluency. I was called before the department head to prove my language skills. The word for interview is *ra'ayon*. The word for pregnancy is *herayon*. Very similar, no? I told the department head that I loved being *b'herayon*. "I think you'd better not take the course this year," he said gently.

That same year I had been saying *pa'amayim* to the driver every time I got on a bus, thinking it meant "stamp my ticket." After all, that is what I heard two little children say every time they got on the bus. I was a quick learner. I could absorb language from my environment, or so I thought. In Hebrew ulpan, intensive Hebrew lab, I was horrified to learn that *pa'amayim* meant... "twice."

I guess I'd paid twice for every journey, and the amused bus drivers let the young woman with the American accent either pay for the person after her, or say some nonsense statement when she got on the bus with her travel card with too many stamps per ride.

A friend of mine told me that when he was in the army as a new immigrant, he was ordered to stand in a U-shaped formation with the other soldiers. The word used for "stand in formation" sounded like the word for bottom, and they thought they were supposed to put their bottoms in a U-shape.

There were not only mix-ups in Hebrew, there was a lack of understanding among native Israelis about what it means to have acquired a new language.

I am studying for my master's degree in Jewish studies. A professor comes into class during the Gulf War in 1991 and hears French and English being spoken in Talmud class. She declares with Israeli bluntness, "What! There are no Israelis in the class?" No Israelis in the class? What am I, chopped liver?

I don't know if I objected out loud or if my indignant rage comes out every time I repeat this story. In any case, my answer should have been: "No Israelis? My husband is away in the reserves, and I have four gas masks sitting on my dining room table; don't tell me I'm not an Israeli because I have an accent." I'm told I'm not Israeli, and I'm told that I'm American when I speak Hebrew. Twenty years after coming to live in Israel, small children, taxi drivers and some shopkeepers will answer me in English or comment on my accent. I am unwilling to switch to English on principle, and because my Hebrew is better than their English. Also, we *are* in Israel.

In fact the MA got me through the terribly thick brick wall of Hebrew, which most immigrants never break through. Most never read a newspaper in Hebrew, certainly not a novel; they miss cultural references to jokes and songs, poetry, literature, theater. They can follow the politics because the media presents the issues in black and white terms.

The first day of another Talmud class, we are told to turn to a page given in abbreviation form. It takes me five minutes to write out the entire Hebrew alphabet, while trying to remain calm and adult, and then write the numerical values next to the letters (letters indicate numbers in Hebrew). My edition of the book is different than the person sitting next to me, so I can't even just imitate. Then the Hebrew laced with Aramaic is so difficult that the only words I understand are "the" and "it." The teacher recommends that we look at the modern Hebrew translation on the side of the page. I can't make that out — my Hebrew isn't good enough. He also suggests that we look at the Rashi; I have never learned medieval Rashi script. I learn it and the numbers by the next day, but need tutoring with the Hebrew. Talmudic logic is also new, and the language simply prevents any kind of following in class. What I dread most, and I imagine the other students dread more than I do, is when it is my turn to read aloud.

A very kind woman with silver hair tries to help me catch up after class. Once I give up, frustrated, and tell her, "Ada, I was intelligent in English!!!" I want to say that at least I knew how to read in English. She understands.

As time goes on, and I read tens of books and texts in Hebrew, the wall begins to crumble. One day I realize that I don't know which language I am reading in, I just understand the subject matter. Afterwards, I realize that perhaps one of the best benefits of the MA is that it has made me a functional adult in Hebrew. I am helping my third-grader with homework, and I think, I couldn't have done this without an MA!

Safta Sarah speaks incorrect Hebrew, but it is the only language she has to speak to her children, to her grandchildren. To her many friends she speaks Hungarian, or Yiddish. She reads fluently the subtitles on TV, she can read a newspaper. I don't think she has time to read books and never has had time.

When I go to America, I miss Hebrew more than I miss the landscape, or the weather, or the outdoor life. I pine for Hebrew.

But I could not write a book in Hebrew.

# Color in the Desert — 1985

Gloomy thoughts of barren deserts come to me as I lie in bed. Why is Israel only one color? The desert seems devoid of color. Yes, for a few weeks a year there are wild flowers, lupines and poppies and yellow *savyonim*. The rest of the year thorns reign and dried grasses, also devoid of color. Rocks and nothing to rest or treat the eyes with.

I am used to the lush green of Midwest America. The rolling glacial hills of green, punctuated by red barns, and a myriad of colors of autumnal leaves, or spring flowers. The winter was a bit like a desert, but it was enchanting and inviting to me. Also I suffer greatly from the heat, and was brought to life in the bracing cold of the winter.

The heat drains me and gives me the feeling that all the energy is dried out of me. A trip downtown is a big undertaking. A trip to Tel Aviv to visit Safta Sarah in her unair-conditioned house is unthinkable. When I am pregnant and nauseated during my first summer in Israel the heat just finishes me off. I vomit and cry and want color.

Safta Sarah never comes to my house. I own a car, I am young and supposedly mobile, and she is past taking buses. She goes out if her children drive her. I go to her.

The mirror looks at me. All stomach protruding out, puffy face, two black circles, almost bruises, beneath my eyes. No life force. I get in the car, and hope that driving will keep me in control, and that I will not lose my breakfast.

I arrive at Sarah's house; the smells of summer salads and pickles and something fried do not make me nauseated, but make me want to cry.

She loves my stomach protruding. She loves my no-makeup young face, looking pregnant and tired. Her whole being lights up to see me.

Complaining about the lack of color in Israel to Sarah, I whine, "I want color, I want lakes, I want hills, I want snow."

She doesn't get a cool washcloth; she doesn't try to make it better.

She also doesn't think I am insane.

Instead, she offers me stories about Hungary, stories about herself struggling in Israel, and loving living here. No car or a phone. No trips to America once a year. No washing machine. No sacred hours at a psychologist, or even an adopted mother to visit. No one helped her. She certainly didn't cry about the lack of color here. She tells me stories about her children.

Then she feeds and babies me. She brings a stool for my swollen feet. I refuse and help her serve. There is cold white yogurt soup with forests of light green dill for first course. Then green and red Israeli salad cut finely. There is purple cabbage with white marbled designs pickled in sweet vinegar. Then golden brown textured fish cutlets. Slices of yellow lemon with their plump flesh pith. And green grapes and pink watermelon sweating beads of water, for dessert. Then a glass of mint tea with lots of sugar.

Before I know it, without planning it and worrying about it, soon I am napping on her hand-crocheted pillows on her soft coach. I don't suffer from the usual endless pregnant need to pee. Sleep remains for a very long time. Sarah knits quietly in her American armchair, while the ghosts of Rafi and the

Holocaust siblings gently go about their business making the garden apartment in Ramat Gan an island in time.

I notice that with each visit, Sarah doesn't speak about her lost child, but rather concentrates fully on me.

# Memories — 1960s

I am a little blonde girl with bangs and a ponytail in a car. My father is driving. Blinding rain makes visibility opaque, and then with a terrifying violence, thunder shakes the car, and a bolt of lightening strikes right in front of us. I scream. My father pulls the car over and parks, and turns to me. "I want to teach you the *brachah*, the blessing, so that you will never be afraid. Thunder is loud, lightning is bright, but they are part of nature. You can say after me, 'Blessed are You, Lord, our God, Ruler of the universe, Who has filled the universe with His power and his glory," my father incants in Hebrew.

"OK, Daddy, I will try not to be afraid, and I will remember. Amen."

# Child Care — 1989

When Danny is drafted into the army, as a doctor he has to serve a year and a half, whereas our other immigrant friends have to serve for six weeks to three months. His basic training is not done with eighteen-year-olds, but with other thirty-year-old immigrants, mostly from the former Soviet Union. "It was a wonder that the whole unit didn't have a communal heart attack every time they had to run laps around the base," he will say later. I know he enjoys the machismo of it — now he can tell army stories with the best of them, about sleeping with fifteen snoring men, and about eating "shit on shingles," as my father called army food in WWII. Meatloaf in cans is served in Israel. The cat won't touch it when Danny brings some home.

He is being sent to an air force base in the Negev Desert for the duration. I guess I have my own army stories. I am being uprooted and sent to a foreign country; call it the Military.

We are given a choice of housing: "American" style, or "Israeli." American is fake wood paneling, fake linoleum in the kitchen. It depresses me no end. So we take Israeli, which is actually quite luxurious with its stone floor, white plaster walls, one outdoor porch for laundry, and one outdoor porch for sitting on lawn chairs and doing cookouts. It is the only place that I have ever lived in Israel with its own yard, so I do some gardening, but my flowers and my lawn are not very successful. We receive orders from the base commander: "Green: Make your grass green." Another FAILURE at a time when I am failing at being an army wife and failing to know where my roots are.

The first Friday night after we have put the beds in the right rooms, and the sofa in the living room, we light Shabbat candles and rest from the trying day. The kids were very undemanding on the drive south to the desert; they were quite excited and happy about the move. Having run around outside and explored the playground they have fallen asleep.

The cultural coordinator for families on the base comes over to welcome us. She brings some cardboard cake and some dried flowers, but she is not happy with what she sees. Nodding at the glowing Shabbat candles: "Give those up at once. There is only one other traditional family on the base. You will be expected to show up at Friday night dances and social events."

I am not sure that I have words to communicate with her. The moving day has been interminably long, with a never-ending maze of stress.

"We are not strictly religious, but lighting Shabbat candles is part of our family life. We have no intention of giving it up."

"You won't fit in here if you do that. It doesn't belong here."

This is a club I didn't sign up to join in the first place! I have no one to complain to.

The lack of control invades many spheres but the hardest for me is child care. It is clear that I am different from the other mothers on the base. Dressed up and fully made up, they take their three-year-olds to day care. Universal child care is the norm in Israel from age two and often younger. An obese nursery teacher dishes out chocolate marshmallow treats (Crembo) very freely. Her charges are positioned in front of the television for over an hour every day to watch bang bang kill kill cartoons. Stationed in the country in the desert, they rarely walked in nature even though this time of year it is in bloom. Their artwork seems to be dictated assignments at age three. This was not my experience in the city, in fact far from it. I complain.

Soon I am visited by the educational committee. This consists of the obese nursery teacher, a very tall pilot, who is the top of the totem pole socially at the base, and the cultural coordinator for families, the one who was opposed to Shabbat candles.

Nursery teacher: "If you don't give your children sweets, they will end up having a weight problem. You have to give them sweets freely."

Pilot: "Violence is very good for your children to watch on TV; it helps them to deal with their fears. The educational message which you are giving them is to be afraid instead of facing their fears."

Nursery teacher: "You are acting like a Flower Child. You want your children to be different from the norm. This is very bad for them; they will never fit in if they don't conform."

Cultural coordinator: "I sensed that you were different from your first night here. This is not good for the army base or for the education of your children."

Back in America I experienced being different as a Jew and felt that I didn't belong. Destined never to fit in, here in Israel, while my husband is "defending the country," I am told that I am different as an American and that I don't belong.

They think they are doing me a kindness by coming to talk to me. To them I am a poor misguided immigrant who doesn't quite get the rules of the game. I envy them all for belonging and knowing what they believe in. I envy the pilot most of all for having a useful role on the base. I am a mother, and now an uncertain one at that.

The year and a half in the desert throws all my relationships into a whirlpool.

Danny is washing the two children in the bath. I laugh at how much soap he has put on them. Bubbles and foam float in piles and turrets above their heads. Each child has a soap beard, soap eyebrows, soap crowns.

There is a phone call. The commander of the air force base has a child with a cough, and Danny is needed immediately. Oh, how I wish I were needed somewhere.

Danny sees that I am standing at the bathroom door watching the kids' antics. Without asking if I will take over, he puts his medical bag on his shoulder, dons a hat and sunglasses and heads out the door.

"The commander's child probably coughed once. Tell him when you finish taking care of your own children and put them to bed, you will be happy to check his child."

I despise the militarism of the air force base. Why does it provide housing for families if it is so alienating for the wives of the male soldiers? Perhaps it would be better for the families not to live here; there seems to be no real connection between us. A siren wakes us up, we receive orders to make the patch of grass in front of our house green, and fighter planes rip the sky in half and shake the house hourly all day. There is a security gate to go in or out of the base.

Romantic ideas of what this exile might mean for us as a couple were my expectation. We have already uprooted and moved to Israel. Now we are uprooting again, leaving our friends and community. I thought we could be each other's best friends, walk in the desert, make love all the time, luxuriate. Danny loves being the doctor on the base; he wears a uniform, has social and professional standing. My name, me the feminist child of the sixties, my name for this time is *ishto shel harofeh*, "the doctor's wife." I don't exist. I don't have a name, I don't have a place, or family, or friends. He is not in harmony with my romantic view of our time together, and I whine and feel lonely. I am also furious at him for *liking* the life on the base.

Danny's family is third-generation British. They are not complainers, whiners. They work hard, make do, have a positive attitude. When Danny was a kid, the family all lived in London close by; one weekend they went to one set of grandparents for tea, and the next weekend to the other grandparents. When I married him I gained two living grandmothers after my own Rose and Sadie were dead. His parents have always been compassionate and warm. Two of their children came to live in Israel: Danny and his sister. Maybe he never really left home. He certainly does not have compunctions about it the way that I do. In fact he does not seem to soul-search or question his decisions.

No local friends actually replace our friends from the center of the country; I miss them tremendously. They come to visit, but day-to-day life without them is grim. The women on the base seem to be permanently depressed and simply do not make friends. Their husbands work all hours of the day and night. Everyone is so neglected that children steal. I see their pockets bulging with Lego when they leave our house. The families are relocated every two years so why make friends? But I take it personally.

I notice that they scrub their houses clean. This is against my nature, but I tentatively try it. They won't come over when I invite them for a cup of coffee. They bake. I try that, but they still don't come. I try wearing makeup; that doesn't help. There is one kibbutznik who dresses like me and seems to be a good mother. I ask her if she wants to come over with her kids in the afternoon and to have some coffee. She seems affronted. "How do I know what I'll be doing in the afternoon?"

The women let me know slowly what they find fault with in my differentness. "Why does a woman your age wear your hair in a ponytail?" "Why does your husband play with the kids at the playground, can't you do it?" "You should go to this great place I know and buy a style."

"What does that mean?" I ask.

"You pay three hundred shekels and receive fashion advice."

"Like what?" That is almost the amount of money we subsist on for a month.

"Like what colors you should wear."

As I walk away swishing my ponytail, I think to myself: "Purple, that's clear. Who needs to pay money for that?"

Extremely lonely, I go to study Judaism at the university. I have to take the base transport. I meet another student, the girlfriend of a pilot. She is young, very bright. She wears an oversized black coat, and arty clothes, scarves, dangly earrings. We are in Modern Jewish Thought class together. One rainy evening bumping home in the desert in the dark, I ask her what part of Israel she is from, which aspect of the class she likes, and she lets me know that it is not the done thing to really converse on the base transport. I sigh, my last great hope of a woman friend dissolved.

The wife of the other doctor on the base loves the army life that I am growing to hate. She has embroidered the symbol of the base and hung it on her American fake panel wall. I resent her, I resent her husband, and I resent mine, all for liking army life.

Still no one will come over for a cup of coffee. There is some possibility that it is me, that my loneliness is so parched and vast that no one can span it.

Raphi and Shira and I find porcupine quills in the desert. We spot foxes. Morning glories grow in the cracks in the desert. We hike, and I teach them how to ride bikes. I teach them how to cross streets as cars are as rare as visitors there in the wilderness. Sandstorms blow with wild whistling sounds. I am like a single mother because Danny is so busy, and because we are on such a strangled budget.

The children and I do their homework, we plant the garden, go on long walks. There is a pool, and a small grocery store, a family "club" where we can buy a small, highly un-nutritious pizza for about a quarter. My children are really flourishing here; I give them the best of me. But there is no supporting social structure, like in Sarah's neighborhood. I let Raphi talk me into adopting a cat. Sharav, which means "fierce hot wind," is another source of love in this desert of a place. We laugh when she has three kittens on Raphi's bed one morning.

I rub Shira's cheeks with hand cream every night because they are chapped; we sing and talk until she falls asleep. Danny gets in late. We have very little couple time together, despite being stranded in the desert. It is always there, like a desert between us.

Danny comes in very late after attending the flight commander's child. He is exhausted and wants to watch TV. The base is showing *Top Gun*. When I see that it is about the air force, I lose all connection with reality.

"You live and breathe air force, now you have to relax with air force? I haven't spoken to anyone over the age of six in two days. I want to talk, to laugh at adult humor, to have some adult tactile contact, to kiss someone who doesn't have yogurt on their face, and you want to watch Tom Cruise bomb someone?"

"I'm tired, leave me alone. Stop whining."

"I have nowhere to go. I am stranded here because of you. We are miles away from anywhere to go and anything to do."

"I don't want to hear that again."

"Fine, you won't have to hear it, I'm leaving."

I grab my knapsack and the car keys. I have nowhere to go. I run through my tears to the end of the dead-end street. The bus stop has had its glass window broken — by bored children, probably — and is covered with shattered glass. I can't even lie down on its bench and cry. Where can I run? I think about my employer, who is very nice, but I don't really know her very well. I fantasize that this would bring us closer. I could go up north, but Danny would find me too easily. I could stay out all night and feign a car accident, make him worry, make him care. That scares me: what about the children? I creep back into the small house. He doesn't seem particularly bothered that I left, that I have been crying or that I have come back.

Pacifists, my parents come to visit on the military base. My seventy-year-old father dangles from the high-flying Omega slide to amuse the children and climbs up to the high wooden platform in the playground and slides down. He swings Shira around in the turquoise chlorine pool as he once did with me. He poses with Shira for a photograph with the guinea pig. My mother hikes in the desert with the children, and reads them books and sings to them.

The year and a half that we spent on the air force base was like being uprooted after being uprooted. And then the Gulf War came.

## The Gulf War, Sealed Rooms — 1991

You hold up thick plastic over the window, and you tape it to the window-sill with brown packing tape. This is supposed to save you from suffocating gas that comes on a Scud missile from Iraq. You are also issued a WWII gas mask, which you put over your face. The gas, however, can seep into your pores, and there are no body coverings issued, although there is a syringe with an injection in each kit to stop mucus production so that you don't suffocate in your own mucus. Babies are issued a bassinet made of thick plastic with one-way air holes, and young children get a gas mask with a plastic bag around it because they can't be expected to tell you if the seal is correct or not.

Danny feels that there is no rush to seal the room, but I feel like I have to *do* something. I also stockpile food that I can't afford after our time on army salary. They say that our food may get gassed too, so food in cans is safe. What would be good to eat in a sealed room, or in a contaminated apartment? I order canned corn, canned tuna — that's protein, canned artichokes because they taste good, canned pineapple. What will the children eat? Canned hotdogs?

Doing something doesn't keep me from going crazy. War, real war — not on television — was not part of my upbringing. At the time I need Safta Sarah the most, I see her least; we have just moved back from the air base, and we have lost touch. I have lost touch with myself.

I start to go see a psychologist.

I telephone Iris, my friend from Hebrew University who has helped with two enormous decisions in my life. The first one was to go visit my Israeli relatives when I was a student. The second is which psychologist to go see. I say that I want someone who is good with immigrants; I want a Hebrew-speaker even though I cannot really speak on a deep emotional level in Hebrew…because my insecurity dictates that I would cause an immigrant to leave Israel with all my doubts, difficulties and sadness.

Iris checks around and says, with an uncanny sense of what I need, that she has a friend with an eclectic approach to psychology who would really understand immigrants.

"Why, is she one herself?"

"No, she is just very professional and has empathy for people."

I tell Iris that I have been raising children without grandparents around, that we don't have any help in the house, that I speak with my other immigrant friends about the approaching war and our helplessness.

My doubts and fears about going to a psychologist come out, and Iris says gently but adamantly: "As an immigrant you cope without relatives, you do so much by yourself. Do you really want to do that by yourself, too?!! It is really OK to have help."

Coincidentally, like my Grandma Sadie, like Safta Sarah and some of my favorite people in my life, my therapist's name is…Sarah. She is young, and quite beautiful. After much work together I tell her my conviction that I would have caused an immigrant psychologist to leave Israel. I tell her that I was probably looking for someone to help me to stay despite the difficulties. And despite the fact that it is such a challenge to do psychotherapy in Hebrew.

She gently asserts, "We *never* had a communication problem, did we?"

But even so, none of my Sarahs is an antidote to the sealed rooms.

At midnight, January 15, 1991, Danny and I listen to the news. I have been "preparing" for the war, which I cannot bear to face. It is simply too frightening to me to think that we might face falling missiles and nerve gas. I am a young mother with a strong instinct for protecting my children. Yet, this is a time when I have to decide where my home is. Sometimes I want to flee to England or America, but Danny is determined to stay. He receives an emergency call-up from the army and he is needed medically. It is a time of feeling very torn, uncertain and scared.

Men with beards cannot wear gas masks; a seal cannot be formed against the gas. But Danny has left his beard long, denying that anything threatening is going to happen. He is stable, calm, secure, whereas panic seizes me more than any other time in my life, and the tiny threads with which I hang on are things like sealing windows and stockpiling tin cans of food. The news reports that America has attacked strategic posts in Iraq. They announce an early victory, of course — all is rosy. Not so in Israel. We know that there will be retaliation for American action.

In the bathroom mirror Danny starts cutting his soft, cuddly, sensuous beard. Then he starts shaving. Soon his face is naked and he looks as though he's been plucked, just like a chicken, and badly! It is truly frightening, facing the imminent missile attacks. He looks in the mirror and sees his parents living through the Blitz. They did not panic and he will not either.

In contrast, I feel that I am sliding down a chute not knowing what is at the bottom. Gas for my children? An apartment building coming down on our heads? Explosions? Starvation? Capture by enemy troops? Slavery in Iraq? There is nothing on this slippery chute to hang on to. Not even Danny, because he is not afraid. Our friends have never been through a war like this one before.

Out of habit, we go to bed.

The first siren rings out at two a.m., a wailing too loud to provoke any kind of reaction except to move! We race from our bed into Shira's room, scoop her up and take her in our arms to Raphi's room, the designated sealed room. I try to "save" the cat Sharav thinking that Raphi will never forgive me if I don't. However, Sharav doesn't want to be saved and I still bear a long scar on my left hand from her clawing me; the siren has terrified her and she escapes out of the room. As I am sealing the four of us in the tiny ten-foot by ten-foot bedroom, and running masking tape along the door, stuffing a wet towel underneath, blood is pouring in torrents down my hand and arm, and I am sad about the cat. Danny is coaxing the children into their gas masks. Shira, age five, says: "But you told me never to put a plastic bag over my head. I won't." Helpless parents, sealing a room against gas that may fall.

Raphi, who has received training in gas warfare in his kindergarten, promptly throws up in his gas mask.

We turn on the radio. It is announced that a Scud missile has fallen in Tel Aviv. That is seventeen kilometers away. We hear some loud booms.

I soon discover what the expression to be "scared shitless" means. I feel that I have to have a bowel movement — yes, right there in the sealed room in front of my family. I use a plastic bucket. Visions of my children being rushed to the hospital with gas inhalation keep appearing. But who will rush them? How many ambulances would it take to take care of a whole neighborhood?

Raphi counts the Scuds falling and then counts the American Patriot missiles shooting back. He and Shira watch the news reports. I am in a state of shock: my children are studying war. Living war.

A Scud lands in Tel Aviv one block away from Sarah and Mordecai's house. The noise can be heard halfway across the country. We hear it seventeen kilometers away. Is this a contribution to Sarah's hearing loss? But they have been vaccinated against the fear of war, by the Holocaust, by the British Mandate, by four major wars in Israel. They have lost a son. A sealed room, and a Scud falling, are nothing to get excited about.

As we have been in Israel seven years by this time, as old-timers we have adopted a Russian family who were at the absorption center. A Scud falls next to their apartment in Tel Aviv. We have shared many meals with them; we have invited them to experience Jewish holidays. We have shared baby equipment with them and discussed the ups and downs of adjusting to life in Israel. We had tea in their absorption center room — I am not sure that spoons or sugar were easy to come by. They worked hard and moved to their own apartment, never complained about what they did or didn't have. But now they come to live with us, indefinitely, which turns out to be for a few weeks. Dalia takes Dina, the baby, out of her gas mask to comfort her during an attack. It comforts us, hearing the baby gurgling to herself and laughing as she cruises around the coffee table, leaving devastation in her wake, and sending the children into fits of laughter as she throws books on the floor with a thud.

# Cultural Differences

We have crossed cultural wires with our closest neighbors, our dear friends across the street, time and time again. That is why they are soul friends, because eventually we have fallen in love across the gaps. They came to understand us better when they spent three years in New York and were immigrants themselves for a while. I love Ariella's stories about not understanding American ways. She talks about being lost in supermarkets. She talks about one day in mid-December when she thought everyone on her street had died. Why? Because there were wreaths on all the doors. In Israel wreaths are used exclusively to mark graves. She talks about her different expectations for entertaining. Middle Eastern entertaining requires about three or four courses, a plethora of salads; go to any restaurant and they slap down about fifteen kinds of eggplant, cabbage, beets, hummus, carrots, and green salads followed by four kinds of grilled meat. She says that American neighbors invited her to dinner, and spoke about it for weeks. She was curious as to what delicacies would be served. The menu was steak, baked potato, "and just one lettuce salad," she exclaims. I laugh.

This couple, Ariella and Yehuda, have been the most generous of neighbors from the moment we moved into the neighborhood. We had no phone, we used theirs. We had no fax machine, we used theirs. We borrowed their car. Our children walked their dog and used their basketball hoop and ping-pong table because we had none. We planted a pomegranate tree in their backyard, because we had an apartment, not a backyard. We decorated their *sukkah*, a wooden hut decorated for the autumn harvest festival, because we didn't have one the first few years. And they turned to Danny for regular medical help throughout the years. For dog-sitting. For watering the garden that we enjoyed so much. *The ironic wisdom in their friendship was that they asked us for help.*

And yet there have been cultural differences. Yehuda was shocked that I didn't take Raphi to Danny's ceremony when he finished basic training. "I don't want him to laud the military."

He is shocked that I am so afraid for our lives during the Gulf War. For him it is a quiet and relatively easy war. He does not see through my eyes the glaring Demons waiting to gas us all.

There have been singing evenings with a guitar where we didn't know the tunes or the words.

There have been endless celebrations that crossed all cultural differences. The first place that I took Shira when she was born was to a Chanukah party at their house. Everyone cooed over the baby. There was a table simply heaving under delicacies from the Middle East, a hundred colors, nuts, fruit, fried goods, baked goods, salads, dips, things I had never tasted with sweet aromas emanating from them. For me it was a terrible strain to entertain guests during the first few years. I couldn't afford to serve more than one dish. I couldn't compete with the generosity of our Israeli nor our immigrant friends. I couldn't afford ready-made foods, nor had I figured out where or what to shop for in Israel.

Our neighbors' sons' bar mitzvahs are the first Israeli bar mitzvahs that we go to. Their summer evening barbeques include us, and we get a taste of extended family. Sometimes it makes it harder to sit next to their grandmother and aunts and cousins.

They invite our entire family together with Danny's sister's family for Passover one year. It is a blend of English, American and Israeli culture, and we feel totally at home. Wherever the hell that is. Whatever the heaven that is.

# Leaving Home, Visiting Home

It occurs to me that if I were blown up by a terrorist bomb, no one from my family of origin would come to my funeral, and no one would fault them because it would obviously be too dangerous to come. My siblings have never seen where I live and eat and sleep and survive and have not met my friends since my wedding. They have never met Safta Sarah nor have they tasted her food. My parents have, though. Once my dad got teary when he saw my workplace. He said, "Now I can picture where you are all day." Once I made a home video of my tiny box of an apartment: "This is the bathroom, this is the kitchen." My mother politely said it was like a *Better Homes and Gardens* tour.

Then I show up at "home" in America and shake their placid routines.

"Hi, Joanne, I'm in town. When can I see you?"

Silence on the other end of the phone.

Friends from the distant past demur when you want to reconnect.

I am not used to the formality of making appointments so far in advance in America.

"Oh, this is my busy season, but I'm free…just a minute, let me look…a week from Tuesday you still here? Oh, for two weeks, great, so on Tuesday for dessert, between eight and nine fifteen at my house?" I pine for Ariella and Yehuda's warmth and open kitchen policy.

The visit doesn't involve Middle Eastern hospitality, the custom that the biblical Abraham and Sarah kept all four sides of their tent flaps open for visitors. In America I am served one slice of frozen cake out of a box: this is fare for the entire evening. When my brother visits my mother, he is expected to bring his own takeout food. You simply could not show up with takeout food for dinner in Israel.

Or you arrive at your best friend's home to find out that she is having exams at university, working overtime at work, her babysitter has quit, and you're the babysitter for the next five days. Or that you have just intruded on her busy schedule so badly, and you want special time with her, and she is overwhelmed that you have arrived with babies in tow. Who don't sleep from jet lag.

"Why don't you just live here?" she moans. "If you did, we could see each other *every* weekend…"

# Mopping Up — 1988

Sarah is still living in her apartment in Ramat Gan, which feels like a house because it has a garden. They haven't made apartments like that since the 1940s; it is all tower block jungles now.

Sarah sees me and immediately starts telling me one of her favorite stories about Yuval. "He was eight years old, and I was pregnant with Rivkeleh. I had no mother here to help me. I worked hard. He had to leave for school but he said to me, 'Ema, do *not* do the sponga (the Israeli way of mopping the floor with a squeegee after purposely flooding it with water); wait till I get home and I will do it. Promise me that you won't do it.' But I cannot stand still and wait.

"To make him happy, I promised, but when he came in from school, hot and tired, he saw me scrubbing the floor. He was mature for his age, but his eight-year-old tears flowed anyway. 'Why, Ema? You promised. I came right home from school so that I could do it.'"

Sarah never forgot this devotion, and told this story, perhaps once a week, all of her life.

"Your Raphileh is like that." That is just prophecy, and true.

Sarah tells me that the cleaner didn't come, and it is her turn to clean the communal entranceway to the building of four apartments. I insist on taking the sponga and cleaning. She watches and coos.


# Heart of Darkness


I play a mind game. I am a creative cook. I make up soups that are thick and healthy. It seems a miracle that by cutting up a few vegetables and soaking some beans, a medley of tastes and delights appear. I play a mind game. I am feeding Holocaust victims. I am making up for the weak broth that they are fed, for their deep hunger over years that makes their teeth and their hair fall out. I am nurturing them in their empty black holes. I am nourishing them. I am also not using expensive ingredients, but am aware of the hunger in the world as I cook... I use simple garbanzo beans soaked overnight, sautéed onions and garlic, as much as I have the patience to peel. Then I cut in pumpkin, leeks, zucchinis, carrots, tomatoes, and then fresh herbs, some pasta, tomato paste (Safta Sarah uses ketchup but I can never do that because I think of it as fattening), lots of salt and pepper and sometimes a bay leaf.

# Immigrant Work — 1950 and 1998

Jews who grew up during the implementation of the Nuremberg Laws, and with Hitler rising to power, experienced a world in which uncertainty and fear were making them outcasts. In states neighboring Germany, uncertainty and fear spread with every newspaper, and with rumors. During the time that Sarah was rebelling against her mother's religious constraints, the Nuremberg Laws were implemented to restrict marital and sexual interaction between Jews and Gentiles. This extended to the workplace; Jews could not employ female citizens of German blood. Jews' citizenship was limited; a big "J" was marked on their identity cards.

Sarah is at home in the Elite chocolate factory neighborhood in Tel Aviv. They have a two-bedroom apartment, the ground floor, with a plot of land on which Mordecai grows vegetables and plants some fruit trees. Four small children and two adults live in two bedrooms. At night the growing children sleep in the living room, boys and girls together. In fact in those days there was no living room; people socialized around the kitchen table or outside while tending the garden, or walking down the street. There is a chicken coop in the backyard; Sarah never really gets over her aversion to chickens, especially at slaughter time.

It is a close neighborhood.

Sarah washes and bleaches the diapers by hand. She is very proud of their whiteness, not a stain ever to be seen on the neat row waving in the wind on her clothesline. She knows that the neighbor in the apartment just above her scrutinizes her laundry and passes on the verdict of its cleanliness to the neighbors along the street. She knows that every aspect of her life is observed. When her neighbor is sick, her complaints are heard through the window, and down the street. Sarah tends the garden with a towel wrapped around her head. "*Voos, voos dis?*" her neighbors ask from the upstairs window. Sarah has a toothache that will not stop her or slow her down; no one would think of going to a dentist.

Sarah takes in children to watch while mothers go off to work in factories, in corner shops. She has her four and usually two or three other children to watch. In these days it is mostly physical care that counts. Years later when she walks around her neighborhood, she looks at the young soldiers and remembers wiping their noses and their bottoms. However, she mostly remembers who had a good appetite and who refused to eat.

Sarah is walking with a walker. I have decided to share my two favorite things: Safta Sarah and my work. I coordinate a program for children with special needs in schools around the country. It is a strange job for me, because as a child I was afraid of authority figures, and here I am working with principals of schools all over Israel. Then there is my accent and different cultural bent. Sometimes the Israeli staff tells me not to be so enthusiastic. The tight lid put on emotions is blown off when I hug them; it is awkward. I always seem to hug and kiss at the wrong time. Would someone please hold up a Stop or a Go sign?

A lifelong fear of conflict misguides me in my choices. One of my roles is to go against Jewish Israeli cultural norms, and promulgate equality for girls and for those with special needs. An inner sense of worth and equality speaks to the educators and parents, but it is new, it is change, and people fight change. I take long train rides and long drives all over Israel in order to do battle with stereotypes.

One such parents' meeting takes place in Acre, a walled port city populated by both Arabs and Jews on the northern coast. A father wearing a knitted *kippah* is adamant: "My son is not having his bar mitzvah together with girls; it is not done." The school principal, a soft and wise Orthodox woman, near retirement age, says, "In my school boys and girls learn math and nature studies together; why shouldn't they study for the Jewish rite of passage into adulthood together?" Avi, the father, huffs and rails against the changes in society.

For Avi, religion is a group of men who pray together, their traditions being forged in societies where women do not take public positions. Only men read from the Holy Torah scroll, open the Holy Ark. By doing so in a ritualistic way, and never changing the way of giving out honors to each other, they feel elevated from their everyday existence.

Avi goes to rabbis all over the Galilee and asks that his son be trained for a bar mitzvah. About ten Rabbis refuse him, saying his son can't represent the other men at prayer, because of his cognitive function.

Suddenly, Avi sees the limits of his holy circle of men. Leaving out the women is not really the important part; rather, they are seeking to elevate themselves and make their lives meaningful. Those with mental challenges too are left out altogether. He decides to go with those who approach Judaism from a more modern and egalitarian perspective, even though it is somehow foreign to him, and not what he previously defined as holy.

Avi's son reads from the Torah. The boy says a personal blessing, "Thank you to Elohim for my father who loves me," as well as the traditional blessings over the Torah. "Blessed are You, Lord, our God, Ruler of the universe, Who chose us among peoples, and gave us our Torah. Blessed are You, Lord, our God, Ruler of the universe, Who gives us the Torah."

Avi has never heard the words in such a meaningful way as spoken through the stammer of his son. Girls also bless the Torah. It strikes him as rather touching that they have entered the holy circle. His new eyes see boys and girls of all ethnic backgrounds joining the circle.

Avi volunteers to come to every teachers' meeting after that in order to convince other parents not to be afraid of something new.

I pick Safta Sarah up at the retirement home. I asked Rivka if I could "have her," or if someone else needed her that day.

"Are you crazy or something?! She's yours as much as she is ours. You don't need to ask permission."

I was delighted. "OK, I just didn't want you to think that she had packed her bags and left."

Not clear on where we are going, Sarah is game to try anything. I cannot park in front of the little synagogue in Tel Aviv. So I call my wonderful friend Susie on my cell phone and she comes out to accompany Sarah across the street. They walk slowly, and traffic waits. I go to park the car, a fool's errand in Tel Aviv.

When I breathlessly join them, I slip into my seat next to Sarah.

She is smiling at the five children in wheelchairs, with CP and developmental disabilities, who are singing and swaying to the music. "This is your work, Yehuditkeleh?"

I did not know that this is why I came to Israel. That only here among refugees, victims of anti-Semitism, the elderly, only in a circle of those in wheelchairs could I dance in a holy circle, limping, flying, at home among the homeless.

# III: Turning Loss into Life

## Laptop Computer — 2001

Part of my job involves taking an hour-long train ride up the Israeli coast-line to Haifa. It sails along by the sea, and it is such a short distance from the south to the north of the country that you actually see the coastline stretched out exactly like the map of Israel. Banana trees appear beside the tracks on the right, and the sea undulates to the left, and hills sprout jagged cliffs as you speed north. My parents give all their children a gift of money, and I blow all of mine on a laptop computer.

I type as the train weaves along the seaside while gazing at the white waves of motion. My fingers find the keys by themselves as my eyes feast on the banana groves, vineyards and green hills.

In the retirement home where Sarah has lived for nine years since Morde-cai's death, I ask her if she has ever seen a computer.

"Yes, I think so." She boasts what incredible geniuses her two great-grand-daughters who live in Tel Aviv are; they play with the computer and under-stand everything about it.

I don't want to spoil it by telling her that most little children who have access to a computer understand all about it.

"I have brought a computer in this carrying case, Sarah, look. I am writing a book about you; that is why I ask so many questions."

She looks delighted and interested. She puts her glasses on the end of her nose.

I take out the laptop, and without plugging it in, turn it on, perched on her bed. She sits in the armchair right next to me.

"Windows," she says, reading the screen, proud of herself.

I am astounded. "I have never heard you speak English, in all the years I have known you," I say.

"It is not English. I read Hungarian; it says 'Vindows.'"

We laugh. I tell her a bit about my writing, which is going extremely slowly.

"I understand," she says. "It is exactly like my knitting. It keeps your hands busy, and your mind active, and then you can't think about your troubles. Or feel the pain too much. I understand."

And she has never seen a laptop before.

"So, Sarah, it is OK with you that I am writing about your life?"

"That way I will live after I die," she answers. She is clearly thrilled with the prospect and takes up her knitting. Perhaps at her age she can look death in the face with equanimity. I am incapable of imagining the fixtures in my life as mortal, finite; and I have made Sarah an important fixture. Death always hurts. It brings loss and I don't want to look at its face as the inevitability that it is.

I have been to the States four times within a few months to visit my father who is under hospice care for his heart. I have terrible jetlag, and relieve his hospice worker at five a.m.; I am up for the day.

The worker, an immigrant from Russia, reports that he took Dad to the commode, the portable toilet that is sitting next to his bed, eight times in the last few hours.

"He hasn't slept much." It occurs to me that I am missing precious time with him while he is awake at night, because he sleeps all day.

I approach his hospital bed, which has taken over the dining room.

His breath smells like medicine. He is cheerful and lucid in the early morning darkness; I am the one who feels somewhat disoriented. "Judith, how is your family in Israel — kids OK?"

I am touched that despite his illness, his dementia, his constant need to pee, his shortness of breath and his palpitations, he can see outside himself and ask about me.

I tell him the latest news. Raphi is driving, he has a girlfriend. Shira is in a theater workshop, and is doing a lot of filming for a local TV station. Ilana can read now in both languages, she is showing up the boys at basketball, and is learning to play the drums.

We reminisce about how Dad used to come to all my cello concerts, and rattle his newspaper in the front row, even during my solo.

"Oh, I did not," he says and makes a funny face, and we laugh. This is the most lucid he has been during my visit. His mind has wandered; he hasn't known where he is, what eyeglasses are for, why his bed is in the dining room, or why I have long hair. I have had long hair as long as he has known me.

He coughs, and then gasps for air. His face turns purple. In the early dawn I haven't turned on the light, but in the shadows I can see his face going dark purple.

"Can't breathe," he says. "Palpitations…" I give him his drug under his tongue, I spray nitroglycerin and give him morphine. Nothing else can be done.

"I will sit with you," I say. He nods that he likes that idea. He closes his eyes for a very long time.

I sit down at my laptop and write but don't like the beginning of the book. Dad opens his eyes. "Judith?" he asks.

"Yes," I say, "I'm here." Then I want some normalcy. My dad is a professor and a prolific reader. At the end he reads and even recites the dialogue of Beatrice and Benedick in *Much Ado about Nothing*.

Benedick: Only foul words; and thereupon I will kiss thee.

Beatrice: Foul words is but foul wind, and foul wind is but foul breath, and foul breath is noisome; therefore I will depart unkissed.

"Daddy, I am having trouble starting my book. It is not dramatic enough."

He struggles for breath. Then this man who doesn't know if he's peed or not, what his oxygen mask is for, says: "You need an enemy. In your case the enemy is the British Mandate. Juxtapose yourself against an enemy."

My mind races off to the myriad of possibilities. I write his idea down on my laptop, and then go sit on his bed and put my cheek on his ailing heart, glad to be so close.

# Aging

One day I will get old too. What changes will be hardest? Loss of people? Sarah is surrounded by people, except maybe at night in the room of her retirement home. Loss of hearing, loss of sight, loss of memory, loss of agility, loss of youth itself and then loss of yourself. There are compensations. Seeing children grow, seeing grandchildren grow. Safta Sarah has seen all her children's children have children, except in the cases of Rafi and Yuval's daughter Dafni, who both died young.

I love walking, I love communicating with people. How long will that last? People who are severely hard of hearing are left out of conversations, don't hear the latest news, unless someone is patient and makes sure that the news gets across.

The telephone is not an option for Sarah anymore. That is not such a loss; people can come to visit in person if they want to communicate with her. I am a telephone addict. Who has time in modern society to visit? Safta Sarah is one of the few people I make time for. Not as much as one would think. Perhaps once every six weeks on average. Recently it has been more. Why? She is among the most loving and wisest friends I have, and that is saying a lot.

Maybe she is an amulet against my aging. I too notice some changes in my body. Lines, needing to exercise more, eat less, my sleep pattern is disturbed. Menstruation becomes harder as I near menopause. Perhaps Sarah is a recipe for aging. Perhaps she is an example of living in the present while assimilating the past even though they get blurred sometimes. I pick up Raphi at the army base and drive him home, I work and write and clean and shop and bleed and cook and exercise and cry and laugh and hug and see that there are first gray hairs streaking my light hair.

Feeling Sarah's pain of loss, I want to surround her with attention. The visits are for me. She is always looking for my children — have I brought them? Not this time. I have come for me.

And for her, because she has had so much loss and I am afraid of loss.

# Cousins — 1985

A trip to the States and back for one person costs just under a thousand dollars. If you are a couple, and have a few kids, and want the grandparents to watch the children grow and have a connection with them, what do you do?

My parents came to visit every year until my father became too sick. They also helped us to fly out to visit them every other year, until the economic noose of moving to Israel loosened, and one day we could pay for our own trips. We became adults finally as we turned forty, about fifteen years after we came here.

I am pregnant with my second child. I have asked my father particularly if he will come take care of me and Raphi and the baby, after the birth. He washed our hair and bathed us as children; he read us long books, way above our heads but very educational; he took us on trips and sledding in the Wisconsin snow. However, he was at work all day, and my mother had the main burden of raising children. As an anachronistic affirmative action move, I ask him to come help me with the baby: "And Daddy, come for a long time. I miss you and I need you." Now that he is newly retired, he doesn't have an excuse not to come. Also, what better way to spend his retirement than to dote on me and my children?

He comes for six weeks; my mother joins him halfway through the visit. I rent an unfurnished apartment for him in a block of apartments in our concrete jungle. I furnish it with Linda's help. We move two spare children's beds in, improvise a sofa out of another bed and some nice cushions, make tables out of slabs of wood, and I put a bottle of bourbon in the kitchen.

I drive to the airport, in the car that they bought for us (just before it got stolen), with Shira in her baby seat. She is three weeks old.

It is mid-winter. After Danny calls to announce her birth to my parents, my dad reports that he is so happy that she is a girl that he "slid up the hill to the university."

Still glowing when he meets her, he takes her, a complete bundle in her baby sling. I help him tie her onto his shoulders and chest, and he cradles her head and says, "She looks just like Bacia"; she is the image of my mother, with her wide cheeks and engaging eyes.

He takes her for a walk in her carriage every day, so that I can have a rest. He walks Raphi to *gan* (nursery school). They hold hands and watch ants on the sidewalk. My dad says, "Look, here's Aunt Minnie, and here's Aunt Gladys."

"Dey aren't dose kind of ants, Zaida!" Raphi says in his Hebrew accent.

We all laugh at how our children count, "Vun, two, tree, four." Jeri, one of my adopted immigrant sisters, jokes that when they say "firty-four," you don't know if they mean thirty-four or forty-four!

In the evenings Dad comes over and we imitate the sounds that baby Shira makes.

One day I drive him to Ramat Gan to meet his first cousin Mordecai. My father is sixty-six years old when he meets his cousin for the first time.

My dad, usually withdrawn and quiet, is jovial and very warm. "Shalom, shalom," he says and holds out his hand.

Mordecai is choked up. All but two of his siblings died in the Holocaust. There is a clear family resemblance. Sarah and Rivka and I watch the reunion with sidelong glances through tear-filled eyes, not wanting to intrude on this private moment but irresistibly drawn to it.

Mordecai tells my father about the letters and packages that his mother sent from America, even during the Depression. "We have loved your mother, Doda Sadie, all our lives. She sent the children clothes and sent us food." Mordecai speaks German to my father, with some Yiddish thrown in; these are their languages in common. I follow, and Rivka translates for me.

"I remember," says my father, looking very far away.

Dad holds Shira, and tells them about Raphi's verbal abilities. "My grandmother had an accent when she spoke English, and my grandson has an accent when he speaks English, and it is the same accent!"

Mordecai is more matter-of-fact than my father. He is ten years older, and has struggled more in his life. "My children say that Sarah and I have an accent when we speak Hebrew. What nerve, when we taught them how to speak!"

"Yes, my grandmother, the one with the accent, taught me how to speak too," Dad says, nodding. (This grandmother of his lived to be 101, so I knew her. She was an immigrant to America, and went back to Europe five times to see her family, almost unheard of in those times.)

Hugging him every time she brings another course to the table, Sarah dotes on my father. Dad loves the chicken soup with homemade noodles. I am holding the baby now and watching the two cousins.

"How is Milton?" Mordecai asks about my Dad's twin. I think back to when I was twenty years old and met the Israeli Edelmans for the first time and Smadi drew a picture of twins climbing grapefruit and orange trees.

"He's fine. He is a professor of industrial relations." Dad says the profession in English and I translate into Hebrew. Many languages are flying in the conversation.

"How's your brother Kalman, in Prague?" Dad asks.

Sarah sits up taller and leans forward.

Mordecai answers. "He gets by. They wouldn't give him a visa to visit Israel for years. And he can't afford to come anyway. He wanted to move to Israel to be with us, but the Czech government said that his wife knew state secrets."

"I must send him something," my father muses.

"Just like your mother," says Mordecai. My dad is much moved. He asks for another helping of chicken which is sweet in its onion and garlic dressing. Some kasha soaks up the juices, and spicy purple cabbage salad and honeyed carrots make the meal sweet and spicy and fresh.

"When did you retire, Mordecai?"

"Oh, fifteen years ago, when I first met Yehudit. I worked in the Elite chocolate factory on the assembly line. I wasn't a professor, except maybe of chocolate! The family was worried that I would rot when I stopped working. My granddaughter Yael had just been born, so I became her babysitter. She is my baby."

My dad winks at me, and says, "Someone here has the same idea!"

"Did you vote for Carter? Nixon? Whom?" Mordecai says, measuring my father.

"I always voted the Socialist ticket, although very few people had heard of it in America. My father was very active in the Cigar Maker's Union; he worked for the eight-hour day."

Mordecai smiles. My father has passed the test.

Rivka joins in the conversation. Her common language with my father is English; I love her accent. "Yes, my father is a socialist too. He marched on Worker's Day, May first, carrying the red flag. He was active in the union too."

Mordecai looks into my father's eyes. "It is good to hear about your father, my uncle. I remember when he died. I was a young man; you must have been a young boy. My father, your father's brother, couldn't stop weeping. It was a terrible loss. My own father had a good death."

In America death seems to be out of fashion. Against the law both to age and to die. "He died of old age and was buried in a private grave. The rest of the family died gruesome deaths in the ovens of Auschwitz, and have no graves."

Silence. Close silence. America, Europe, Israel, different lives, joined in common deaths of common relatives.

I pull Sarah into the kitchen. "Mordecai has another brother?!"

"You do not know about Kalman?!"

"You could write a whole book about what I don't know about this family."

"Why did my father say that he'd send him something? I remember that my father and his brothers always sent checks to someone. Who was that?"

Sarah's eyes meet mine deeply. "Kalman was out of work for fifteen years under the Communists. Perhaps they helped him."

Then she pauses and says, "Kalman is the reason that I married Mordecai."

Why is that? I do not understand and she does not elaborate, then.

I will not meet Kalman or understand until Shira, the baby, is ten years old.


# The Rift — 1950


Three brothers survived the war: Kalman, Mordecai and Tuvye. Tuvye came to live in Israel, but the two brothers feuded. When I finally did meet Kalman, in his own home, I saw pictures of the weddings in Israel, and both brothers.

Some say they fought because Tuvye's wife Sarenka, a survivor, and Mordecai, both had very strong opinions.

Some say they fought about nearly everything.

However, Mordecai himself revealed the real reason to me once.

It was after the war. You are supposed to love your siblings, yet most people compete more with their siblings than with strangers. All the more so after a world war when six of our nine siblings died at Hitler's hand. Tuvye made his way to Israel after we were settled, after enduring the camps in Cyprus. We both loved our little brother Kalman very much. Both of us held on to him, the remnant of our family in Europe.

We fought about Kalman. Tuvye said that Jews should not marry non-Jews after Hitler. That it was continuing their work for them. Kalman married a non-Jew.

I totally disagreed. I felt that one could not judge anyone who had survived the camps, and who had found love. So we fought. We never made peace after the war ruined our lives.

There was silence for a moment, and then Mordecai spoke again.

Maybe it was really about survival; maybe we couldn't stand being the only living brothers in Israel after the war.

# Immigrant Daughters — 2001

"My biggest dream is to go to America. Can I pleeeeeze go, Ema," Shira begs, pleads, demands. America?! Representatives of a five-month exchange program look for eager students at her school. The grandfather who came to take care of her as a baby has left some money in his will for her. Can she please use it to go to America?

I want to say no. I say yes. I want to say, *but I encountered so much pain and loss coming here. It has been so hard. You speak Hebrew. You were raised on the language of the Bible. You have a good life, with stability. I have shielded you from the upheaval that I have known. Go and see what I left and what I was looking for.* But the rules of mothers and daughters dictate that I don't say any of this.

It seems right for this particular fifteen-year-old to go experience the world — she so much wants to breathe in the horizon. I step into the waters of the Red Sea without knowing whether they will part at all. I want her to stay; I want her to love me; I want her to spread her wings and fly.

The Red Sea parts and I jump in like the biblical figure Nachshon son of Amminadab. He jumped in, believing that the waters would part, but he had no inkling of proof. After a four-day seminar in Tel Aviv Shira says: "Thank you, Ema, for making aliyah to Israel. It seems the only possible decision to have made."

I cry when she leaves to go up the stairs at the airport. I have tucked a love letter in her knapsack to be read after takeoff, a tradition cultivated by my women friends and stemming from my fear of flying. If you have letters from people you love, the plane stays in the air better.

She calls me from her grandparents' house in England. "Me, too, Ema. I love you, and thank you for helping me live my dream to go to America."

I know about blessing children on their way. My parents did not succeed in doing it easily. *Don't leave, Shira, don't like it there too much, don't forget where your home is. Will you ever find your way back? How can I reach you?*

# Healing with Food

Until I came to Israel I thought that my culinary heritage was meatloaf and potatoes, hamburgers and French fries, spaghetti with tomato sauce. I hadn't tasted the food of my grandmother — we lived far away, and by the time I was conscious of such things she had stopped cooking. My mother did tell funny stories about herself. Mom tried to make Grandma's chicken soup as a young adult at home and forgot to remove the feet from the chicken.

Sarah brings me the taste of my foremothers, of Europe, of the Sabbath, of holidays, of survival, of humor, of travel.

The most heavenly and divine dish that she makes, a magical one for me, is made of a vegetable with which I develop a love affair. If you know how to make fifty kinds of eggplant, you are a Middle Easterner.

You boil the cabbage until it is soft and then give your full attention to the eggplant. Meanwhile slice the eggplant into circles, about a half-inch thick. Then take a knife and make a pocket in the black skin around the side by slicing the round in half but leaving it intact. Like so. Salt the eggplant and leave it to drain the brown juice while you make the meat filling.

The meat filling is ground dark turkey meat, or lean turkey meat; it is very healthy for the heart. Mordecai has to be careful how much fat he eats. This is very lean ground meat and we don't use beef.

Take a pound of meat, chop in a large onion, add an egg, ground black pepper, one glove of garlic chopped, and a pinch of salt. Add a fistful of matzo meal and mix.

Then you fill the pockets in the eggplant circles with the meat filling, and dip them in beaten egg. You fry them in oil until brown. While they are frying, take your largest pan, and fry an onion in oil. Then add a can of tomato paste, about a quarter cup of brown sugar — Ilana uses artificial sweetener — and about a cup of vinegar and a teaspoon of cumin. Fill up about half the pan with water. All the stuffed vegetables will cook in this sweet and sour juice. Add a cup of uncooked white rice to the meat mixture now.

Start with a layer of stuffed cabbage. Take one leaf at a time, separate it, cut off the hard vein in the middle, and fill and fold with a generous tablespoon of meat mixture. But use your hands. Make a nice neat package folding in the sides, and lay these in the simmering juice.

Core a few red peppers about the size of your grandfather's fist. Fill them with the mixture and put them in the pot.

Now hollow out a few zucchini, make them like hollow tubes with a knife. Fill them with meat, put on top of the cabbage. Now lovingly and gently lay the eggplant rings. Make sure all the vegetables are covered with the juice of the tomato paste and the water. You can add more water, vinegar, tomato paste. Then cover. Safta Sarah uses ketchup sometimes and then you don't need the sugar.

Cook for about an hour or more until the rice is cooked.

Now sit down and rest, and later we will eat. Safta Sarah fries a few breaded turkey breasts in the leftover oil from the eggplants. They are sumptuous. They are beaten flat and dredged in beaten egg, and then in matzo meal with salt, pepper, and paprika. Then fried until crispy and brown. Together with a chopped cucumber and tomato and onion salad, with a little parsley, this is a whole meal. Of course Sarah has some of her golden chicken broth on hand.

Delicious food prepared with care is the mother's tenderness and nurturing that I crave. Eating too much, pigging out, is a mother criticizing me for gaining weight. So eating serves all mothering voids. And it temporarily fills the empty space of loss, leaving home, sadness.

# Terror — 2001

On Erev Rosh Hashanah, I go to see Safta Sarah at her retirement home. She is surrounded by a throng of elderly residents waiting for the elevator, perched on her walker. I hug her from behind and let her get a good look at me, to get oriented. "OOOOooh," she says. The crowd of disheveled white-haired women, and one man, watch as I produce a homemade honey cake, and some honey-sweetened carrots, her recipe, and wish her a happy new year. "Who are you?" says a woman who has seen me a dozen times, but cannot place me. "I am her daughter," I say, playing to the crowd. Sarah chuckles at our private joke, and says, "Yes, yes, there are some children who are born straight from the heart."

The old man, much thinner than the last time I saw him, smiles and says, "Your sister was here yesterday." I have passed as Rivka and Ilana's sister. This is great. Danny nudges my arm. We are late for our play in Tel Aviv, and this was to be a quickie. I bend down and kiss Sarah's forehead. It is hot. She says, "How did you find me, do you know where I live?" Have I confused her with my joke? I ask her if she is ill. "Yes, I haven't been feeling too well." I leave feeling uneasy.

Yuval tells me that she has been in the hospital unit in the retirement home for a few days, following a shot for the pains in her legs. I am very troubled.

My world is caving in around me. Israel has been suffering from one terrorist attack after the next, getting closer and closer to home for the last twelve months. Teenagers are blown up going to a disco for new immigrants with low incomes. Parts of families are severed in a pizza parlor in the center of Jerusalem, just minutes from the headquarters of my employers there. Two train stops that I frequent are blown up, one with human casualties, one without.

And then the World Trade Center is attacked by terrorists, thousands of people die, and another world war is looming. Sarah is always hoping for peace, despairing of war, worrying about the future for her family and for Israel, for the troubled world. And now she is sick, and I am worried about Raphi, who is to be inducted into the Israeli army in March 2002. I take the attacks personally: will there be a war raging when he is in the army? It is dangerous to be a civilian; every time there is a bomb attack my teenagers check the papers and call friends in agony, waiting to see if their friends were caught at a pizza parlor or at a discotheque at the wrong time.

And what about the Palestinians? They have teenagers too. They have young people who want a future too. Neither side can back down and talk peace.

The Gulf War in 1991 shook my early tentative tendrils into the ground here, and uprooted them, stunted them. During the wave of terror, however, I make a leap in feeling more at home in Israel when I decide not to cave in to terror, but make a conscious act of riding the trains and buses. I choose to go to the city center of Jerusalem which is blowing up every week, during the heat of the Intifada. Why do I do it? I, the woman who's afraid of flying, who gets sea sick, who doesn't like cliffs or elevators? No one can accuse me of bravery. I think it is a decision to choose life. My work is my life. If I stayed at home I could not do my work. I also decide not to ruminate on the trains and buses and city centers. Humor helps. On a Jerusalem morning near the bomb epicenter, I say to my colleague, "You sit by the window, then when the bomb comes, you will get it."

Without missing a beat he says, "You will get the after-blast."

We go on with our meeting. Weird strains of shofar-blowing and the sweet violin strains of a new immigrant blast through the window. Smells of the local schwarma stand penetrate our nostrils, our senses poised.

# Displaced Person with Eggplant — 2002

Safta Sarah *hates* the food at her retirement home. It is institution food, cooked in great quantities with a heavy hand on the oil, light on the spices. She is not a complainer, but don't get her going on the food at her home.

I make Safta Sarah's stuffed vegetables for Shabbat for close friends, to express my love for them. So few people cook like that anymore, a dish with more than two steps to it. I save the most perfectly shaped eggplant wearing a dressing of its red sauce in a recycled plastic container. I also freeze some of the homemade challot made for Shabbat. I choose a medium-sized one, too big for one person.

"How are you, Sarahleh?"

"Not so good, my leg gives me no rest, I have shooting pains, and…"

Never very good at surprises, I can't hold back. "I have a surprise for you, the only thing that could possibly make your leg feel better."

I take the plastic container out of a bag with cooling packs. I open it partially, and wave it under Sarah's nose.

Her eyes and ears do not absorb stimulus the way they used to, but her nose is in full gear. "EXACTLY! Exactly like mine. You got it just right."

I think this is the biggest compliment that I have ever received. Then I wave the challah under her nose, and put it in her hand for her to feel the soft but firm texture. The aroma is sensual and sweet; it fills up her small bedroom.

"That is not store-bought," she says in amazement, "ooh, you brought me real bread."

"Please eat some, dip it in the gravy. I want to see you enjoy it," I say.

"No." She is determined. "I am going to have a party tonight and show it off to all my friends."

"Yes, tell them that it is YOUR stuffed eggplant and challah."

We love the conspiracy.

Sarah rewards me immediately with new stories. They are never actually new stories, but a new telling of the old stories, lighting a lamp in a way that illuminates them and lets me into a darker corner where I have not been taken before. And lighting up the past for her, when the present is crumbling in osteoporosis, loss of memory, loss of hearing, loss of clear speech, fears about the future with the Arab-Israeli conflict.

It is winter. There is no electricity and no running water on the farm. The outhouse is a cold walk out in the snow to near the barns. Sarah fetches the water from the train station which has a pump. There are stairs cut into the sharp hill up to the station, but when it is icy there is no way to get a toehold. Sarah falls hard on her way back down, spills the water, tears her dress and bruises her thigh badly. She is not a complainer. She is angry at nothing in particular and kicks the ground. She climbs back up by crawling. At least she will return with water, so that Preva won't worry too much.

Preva is distracted when she gets back. More laws against the Jews. This time the authorities want to make sure that there are no marriage or sexual relations between Jews and Gentiles. The neighbors are so kind and accepting of them, this seems out of synch with their everyday lives. They trade, buy their milk and apples. But on his delivery rounds there is a new cold correctness behind the neighbor's eyes.

Preva tells Sarah to leave on her stained work dress because there is a calf being born in the barn; that is messy work and Sarah is so good at helping with births. Sarah dislikes birthing calves in the early spring; it is cold with all the liquids coming from the cow into the fresh air. The animal cries and Sarah strokes her and speaks soothing words to her. Sarah's father can't understand how she knows intuitively what to do.

When the new calf lies in the straw, the cow lows in pain. The new calf struggles to stand up but will not suck. Sarah puts her fingers in his mouth. He sucks, and she guides his soft mouth to the cow's udder. After several attempts he is rewarded with milk. However, he has already imprinted on Sarah. Whenever he sees her after that he chases her around the barn and lows to suck her fingers.

Sarah is thinking of these memories which seem to be in the present tense for her. The week before my visit she makes her great escape. She wakes up and looks in the mirror and sees an older version of her mother. Her mother. Left behind, begging to be taken. But she objected to the idea of leaving Europe just three years before! Sarah takes her purse, her walker, her hat and shuffles to the elevator. No staff notice as she disappears behind the automatic doors. As she looks like she has a determined purpose, no one questions her as she leaves the front door of the home. On the main street a cab crawls slowly along the curb. "Where to?" the young immigrant driver from Russian asks.

"The train station. " He hops out to arrange Sarah's red frame walker in the back.

The cab driver takes her arm. The fare is twenty shekels. Sarah hasn't used money in quite a while. She has one fifty-shekel note, folded into her purse by Yuval.

At the ticket office in the train station the teller asks her, "Yes, what is your destination?"

Sarah fingers the change from the taxi. After the tip she has twenty-five shekels. "Where can I go for twenty-five shekels?"

"Just to Hadera."

"I'd like one ticket to Hadera, then. Where is the platform?"

She is pushed aside and it takes her many attempts before finding Platform Two.

In Hadera she wanders around aimlessly on the platform. She doesn't think she is much closer to where Preva lives, but maybe her daughter Ilana is nearby. A young train guard, just out of the army, notices a very elderly woman with a walker wandering up and down the platform.

"Where are you going?" he asks her helpfully.

"I don't know," she says, hoping for direction. He radios the police and asks if there are any elderly women who have run away from home. There is one who fits her description. Rivka is at the police station and is frantic. They tell the guard to make her a cup of tea and wait with her until they can drive north to Hadera to rescue Sarah from her last solo flight.

# Knots: Tangle, Puzzle, Problem, Cluster, Tie, Bind, Fasten

Grandma Rose kept kosher *style*, my mother Bacia didn't, I do, my daughter Shira did. Past tense, although now in the army she does again. The host mother in Oklahoma promises me that she will respect our dietary laws — she once hosted a Moslem girl who also did not eat pork — but she adds her hesitations. "She could learn our ways while she is here."

"But that is not cultural *exchange*," I protest. "Each should learn from the other, not neutralize the other. You need to have your own culture in full blossom before you can share and exchange it." Exchange is education, not reeducation, I add to myself.

The host mother feels ambivalent about Shira missing school for the Jewish New Year and Day of Atonement. "She will miss the very beginning of school."

I remember the days when I missed the very beginning of school every year; then every other day I missed school for illness, my classmates asked, "Was it *another* Jewish holiday?" Their question was pointing out difference. The host mother is intolerant. Perhaps she is ironing out the differences between Shira's practices and her own.

Shira isn't allowed to telephone home more than once every two weeks. This, by Israeli standards, where parents and children check in to share important news hourly, like: "Please take out the schnitzel and heat it up for your sister."

My mother did not feel comfortable with heart-to-heart talks. She was worried that I would be delinquent with boys, smoking, and parties when I was a teenager.

Nothing that my teenager can tell me would dissuade me from talking to her. Shira cries from homesickness when she talks to us. I can hear the host mother hissing in the background telling her to keep it short.

Shira is like the baby that King Solomon had to divide between two mothers.

My uncle Milt's grandson is becoming bar mitzvah. Shira is, relatively speaking, within visiting distance, and I ask that she be allowed to attend. The host mother balks and dissuades her. "It isn't safe to fly after the terrorist attacks in New York and Washington, and Philadelphia," she says, sounding competitive.

Power struggles ensue. I lose.

I found solace as a teenager in my Jewish youth group. My mother hated Hebrew school, which Rose, as an immigrant mother, forced her to attend. Pretending that she'd been at Hebrew school, she hid up in the attic.

My parents were not affiliated with a synagogue; they were not enthusiastic about paying my dues. I paid for some of the weekend retreats myself, and got synagogue assistance for others.

The host mother starts teaching the Gospels to Shira at nights. She asks permission for her to attend a Christian youth group; she promises me that there isn't religious content. "Shira is isolated, she doesn't have friends. This is a social group."

I ask that she be sent to a Jewish youth group. The host mother lodges a complaint to the program, to the effect that "Jews" are interfering too much, and some youth worker is harassing Shira to join a Jewish youth group, and inhibiting her adjustment.

My mother is upset. "Tell her that you don't allow it."

I speak to the host mother and cry. "Please don't teach her the Gospels. She is alone, isolated, uprooted, young, vulnerable."

The host mother retorts, "If I sent my child to you, he would be strong enough to learn your teachings."

"Well, we are not Fundamentalists," I reply. Shira is very far away. I am used to missing my parents, but not my child.

Why did I come to Israel? As much as I love diversity, that diversity has not always made room for me. In *chutz la'aretz*, outside Israel, I suffered anti-Semitism, and so did Sarah. My mother encountered signs that said, "No Blacks or Hebrews need apply." True diversity is respect for other people's differences. There was no diversity for Shira in Oklahoma.

I came to Israel and taught diversity and acceptance towards those with special needs, who are part of the immigrant experience because a third of them are first-generation immigrants. We take so much with us when we emigrate. We lose something. We gain something. Both Israel and America are melting pots, but melting pots have to make sure that they are not a blended stew, but rather a bouquet of divergent flowers that retain their individual color and fragrance.

# The Guide — 1995

Yuval telephones me to say that his uncle, my father's cousin Kalman, is coming to Israel. Rivka calls with an invitation to a party in his honor at her house. I do not have a clear picture of who this is.

We plan to meet at the Museum of the Jewish Diaspora in Tel Aviv. This was my first job and therefore *home* in Israel. I spent the first several years that I was here telling people the story of the Jews for the last two thousand years. Behind me were props, and reconstructions of walls, cities, symbols, life-cycle events in film and models, moving and still. I loved guiding Jewish and Christian tourists.

Yuval and I meet Kalman in the lobby of the museum. The black marble floor mirrors the three of us meeting and embracing, and tingles shoot down my spine. So much like my father. My father is diminutive, while I am quite tall; Kalman is slightly taller than me. He does not seem shy or retiring, but gracious.

Two thousand years hold their breath as Yuval and Kalman and I enter the dark passages of the museum, the landscape of our common history, even though we were each born on a different continent.

Although there is nothing missing in my familiarity with the museum, within three minutes it becomes apparent that it is Kalman who should be guiding. I hadn't known that he was a professor of history, specializing in labor movements. My father, his twin brother, and my brother all specialized in labor relations in some form! Humbled, thrilled, delighted, I step back and wave him ahead with a laugh at myself. Yuval and I listen to his learned discourse; even though he has never set eyes on the museum architecture, he jumps right into its symbolism.

We stand in a dark hallway with a luminous wire cage column hanging from the ceiling. The room calls out, "Remember!" It is a memorial room for all the times that punctuated the centuries when Jews were slaughtered by the Romans, the Crusaders, by the Inquisition in Spain, the Polish lords, the Holocaust. For Kalman this is not an exhibition as it is for me. He stands under the wire cage, with lights casting their remembrance through the bars, and he turns to Yuval. "I remember when I received the telegram that you were born. It was like a light at the time of darkness."

*So that is the person to whom Mordecai's telegram was addressed. So that is who was alive to receive it. One brother lived through WWII and remained in Europe. What did he see there? Is there a number on his arm?*

Yuval and I trail behind him, like the two children — male and female — that he never had, because of his personal history.

I was enthralled with Kalman during that visit, but we did not have enough time alone to establish a personal relationship. What was he really like? Who was this man? I would find him when my world came crashing down in 2001 when my father died, Shira went to Oklahoma and Raphi left home about to be inducted into the army, terrorism spread and the threat of war was breathing down our Israeli necks.

# The Breakdown — 2000

The army envelope that arrives at our apartment building might as well be a letter bomb. An army envelope explodes in my post box sending my entire building up in flames and my life crashing down. An army envelope enters my body and begins to turn my light hair to white, my muscles to fat, my sleep mechanism to "hold." The official command expects my son to go take a gun and learn how to shoot it. He is commanded to exchange his jeans and t-shirt for a khaki green uniform with stiff buttons and stubborn wrinkles. He is commanded to relinquish his free choice and to submit to young officers who will tell him to wake up after four hours sleep, to run for six hours, to sleep under the sky on rocky ground, and to guard outside in the rain, in a ditch with no waterproofing.

Shira is going off to Oklahoma this same year. A home full of teenagers will now become a home of two unglued parents and a nine-year-old.

My father is lingering and there is no predicting when he will slip away. Raphi is about to be given his gun. Life hangs in the air, without breathing.

My friends and near ones can't possibly reach me, or make me happy. And who wants to be with a person who can't have joie de vivre?

I came to Israel to build a family that was rooted in promise, in light.

Someone has turned the light out.

I have nothing to hang on to.

They have sent me down a large chute, the speed has increased; there are no hand grips, no breaks, and no end to the sliding down.

No one could have predicted just how a graveyard, a dead grandmother and two aging distant relatives could help with the task of living.

# Prague — 2001

Safta Sarah says that she married Mordecai because of Kalman, Mordecai's youngest brother and my dad's first cousin. She has repeated that to me so many times like a clue to a puzzle. Every contact with him brings me closer to putting together the pieces.

Danny attends a yearly medical conference abroad. Where would I like to go this year? I ask for Prague, and luckily, there is a cardiology conference there during the autumn. Yuval lets Kalman know that we are coming. A day before we fly out, I telephone him to set an exact time and place for our meeting.

He says on the phone that his English is not very good. It does sound chancy on the telephone. I wonder how we will communicate. We make a date to meet at our hotel for the following day.

Kalman knocks on the hotel room door. He hugs and kisses me warmly. Wearing a suit jacket and tie, with an ironed button-down shirt, Kalman is neatly attired and smells of cleanliness. He has a large bald spot on the top of his head and a white circle of hair around the sides, and some age spots on his skin; otherwise there is no evidence during the week that we spend with him that he is elderly as he has a lot more energy than I do! His eyes are clear and piercing, touching, and he has a smile waiting to crack open at any time. My love for him seems to have been born before I was. His love for me is rooted in centuries of Edelman immigration stories.

Danny asks him what family he has. I wince and try to ward him off, but it is too late. I know that he had a wife whom he loved very much, and that she died of Alzheimer's disease, that they had no children, and that he is alone in the world.

Kalman answers the question seriously and with warmth. "I have my brothers who died (Mordecai and Tuvye) and their wives (Sarah and Sarenka) in Israel. I have their children (he names them all: Yuval, Ilana, Rivka, Shlomo and Alex), and I have family in America. I have Seymour (my father's oldest brother), dead, and I have Milton, and I have Murray, dead this year." He has planted the seeds of connection between us, by listing my father and his two brothers, his first cousins.

I have brought him Elite chocolate in a gift box with the picture of a Monet painting on the cover, a huge can of Elite coffee and an Osem nut cake. As I start to explain to him why I brought these things, he looks deeply into my eyes and says, "Because Mordecai worked at the Elite Chocolate Factory."

His English is somewhat broken, but his vocabulary is rich and studded with diamonds. Language is not a barrier, and we proceed to speak and tour Prague for many hours every day. We ask him to stay for dinner but he has to go give a urine sample at home as he is being checked for prostate cancer.

# Gifts — 2001

"He ran to meet them from the tent door, and bowed himself to the ground.... Let a little water, I pray you, be fetched and wash your feet, and rest your-selves under the tree, and I will fetch a morsel of bread, and comfort your hearts."

— *Abraham receiving guests, Genesis 18:2, 4*

The next day in Prague, Kalman runs outside in the dark to greet our taxi. Hugs and kisses. His apartment looks much like apartments of immigrants to Israel from Europe. It is quite modern in its design with a colorful abstract painting, furniture from the 1960s and walls lined with books. For a moment I feel a time warp, and I could be in my father's study when Kalman approaches me as I am reading the titles of his books. He points out his name on scholarly books in Czech, French and German.

Our last two nights are spent at a spa in Carlsbad. Kalman tells us that he is sent there for a fortnight a year as part of his reparations from Germany. We have two days and nights of romantic hikes in the autumn leaves, and luxurious spas and a hotel that looks as fancy as the Titanic before it sank. Then we return to Prague for our last night.

The greatest surprise of all waits for me. Kalman has made us dinner. An eighty-three-year-old man has never made me dinner before. He tells us that he koshered a chicken especially for us! He salted it himself to draw out the blood as it is forbidden to eat the blood of an animal.

"But Kalman, how did you know how to do it?"

"My mother taught me how."

"That was over seventy years ago!"

"Yes, but what you learn at home, you never forget, even if a world war comes and takes away the home."

We start with homemade chicken soup with noodles. He bounces between his little kitchen and the dining table, which is in a corner of the living room, just like our apartment in Israel. Then he serves us beautifully browned and succulent chicken. He asks me which piece I would like. I say just a wing. He says, "Not enough *fleish* (meat), take this piece," and gives me a huge piece of white meat. On the side is compote made of raspberries. I think about the amazing combination of meat and fruit, a winning complement of tastes that I decide to adopt. For dessert he brings fruit, which, surprisingly, we find room for. We can't touch the cake. He says that the cake I brought from Israel was very good.

During dinner, he, like me, can't keep surprises, and gives me a green folded napkin with a hand-embroidered monogram on it. It says "P. E." Pepi, or Pessy, Edelmann — his sister who died in the Holocaust. Kalman has no daughters, no sons, and he has given this priceless gift to me. Most survivors of the Holocaust have no mementos from their homes before the war. They couldn't keep anything. I am already speechless and overwhelmed from the gift of the embroidery, and now Kalman gives me a small box, wrapped. I look into his eyes, amazed at the connection that we have formed in just a week. I open it, and inside is a Jewish star, about the size of a quarter, studded with red garnets that are characteristic of the Czech Republic. We, two orphans, have adopted each other. So many gifts at once!

I am a person who loves gifts like a child. My mother's mother sent me big packages with wooden dolls and homemade doll clothes. Once Grandma Rose cut up her own wedding gown in order to make my doll a wedding dress. A box of earthly delights. Coffee candies that were smooth on your tongue. There was delightful stationary with horses or cats or gardens in the countryside. Martha, my lifelong friend, sends me packages of everything that I miss from America: Peet's gourmet coffee, the lastest James Taylor CD, the book *Traveling Mercies* by Anne Lamott and a new paper hat that looks like straw, as well as Carl the dog books for the children and Ghirardelli mint chocolate for Danny.

My own mother once had a cello waiting on my bed for my tenth birthday. It was honey-colored and just glowed. The best present that I ever received, it set the standards very high. And then there were the frustrating presents. Like a plaid autumn jacket, very much in style, which came with the words, "This was so expensive that it is your Chanukah present, your birthday present, and next year's Chanukah present." It left me with a sense of deprivation. No presents to look forward to. Safta Sarah's presents were always exactly what I needed for comfort: a bag of homemade sugar cookies, homegrown oranges, and home-knit sweaters. Her children were giving in the same vein; Ilana gave us a tricycle for Raphi when we moved to Israel, a brand new one, which we couldn't have afforded at the time.

Kalman's gifts are the gifts of filled-in family history, of his sister's embroidery, of his cooking, of a necklace that is like a blessing, because he sees me and what is important to me: not gold and garnets, but the symbol of Judaism and a symbol of his giving. Kalman's gifts are gifts of seeing me and hearing me, loving what I love, connecting me to my history of scattered immigrations. Cups of coffee ensue. Kosher lunches at the town hall in the Jewish quarter. Tram tickets. This must surely fill up the empty spaces in the black holes of my history. My hunger for sweets, for food, for connectedness to family, my longing for my deceased father, my collective historical consciousness of the Holocaust which is a bruise in my psyche. My son in the army.

Having cleared the dinner dishes, we sit before a stack of photographs and envelopes. I see from some of the modern ones that my first cousins, my uncle Milt and Aunt Esther, all my relatives from Israel are featured. Then he takes an oblong black-leafed album off the table. Very few European Jews have their pre-war photo albums.

"I gave it to friend of mine. They hide it for the war," Kalman explains.

He points to a beautiful young woman. "My first girlfriend." He looks like he is full of secrets. "She not come back." I am stunned; she looks too beautiful not to be alive and still young.

Before I have a chance to recover he points to a girl with dark hair. "She my second girlfriend. She not come back."

Then there are photos of young boys and girls playing guitar around a campfire. There are tents in the background. Some of the boys are wrestling, and one of them with a wicked grin...is Kalman.

"They not come back. I am the only one to live to tell the tale."

They look just like the young men and women in Raphi's youth group.

In the stack are a few letters. Kalman hands me three airmail letters written by his Aunt Sadie, *my own grandmother*. One and a half of the letters are written in English. Sadie died when I was two, but I realize from this letter how intelligent and able she is. I can see why her sons were all professors and scientists.

Mordecai had also shown me her letters and spoken of the packages she sent. My new narrator tells me that she sent food, coats, cigarettes which could be used for trade. Marriage and history and kindness had woven them into family, not blood ties. And I am woven into the family also, sharing a letter that was received a brief fifty-three years earlier, in response to Kalman's announcement that he has survived the war.

Just at the time of my father's death, I meet his mother in Kalman's letter.

Sadie writes: "Surely it would be better for you to join your brothers in the Land of Israel, rather than to remain in Prague..." I feel that I have received a blessing from my grandmother whom I never knew.

February 28th, 1948

Dear Kalman,

We were happy that your trip proved both instructive and enjoyable. I'm sure the contacts you made and the experience gained will prove beneficial to your work. Did you find many changes when you returned? I am also curious to know whether your discussions with Americans in any way affected your opinion of the U.S.A. Naturally it depends on the type of people you met.

Here there is a division of opinion about the Marshall plan and European help. In view of your state of health your decision to continue your studies is wise. Will you continue to receive help from the government or else how do you expect to finance yourself. That is exactly what my Milton is doing. He teaches part time, which pays him a salary. That with his veteran's allotment gives him an adequate income. His wife works too, she is a secretary to one of the department heads in the university. It will probably be another year before he will receive his PhD. Murray is doing nicely. Milton will complete his studies soon. Seymour and his wife are well, they are both working for the government and both attend classes evenings.

It seems to be an Edelman characteristic to want to increase one's store of knowledge. I do not expect any of them home until summer vacation time, when they take turns. Our home is too small to accommodate all simultaneously.

General conditions have not yet come back to normal. Both employment and the cost of living have declined somewhat, but barely enough to make a real difference. There are still shortages but gradually supply is catching up with demand. Taxes are high and will undoubtedly remain so while there is this confusion and uncertainty — although there is considerably less tension. If only the futility of war could be brought home to all concerned and the wonderful progress of science and technology be applied for the good of humanity instead of its destruction what a grand world this would be.

Let me know where you have any difficulty reading and understand this letter.

Love, Aunt Sadie
New York, New York


The photographs look at us. Each of his brothers and sisters are brought out in sepia color to meet me. Liebe was still a young woman when the Nazis killed her. Rachel had two little girls who were actually stepdaughters, from her husband's first marriage. They were so loved by Kalman, his first nieces, that he has now blanked out their names entirely. Simon, the oldest brother, went to the concentration camps with his mother so that she wouldn't be alone.

There are photos of my cousins, my aunt and uncle, the Israeli relatives. We spend quite a time looking at a photo of Kalman standing by Mordecai's grave in 1995. They have engraved the names of all the sisters and brothers on his tombstone. They didn't have graves because of mass burials, or because of being burned in ovens at Auschwitz. Simon, Rachel, Pessy, Esther, Yaakov Moshe, and Liebe's names rest on Mordecai's grave.

Kalman leans towards me. "I am asking a big desire. I would like to be there too. When I die..." He pauses. I sense that he doesn't talk or think about his own death much; he is so young in his actions and style. "I would like to rest with my brothers and sisters."

I listen, somewhat dumbstruck, and at first cannot respond. I look at him and say, "It is beautiful that the names of your brothers and sisters rest together. We will put your name there, too, when the time comes."

"Not just the name."

"You would like your bones to rest with Mordecai's?"

"Yes, my bones too."

I take Kalman's hand and squeeze it. "When the times comes, I would be honored to accompany your bones to Israel. I will check with Yuval about burial."

"There is complication. I want Alena to be buried with me. Her ashes rest in an urn in the other room. She is not Jewish. Perhaps this is liberal graveyard? I have seen flowers there, and flowers are not Jewish custom."

"I will bring Alena too. We will find a solution. I am honored that you have asked me, and will do anything to fulfill your wish."

I have thoughts of sprinkling Alena into Kalman's grave when no one is looking! Or sneaking the urn into the graveyard and burying her myself when no one is around. Kalman's wishes are more important to me than Jewish custom or law, although I know this question would have to be pondered carefully.

Such a lot of gifts that Kalman has given me. Among them, total acceptance, love, a history, a family. I want to tell him that I will say Kaddish for him too, but somehow can't, yet, not until the opportunity arrives at another visit.

A messenger with a box of Czech chocolates for Safta Sarah: I can't wait to see her face when I give them to her. Her wish was to have a brother-in-law like Kalman. I am bringing chocolates from Kalman to Sarah. As I pack the generous box of chocolates in my overstuffed suitcase, I wonder what size box of chocolates he gave her a lifetime ago when he first met her at the Hachshara farm. When we embrace and say goodbye I feel a sadness and a sense of completeness. Just when I am in total despair about the security of my child, and the whole country, Kalman walks out of the past and into my life.

# Masaryk Saves the Jews, Kalman Saves Me

"It is easy to write what you are passionate about," states Kalman. He saw in the early 1990s that there was nothing written about Masaryk and the Jews. He took it upon himself to research this question, about which he has now written some two hundred articles. He was especially fascinated by Masaryk's historial trip to Palestine. Before the whole world let Jewish refugees sink at sea, or burn in concentration camps, Thomas Masaryk, the president of Czechoslovakia, saw a positive answer to the refugee question of Europe's Jews.

My dear Judith and Danny,

For all I come to thank you — Judith, Danny, Raphi, Shira, Ilana — very very much for the splendid card, with all the good wishes to my birthday, and for the beautiful pictures. At once, I must thank you for your so much costly and precious gifts, which you bring from Israel.

Your personal letter, dearest Judith, wrote with so much love, nobleness, and sensitivity, touched me profound... You used towards me so kind and warm words — I am at fault; but I can assure you, that the affection and consonance is mutual, as to my next being and relative. All the time that spent with you was to me so nice, cordial and attentive, so that I never shall be able to forget your visit in Prague. I feel me with you happy! And therefore, when you left suddenly in the evening on Saturday my flat, I feel me isolate, and around me emptiness...

I remember of you, Danny and Sharon (*Danny's sister who lives in Israel*) very often now, I think of you fly to New York and Los Angeles, hope that all passed well, and you came just back happy at home. The last week I became [received] a letter from Milton, but I debt [owe] to answer him.

Of your book, which you write about our family, dear Judith, I enjoy much — I don't doubt, she shall be interest, wise and attractive...

I should be glad, when I should receive from you again news: about you, Danny, and particularly your children.

The advice, relative other death of my sister-in-law Sarenka (she wife of

Tuvye), mournful me very. She visited me all the year, when she visited to Karlovy Vary, and was here happy and good.

With all my love and best thanks, I embrace you —

Your
Kalman

P.S. Excuse my bed English!

# Threat of War, Or Death Approaching — 2001

The war in Afghanistan has begun; echoes of the Gulf War reverberate on the TV screen. CNN shows rockets of green lights gliding across the night, and we're supposed to understand. It just signals war to me. There are threats of more terrorism in America. I have always been afraid of flying and I have a trip scheduled in November.

Shira is getting more and more into American culture. She asks if she can stay. She has been told that the Jewish community is not welcoming and that the only other Israeli there is not respectful. I feel that they are cutting her off from herself, and want her to come home before she forgets who she is. She says that a host mother of someone on the program was shot to death with five shots to the chest this weekend. The world is threatening everywhere.

And Safta Sarah's life has spanned the century. She grew up on a farm, and she embroiders and knits patterns of another place and time for her Israeli great-grandchildren with names that are so modern. *Shaked* means almond tree or almond, or almond blossom. *Amit* means friend or colleague. *Noam* means pleasantness, *Bar* means wild, *May* for the month of May, *Nadav* means one who gives, *Noa* means movement, *Omer* means the barley harvest of the field, *Yannai* the name of one of the Hasmoneans, and *Yonaton* God gives. We have *Levi*, an ancient tribe; *Harel* means mountain of God; *Amir* means treetop; *Gal* means wave. We have trees and friends, the ancient field of Israel and the wildness of hope. She is so proud of the growing number of them, and one more on the way. Maya is pregnant for the second time. When I first came to Israel, Maya was a toddler.

"I feel that Mordecai is closer than ever now. I feel that he is calling me. He comes to me at night now, he visits, and is waiting." Sarah is not superstitious. She is reconnecting with her life with her partner, even if that means joining in death.

Someone told me once that rarely would anyone choose cessation of pain over the life force. The pull of life is too strong. Sarah has lost a child first, then a husband, then a granddaughter. The pain in her leg, hip and foot is torturous and incessant. Yet the fruits of her labors are tangible. This restaurant is full of offspring and everyone has a source of income, a place to live. There are some divorces among this bunch, but still statistically low. On balance, she would always choose life.

Sarah lives alone in the retirement home. She doesn't like the food or being alone at night. Mordecai, who has been dead for nine years, sits with her; she talks to him.

She does not seem afraid of death when she speaks to me. What is more frightening, death or feeble old age, with pain and loss? Sarah cannot hear without the latest model of hearing aid that Yuval has fitted her with.

"He has thought of everything. A telephone that lights up because I can't hear. Speed dial to all the relatives. Wireless headphones for the television so that I can hear. The walker with the basket and brakes and handles. What a son. Who has a son like that? You do, your Raphileh." I think, oh, Yuval is the one who lived, and she says Raphi is like *him, the one who lived*. Or I think, Sarah remained with three children and I have three children, so I needn't lose one.

It must be her close tie with her children that keeps her alive. They nurture her, take her to doctors, see to her every need, take her to their homes for Shabbat.

She tells me that she is ready to leave the world, and I tell her that I am not ready for her to go. I need her to tell me her stories.

Old age frightens me, yet I stay very close. Sometimes there is a smell of urine in the retirement home. Sarah no longer heats up or serves food of any kind. She can still knit for all the great-grandchildren. She can still give, so she has that to live for. Drugs sometimes make her groggy and only dull the pain.

Sarah doesn't want to see another war.

# Immigrant Daughter — 2001

I am an immigrant mother. I left my mother and my father, my town (with lakes and forests and a hip university atmosphere) and my country, and came to live in Israel. It was hard to raise children with not enough money for toys, clothes, the phone bill, an apartment, travel abroad. Safta Sarah fed the empty missing black holes in me, which were crying for nurturing, for care, for having given something up, even when I felt appreciative of what I had here in my new country.

Economic stress was relieved but the black holes remained, and a visit with Safta Sarah always felt like a remedy. She is an immigrant mother; her leave-taking of her parents, her country, her economic noose were all so much more traumatic than mine. I see her as a survivor, as an example of someone who has managed a positive response to survival, to loss, to aging. It is healing to be with her. I feel that I am staving off her loneliness and preserving her specialness by seeing her being through her wrinkled skin. I am staving off my loneliness.

Shira's six months in America are coming to an end. She has loved her church group, her new mother, her school, her life there. Yet in this new life perhaps she is discovering what she has to offer from her other life across the ocean. She was asked to teach about Chanukah to second-graders. She took in the menorah and candles, the dreidel and chocolate coins that I had sent her. Chanukah in a box from Ema in Israel. She says that there was one little boy in the class who was Jewish. His name was Nathaniel and he was extremely excited that she was teaching *his* holiday.

"I was just like that little boy, Shira. I was the only Jew in my class. Except that I didn't get to have some cute teenage girl from Israel come to tell me about Chanukah. Baba always gave me a menorah to take to class. One year I heard someone say: oh, there goes Judith with her menorah again. You did a wonderful thing by going to that class."

Shira celebrated Christmas and New Year's. Both Shira and her host mother tell me how close they are, how they speak late into the night. They sometimes speak about the New Testament. I ache, that Shira is so far away, from me, from Israel, from Judaism. I ache that she has found someone to talk to, when she has used her teenage prerogative not to share her joys and pain with me.

Then after months of pain, it hits me. Her host mother is like her Safta Sarah. Shira is cut off from her roots, and her host mother makes sense of it all. I can now welcome Shira back with understanding and with empathy for her experience. As she is, who she is. I arrange for us to go to Europe together, to ride bikes, to play, to eat spaghetti with pomodoro sauce just for fun, and to visit Kalman who knows the depth of Jewish history and loves to tell it. Maybe she will get to know me, maybe she will get to know what is valuable about her, and maybe she will see how much I value her.

# The Holocaust Siblings: Yaakov Moshe

Yaakov Moshe is taller and thinner than Kalman, Mordecai, Tuvye and Simon. Just before the war, he fell in love with a young woman from his village. In 1942 when he was deported, Yaakov Moshe was twenty-eight. His younger brother Kalman was only twenty-three when his family was being deported one by one, two by two. Kalman stayed in touch with the remnants of the family of Hannah Gluck, who barely had time to be Yaakov Moshe's bride.

The Gestapo entered Hamborek. They marched the town's Jews to the station. Yaakov Moshe saw that they were coming for him and his family. He had to tell Hannah that he was being taken. His Hannah. He looked frantically around the yard. He saw his little sister Liebe's kite in the yard. He was so good at flying kites; he did it to amuse his sisters and to flirt with Hannah over the shared fence that divided their two houses before they married a few months ago. He took a pen out of his pocket and scribbled a note on the kite.

Hannahleh, my dearest love, my closest friend, my wife,

They are coming for me now. I want you to know that I have been taken. Do not fret, only take care of yourself, and protect yourself from harm. I will fight to survive this terrible hatred of Jews, so that I can come back to you.
    You are my love and my life,
    I am so terrified, and so happy that your love goes with me,

Your Yakub

Yaakov Moshe ran towards the wind and his kite went straight up. It bounced over the fence and floated for a few minutes after he was taken, the string dangling… Hannah cried out when she read it, and ran to find Kalman to tell him. That is how the family knew.

Kalman watched from a distance as Rachel and her husband and two little girls were taken. He couldn't say goodbye, he could not save them.

Kalman Edelmann (the name was spelled with two n's by the European Edelmanns, but was simplified to Edelman at Ellis Island in America) was born into a practicing Orthodox family. His father served as a *chazzan*, a prayer leader, in order to earn a few extra crowns on the high holidays; otherwise he ran a small shop with dry goods. "We were very poor," remembers Kalman. Every day in the morning, Sandor, the father, and his sons put on tefillin and davened, swayed as they chanted the prayers. There was no synagogue in the village. On Shabbat they walked two kilometers to Brezovice. There was no *cheder* (Hebrew school) in the village, so from the age of four, Sandor taught Kalman *Chumash*, the first five books of the Bible, the Torah. "My father was a good teacher." This is evident in both Kalman's academic prowess and in his emotional strength.

"*Bereisheet, bara Elohim et hashamayim v'et ha'aretz,*" he chants to me eighty years after his father taught it to him. This is the opening line of the Hebrew Bible, "In the beginning God created the Heavens and the earth…"

"Did he teach the girls, too?" I inquire.

"Mainly the alef-bays," the alphabet. "My sisters went to school."

> The Sabbath in our house was like a paradise, even for the children. My mother made kugel that was full of cinnamon and sugar; we had a meat meal, which we couldn't afford the rest of the week. Mother put on her good dress and baked the bread for the Sabbath and for the whole week. Also homemade pastries.

Kalman closes his eyes as he tastes the past.

> Later I left Orthodox Judaism and joined Tchelet Lavan (Blue and White, a youth movement which is an offshoot of Hashomer Hatzair). I believed in the Zionist ideal. This was my first transition. The Jews of Europe were hated, despised — you cannot imagine such hatred. It makes sense that we build a homeland of our own if we are not wanted elsewhere. I was a partisan, I changed my name, I did not exist! I lived more as Reform Jew, less observant, but I knew that I was a Jew and I had Jewish learning. The Holocaust came. It changed me; it changed my values with regard to meaning, God, religion. I was more of an existentialist and sidled away from tradition. Mordecai wrote to me, "Come to Israel."
>
> In the second transformation of my life I remain as a Jew with a non-Jewish name. I came here to Prague — was active in a group with Alena and others. We not practice, we go away from all connected to religion. We see democracy as a higher point of view than any particular religion.

When the Communists took over the Czech Republic in 1968 both Kalman and Alena were ousted from their jobs for the next fifteen years!

Kalman doesn't mention a further stage. His work (at age eighty!) shifts from general European history/philosophy to writing many articles about Masaryk and the Jews. He is an ardent researcher of Czech/Jewish relations and the Holocaust. Thomas G. Masaryk was the Czech president before the rise of Hitler who publicly stood up against the growing anti-Semitic scapegoating in Europe in the 1920s and 1930s.

Unlike me or Sarah, Kalman did not build a new life by immigrating to a new country. He stayed in Europe, as a European Jew. His Jewish identity became more and more important as he grew older, but he decided to be buried in the New Jewish Cemetery in Prague and not with his brothers in Israel. After much deliberation, and with the help of Lena, his doctoral student, he buried Alena, who was not Jewish, in the New Jewish Cemetery in Prague. Together they designed a black granite gravestone to mark the spot. Kalman wants to die and rest as he has lived, as a Czech, as a Jew, as a survivor in Europe. In the absence of family, the meaning in his life became his students and his colleagues, and his work; therefore, he chose to be buried where he lived. Just because I write so freely about his death do not think that I am at peace with the thought of it — no, I cling to Kalman.

Unlike me or Sarah, he did not make his Jewish survival his first priority, but rather his survival. He defied the Nazis by surviving the war. He defied the Nuremberg Laws, years after they were not dictating life anymore, by working in Europe and by marrying a non-Jew. He chose his own civil liberties. But he did not define his civil liberties by defending the borders of the Jewish state in a world that does not accept Jews. Alena accepted Jews, and he was loved. His books were well received. And he contributed to the Jewish people by permanently marking the contributions of Thomas Masaryk who defied racism in all its forms.

Unlike me or Sarah, Kalman could not have children. But he has me.

# Graveyards — 2003

Raphi is not going to be released from the army for Yom Hazikaron, Remembrance Day for the fallen soldiers, this year. He is being punished for sitting down three minutes too early while on guard duty in the most grueling of postings. I ask him if he can explain to his officers that he was named after a soldier. He laughs cynically. "Do they care?" he says.

"Tell them that Sarah is ninety years old."

"Yeah, right," he says.

I am despondent.

However, Raphi calls me early on Tuesday morning. "I am already at the bus station in Jerusalem." We agree to meet at the graveside. I am in awe that he worked so hard to get out.

A dusty, tall soldier is waiting for us at the graveside as we hurry there, his sisters and I. Shira has taken a morning off from high school and Ilana from elementary school. The three of us, the women in his life, spot him from afar. He has grown a beard. Big hug. I can't let go. We tidy the grave a little, put water in a jug, scrape the bird droppings off the lantern that holds a memorial candle. I decide not to light the candle, but to let Rivka do so. The hot May sun is beating down, so we move to the shade to wait for the rest of the family to arrive.

The girls and Raphi chat. Shira is going into the army soon. I have started experiencing flashbacks of her as a little girl with a pixie haircut and purple spaghetti strap dresses, or as a baby in my arms, so I know that she is about to leave home. My reaction to my children leaving home is to try to memorize their babyhood.

The girls ask Raphi what all the army insignias mean and what color berets stand for which units.

Sarah and Mordecai no longer stand physically around the grave. Mordecai has been dead for eleven years, and Sarah cannot be transferred from the retirement home to be in the hot sun in the crowds. The section around Rafi's grave is a section of soldiers who fell in the Six-Day War. That was thirty-six years ago and the people have aged and become weathered, like the twisted trees that provide little shade from the Israeli sun.

The Edelman clan all know the people who come to the grave next door intimately, although we do not know their names. I can picture the father who used to wail and scream and wash the grave with perfume. He died many years ago. We are told that the mother, his wife, died a few months ago. I remember her quiet grief, her hair turning grayer every year. Now the sisters and brothers of the deceased remain, and they themselves show some signs of aging.

The entire field of graves is overflowing with relatives. There are few left to visit the soldiers who died in the War of Independence in 1948. There are more living friends and relatives around the graves of those who died in the Lebanese War in the 1980s. We had to walk past the fresh graves from the extended parking lot, and at the newer ones, relatives are keening and crying; dozens, hundreds of young friends crowd the graves. Not so at ours anymore. Our graves have seen two generations change over; they have seen their living siblings grow into grandparents.

Rivka and her husband Jack arrive first. They have walked from their house. Rivka is delighted to see Raphi, and she asks each of my children in turn about themselves.

Then Yuval arrives with his daughter Lital. She is overwhelmed, as I am, to see Raphi, in uniform, standing by the grave of his namesake. I notice for the first time that my dead cousin's rank is the same as Raphi's. Also, his age: Raphi will be twenty in July, in two months. The proof that the army is dangerous and potentially fatal is etched in stone. The tens of thousands of cars parked for miles around, the crying men and women, the flowers so thick and so sweet that the air is all sweetness — the cemetery is alive today, mocking its everyday empty quietness. Sweet denial is not possible today, and it hurts.

"How can you stand it that he is in Hebron? Can't you DO something?" asks Lital.

I know she's right; she has expressed what I feel. Yet I state my helplessness. "What can I do? Chain myself to a tank? What will that do to support my Raphi — how will he cope if he knows how much I am suffering?" Chaining myself to a tank in front of the prime minister's house is definitely a consideration for me. Instead I go to peace rallies almost religiously.

Lital asks for my cellular phone number in order to call me for Raphi's address. She wants to send him a package of her special baked goods. It is clear who her grandmother is. In my thirst for relatives, I feel a deep sense of joy to be a cousin to all generations of the clan.

She tells me that she is thirty-six years old. That she was born ten days before Rafi was killed. I can't believe that she is only nine years younger than I am; she is one of the "children." Lital is the younger generation, but the oldest of the grandchildren. We talk about how her sister Dafni is missing, having died in a traffic accident at age twenty-five. Yes, traffic accidents happen here as well. Even more than terror. We can both picture her here around the grave. We talk about being mothers to soldiers. Lital has two sons, and all her life she has known the fate of her uncle Rafi, the soldier.

Lital's father Yuval is speaking at length with Raphi. Rivka introduces us to another Rafael, the son of Rafi's friend, who was also named for Rafi. I say, "I am a distant cousin." Yuval objects. "Distant? You are a very close cousin. Never mind that few others survived — you are as close as can be."

I feel the same way and am very touched. I see that Yuval, who has had white hair as long as I have known him, has aged. "My brother Rafi would be fifty-six years old now."

"No!" objects Lital. "He couldn't possibly be. He is twenty, he will always be twenty." We all feel the strangeness of the fact that Raphi is a soldier and is twenty years old. Yuval himself is over sixty years old. We are aging but we are also living. We feel loss, but we gain the pleasure and pain and fear of every day.

I have always loved being with these people around this grave, with the strange comfort of the sweet smell of tens of thousands of bouquets of flowers, and the sweetness of my children next to me. Meanwhile, somehow Rivka has zipped light years ahead to being a grandmother, and Lital has become my age, Yuval is heading towards his father's age, and my children are all taller than I am, Raphi with a beard. In my mind I remain the same, a twenty-six-year-old new immigrant mother of young children. I think of Safta Sarah saying how she is really eighteen in an aged body. I understand.

But we fool ourselves that we are young. We have all moved ahead and Rafi hasn't. He has not had a love, he has not married, he has not had children, he did not study at the university and he did not have a profession. He has remained a daring, fun boy with a rascally smile — a boy I never had a chance to know.

I realize that I have romanticized this meeting place. His siblings are hurting thirty-six years later. I see how close Raphi and Shira and Ilana are. I pray: "Keep them together to enjoy each other's children, to enjoy holidays. Let all three of them comfort each other when I die." Death is not romantic. Remembrance is not to be idealized. Perhaps I have liked my role in the graveyard too much, as the cousin who came from afar and comforted them. But death is really sad and painful, for as long as people remember. I am quite certain that my children will keep coming here when I am too old to be able to stand in the May sun.

# Army Buddies

One of the young men in Raphi's unit was considered a "lone soldier," because his mother, like so many other rabbis, had to leave Israel for financial reasons. I feel for her. It is so unbearably hard for me, but at least I have the fantasy of being able to protect Raphi with my love. Of course there is nothing that I can really do. So I write to Amy, his mother, an American immigrant who had to leave Israel so that she could earn money for her pension and to be near her elderly parents, and to work in her profession.

From: Judith Edelman-Green
Subject: aryeh and the garin

Date: Thu, 11 Apr 2002 15:49:42 +0200

Dear Amy,

I want to send you a fresh report, I thought of you so much yest at the boys' base. Aryeh looks good, very different. He has short hair, it actually suits him, and he has lost some weight. He was smiling and was getting a lot of hugs from his girlfriend Aviva. (The boys live in a tent, it is almost a biblical image of Yitzhak being comforted by Rivka in a tent!!!)

They are very much a group, they are really there for each other. Raphi loves the youth group that he will go through the army with, so much.

I am not a spoiled person, I have gone to summer camps all my life, and camp for recreation, yet, I was a little surprised at just how basic this camp was. The tent holds 15 beds, and is as basic as basic can be. The toilets and showers are even more basic. There are a few buildings on the base. The work day is long. They sleep six hours, and have one hour in which to take care of their physical and emotional needs (phone calls, snacks, showers.) The group have decided to pray together every morning and not shave for the allotted mourning period in the spring. This is not to be taken for granted that they would observe this particular custom. They joke that they do it so that they can recharge their pelephones in the synagogue, but Raphi says they have really "connected to prayer." This is the first time that this connection has been a reality for him.

I offered Aryeh some home-cooked food, but he was fine, wasn't hungry and only had a few grapes. The togetherness is really beautiful.

I will send you reports whenever I see them, and if there's anything you'd like me to buy or give to Aryeh, just let me know. I am planning on sending weekly packages to Raphi from Telesal, my telephone order shopping. Let me know what Aryeh likes. I have their address if you want it. I don't know if it is top secret or not. You could write a book about all that I don't know about the army...

With love and a hug, Judith

At 15:27 11/04/02 -0400, you wrote:

> Dear Judith,

> For the first time since Aryeh started basic training I let myself cry when I
> got your e-mail. Thank you so much for helping me have a sense of how he
> is. I know that about that precious hour they have every day and I leave a
> message on Aryeh's voice mail every day telling him how much I love him
> and how proud I am of him and how happy I am that he has his youth group
> close friends with him to support him. But it's so hard that I never get to
> hear his voice.

> I would love to have the address so I can send him packages. It would be
> one more way for me to touch him. Does telesal have a website, too?

> I am so proud of the garin for establishing daily prayer for themselves. I am
> grateful that it is helping them.

> Judith I can't thank you enough for reaching out to me like this. God bless
> you.

> Love,
> Amy

# Floods — 2002

A dream about flooding comes a month after I have returned from
Prague, which in real life experienced the worst flooding in a thousand
years just days before Shira and I arrived there. In the dream, I have to go to
the hospital for a minor operation. While the surgeons are operating they
discover that my digestive system is seriously faulty and I will have to come
back for another operation. My mother and younger brother accompany me
and stay with me throughout the operation. I don't have to go through it
alone. The staff and the surgeon are either warm and loving or evil, but it is up
to me to decide. I ask Sarah if I should look at them positively or not. Then

when we look for the clinic for follow-up care, the city is flooded, there is a swelling lake, and the gate and stairways into the city are blocked by plywood.

When I wake up I puzzle through the interpretation: My mother and brother accompanied my father on his last night on earth; I did not. I do not want them to be alone; I do not want to be alone. Sarah is my guide for positivity in life.

Just before I go to sleep, and dream this dream, we are notified that Raphi and his gang were called up in the middle of the night and taken to a place where a terrorist attack has just taken place. It is a place notorious for "incidents," which end up with blood being spilled. Hebron, where the Patriarch Abraham buried Sarah. Where today people are killed unnecessarily. Even very right-wing politicians have wanted to wash their hands of it. My son is there. My son who is named for Rafi. My son who was just a baby yesterday, and such a roly-poly one. I remember him laughing a great deal. I remember his interest in books, in nature, in people. I remember how sweet he got when he left home, and how he always kisses relatives and our close friends, the men and the women; he always smiles and has a friendly chat with them. Whenever the computer wasn't cooperating I yelled out, "Raphi, come quick." I still call out "Raphi" at work when the computer acts up or if I don't know how to do something. Raphi, Raphi.

The floods came and brought mud over the banks of the Vlatava in Prague. It floods the week before Shira and I are due to arrive there, and television images of buildings knee-high in water, the river flowing through the streets, have kept most tourists away.

Our friends send worried e-mails asking, "Is it safe to go there?"

*Since when is life safe? Was it safe for Kalman and his family during WWII?* Is it safe for Raphi in the army? Sarah has seen untimely death in each of four generations. Her mother and father died when the Nazis marched into town. Siblings died in the camps. From her body, Rafi, her son, died in the Six-Day War. Dafni, her twenty-five-year-old granddaughter, died in a car crash on her way to work as a fifth-year medical student. One, two, three, four. Sarah hurts about her mother her whole life ("take me with you"); she has a needle in her heart about Rafi and doesn't stop working till work stops working her; she can barely take in Dafni's death, coming in her extreme old age. It serves to remind her of the other losses.

We arrive a week after the deluge. The streets are dry but there is a stench of dampness and rot emanating from the underground train stations and from the flooded sanitation system. On our first day, we meet Kalman in the Jewish Quarter, right near the pregnant riverbanks. On our previous trip, he suggested that we tour the Jewish Quarter on our own. A flood of too many memories? A flood of Jewish associations which fill his head with tastes and smells, the soft hands of his mother, the practices and repeated sentences of his father teaching him prayers and the Bible, the sight of spice holders — lacy silver filigree with a flag on top, the holy ark, the embroidered velvet cloth, stories of his childhood, the Golem of Prague. As if drowning him, the memories threaten to cut off the air that was given to him by his life at the university, by his couplehood with Alena.

However, for Shira, his cousin Murray's granddaughter, he is willing to venture in and to make it her history as well as his. He points out the Altneuschul, the oldest surviving synagogue in Europe. The Nazis used it as their headquarters. They wanted to create an exhibition to show the race of people, the Jews, whom they had wiped out. The clock tower in Hebrew stands out above the thirteenth-century synagogue, which is slight in stature because of a medieval edict prohibiting synagogues from approaching the height of churches. To gain grandeur inside, its base begins underground so that the low ceiling will seem heavenly. The Hebrew letters of the clock tower and the hand go counterclockwise, because someone made the mistaken assumption that it had to be so as Hebrew is read from right to left.

As the legend goes, a being made out of clay by the great rabbi the Maharal of Prague was created to protect the Jewish ghetto from the onslaught of killings and beatings. This unseemly being could not be controlled, and was called the Golem, or "Being." He may well be lurking still in the attic of the Altneuschul. Nazi officers were said to go mad when they tried to approach the attic during WWII, proof that the Golem still protects the community with his magical body of clay.

Red and white tape closes off the entrance to the Altneuschul, and there are notices on all the synagogues that say that they are closed until further notice due to the flooding. The Jewish community center where Kalman and other older community members eat their noonday meal is also closed, and they have no alternative venue.

Kalman has lived through the fearful darkness of Jewish history, without a country of refuge to go to. Today we have a country of refuge, but young lives are at risk — *my Raphi's life is at risk* — while offering safety and refuge for others. Water floods out of my eyes. I am bloated with overeating, filled up with water. I have to release some messages that play in my head and have emigrated from far-off lands from before I was born, the Golem of my soul.

And my daughter is falling in love with Jewish history, told by a Jewish historian with a curriculum vitae of six concentration camps and two death marches.

# Journey to Germany — 2002 and 1945

Soaring on bicycles to the top of Petrin Hill in Prague, which lies like an alluring woman above the city, my daughter and I race to the top of the world. Bicycles carry us back and forth across the bloated river under the hot August sun.

Shira wants to visit with some German youth who were exchange students with her in Oklahoma, to compare notes about coming home. I plan to stay on in Prague, to write.

The afternoon that she is meant to leave for Germany, Shira's ticket is pick-pocketed on the tram. Lena and Kalman warn against a young girl traveling alone to Germany by train. Warnings of people who would prey on young girls, of pimps who try to tempt young, pretty girls into prostitution ring in my ears. Shira doesn't exactly look like the Golem of Prague; strangers might be attracted to look at her.

"I'm not stupid, Ema." Shira protests. The train line through Dresden is under water with the recent floods. Lena advises that a bus would be better anyway; it is the same group of passengers the whole way, so that she couldn't be easily kidnapped. Shira paid for the bus ticket with her own money, and now it is missing. She is frantic. It is four o'clock, the travel agency closes at six, and it is across town from the hotel, where Shira's unpacked clothes lie in heaps.

Shira, independently taking the initiative, calls the travel agent. They are unyielding: she will have to buy another ticket, and there is no such thing as a replacement ticket.

"Let's go back downtown together," I say, trying to be calm, comforting and supportive, when I had other plans for the afternoon, like a nap. I get grumpy when I am tired.

I coax Shira to stay calm, which I do not feel, and to return to town. We arrive at the travel agency where the tellers conspire against us in Czech in order not to produce a replacement ticket.

"If you get a note from the police, you can get a replacement ticket for free."

It is five o'clock and ticking; the agency closes in an hour.

"How do we know that we can get back here before you close?" I ask. Israel has seasoned me to bureaucratic labyrinths.

"Oh, you cannot get a replacement ticket here but only at the bus station."

"Will it be open?" I inquire suspiciously, thinking of all the worst-case scenarios.

"Absolutely, I just spoke to them."

Dubious, I turn to Shira. "I'm just going to pay the money so we can rush back and pack." The sum in question is only thirty-two dollars.

"It's the principle, Ema," she says, "We're going to the police. I was robbed."

First we have to find the police. At the first police station they don't speak English, and don't deal with tourists. In non-English, they send us to a second station. At this station there is a big sign outside: "Foreigners' Complaints." The female voice on the intercom won't let us in because she doesn't understand English. Five minutes later a policeman also wants entry, so we sneak in after him.

It seems that all of Prague's tourists are in the waiting room. Both doors for reception are marked "Do Not Enter." The line doesn't seem to move at all. As the clock is ticking, we become intimately acquainted with a French-speaking woman whose whole knapsack was taken, and a Dutch-speaking tourist who can't stop her hysterical laughter, whose purse with all her credit cards, money and valuables was taken.

"You see, we only lost a ticket," I encourage Shira, in Hebrew, so that our new best friends won't understand. For once we have the correct documents at the right time; we have her European Community British passport *and* a photocopy of the receipt of her ticket which we managed to procure from the nasty tellers.

At five minutes to six, I say to Shira, "We're not going to make it, let's just go buy the ticket." We jog to the ticket office, me on my swollen tourist feet. She tears ahead, and meets me coming back, face red. "They have sold their quota of reserved seats. They wouldn't sell me a ticket."

To avoid panic, and to try to make the nine o'clock bus, I delegate responsibilities. "You go back to the police station, get the document that your ticket was stolen. Then hightail it to the bus station and buy your ticket. I will go to the hotel room and pack your things," I say with trepidation. "We will meet at the bus. Oh, God, how will I carry your knapsack?" She has a backpack that would house a baby elephant, hand luggage and a guitar.

"Take a taxi, Ema." We run off in opposite directions. I take a tram back to the hotel, take an elevator up to the eighth floor and stare helplessly at the overflowing pile of clothes, and the flaccid, gaping knapsack. I begin to stuff, roll, and stuff.

I call a porter, not my habit, and heave the bursting backpack to the door. My back muscles tense and ache for the rest of the evening. I have moved the backpack about three feet. The porter arrives and does the rest. The taxi doesn't come. The receptionist at the hotel desk has just been inundated with two busloads of new guests; she cannot help me and I cannot even check if she has really ordered the cab. I do not know Czech. Some kind, elderly British women watch Shira's bags as I helplessly zigzag between the taxi stand and the hotel reception desk, which is swarming with tourists.

The taxi driver eventually arrives. He wildly overcharges. However, I take revenge by letting him unload the backpack.

Shira and I have agreed to meet at the ticket office. There is NO ticket office. The driver says he can't wait because it is not a stopping zone; he has to let me out. Never mind that I have paid just about a week's rent for him. I cannot wander around looking for Shira with a bag made out of cement. I tell him that I will pay him to wait while I look for her. He refuses. Just then I hear Shira yelling for me. I don't care about anything anymore, only that I have found her. It is a quarter past eight; we have forty-five minutes to spare.

"I don't have the ticket, Ema. The ticket office is closed. Information is also closed, so I don't know where to wait for the bus. But I have the police report," she gloats hopefully.

I react as any caring mother would. I completely lose control of myself. "I TOLD you we should have paid the thirty-two dollars. I have LIFE EXPERI-ENCE — I KNOW these things. You can just forget Germany. NO WAY they are going to let you on the bus."

We spend the next hour trying to find out which bus stop is the right one. The passersby speak either Czech or German, or have never heard of the bus that we want. The stop is not marked by destination.

"They said you can't miss it…" Shira says hopefully.

I look around and see twenty buses and forty stops; it is getting darker and darker. You can't miss it?

I try to appease Shira, who is crying. I offer her food. I irrationally offer her a guitar lesson. She looks daggers at me, justifiably.

"It'll be OK," I tell her, convinced that she will not be going. Her exchange program friends are waiting for her. They have planned to meet her in the middle of the night, five hours from now, in Germany. They are going to miss a night's sleep for nothing.

Fifteen minutes late, a bus pulls up; it turns out to be heading for the right towns in Germany. With no ticket, Shira is first in line. I remain behind, guarding the cement bag. The driver inexplicably agrees to take the police report and the photocopy in lieu of a ticket. No charge. She is triumphant. I feel like a jerk. I try to placate her once she is in her seat, but she is so tired that she is crying. I am sure that she will sleep through her stop and no one on the bus is getting off at the far-flung town that she is going to.

Miraculously the bus doors close; it sets off. Shira tries to smile at me and to wave. "I love you," she mouths.

Blowing kisses and waving, I draw a big exaggerated heart on my shirt. I feel flooded with love for her. We have had an exhilarating vacation together and now she is gone. I am totally deflated, but relieved for her sake.

I decide to walk the three kilometers back to the hotel. I pass the Jewish cemetery with its six-pointed star on the gate. Kalman's narration of his trip to Germany follows me through the dismal night walk.

We were on the train to Saxenhausen on the thirteenth of January, 1945. The transport took five days; it was winter, and bitterly cold. A small group of men tried to escape. They tried to pry loose the sides of the train, to break a hole in the floor boards.

I am glad somehow that Shira has not traveled by train to Germany even though the bus journey seemed impossible to arrange.

At the next station the guards discovered their efforts. They demanded to know which individual or group had attempted escape. No one would tell on their comrades, even if they were unknown to each other.

> There were two Gestapo officers. They walked around the crowded cars and took our heads one at a time and smashed them into the floor. They kicked our backs and stomachs with their boots. They spat us. Then they proclaimed, "Unless you hand over to us the prisoners trying to escape, we will randomly choose ten men, and shoot them."

One officer looked at Kalman grimly in the eye. Kalman tried not to show disdain, or fear, or defiance. "Wait here," he hissed at Kalman, clearly marking him as one of the ten.

The prisoners could hear a phone call being made from an office by the platform. Indeed the officers were asking for permission to shoot the prisoners. Without further harassment or explanation, the train door slammed shut, and the train proceeded, to Kaufering.

Before Kalman was captured he had hoped that by taking a non-Jewish name and identity, and with his looks, he could perhaps survive the war undetected.

> I rest with [keep] the name Gajan. Jan Gajan, I say thank you to this name for keeping me alive during the war because they didn't know I was Jewish while traveling with this name. I could pass as a non-Jew, and get work and lodging. My physiognomy is not Jewish.
>
> I went missing. I did not exist. They can't find me.
>
> I traveled illegally from Prague to Slovakia. Rachel, my eldest sister, lived there. My two youngest sisters had just been deported. I was in the train station. I asked someone, "What is that?!" They said, "Jewish girls," dismissively. Nobody would say where.

Kalman's eyes tear up and it is hard to speak. This is a great strain on him, but he knows that I want to know.

I caught glimpses of young Jewish girls, with braids, with embroidered blouses, skirts. I could see them as the cattle car doors were opened and closed. I could hear them. I sensed that my younger sisters were on that train. I might have quickly seen them.

Rachel bought a document with the name Jan Gajan. People would come to her Jewish ritual bath, used by women before sexual relations after menstruation, and by men for spiritual cleansing before the Sabbath or after nocturnal emission. The villagers would bring her eggs, butter, and fresh milk from their farms in the country. Instead of the usual barter she asked one of her clients to bring her a certificate of baptism. With this documentation Kalman could travel, live, and save himself from capture.

> Jan Gajan was younger than I, born 1925, so I had to illegally change the date so as not to go to the military.
>
> Rachel saved me, but could not save herself or her daughters or her husband. They were deported to a concentration camp.

Another name for Kalman is: # 144125.

It is not tattooed on his arm because the Nazis were on the run from the advancing Allies when he was captured.

Kalman gives me a photocopy of the International Red Cross document which states, in German, that Prof. Dr. Gajan, born Edelmann in 1917 in Hamborek, had been in Bergen-Belsen, Dachau.

> International Tracing Service
> October 1971
>
> Ref. Prof. Dr GAJAN (previous: Edelmann), Kalman, born 7th November in Hamborek
>
> Gentlemen,
>
> We refer to your above-mentioned communication, and please be advised that based on your declarations, we have researched all relevant documentation available to us.
>
> Based on the given personal description, no ascertainable information could be determined.
>
> Prisoner number 144125, as presented in your request, does not appear to

us in the available (incomplete) documentation with respect to concentration camp Sachsenhausen.

We were able to determine that the abovementioned prisoner number was issued later than 10<sup>th</sup> Feb 1945.

At concentration camp Dachau, the prisoner number 144125 was issued to the following person:

GAJAN, Jan, born 12<sup>th</sup> Jan 1925 in Hamborek. Citizenship: Czechoslovakian. Religion: Roman Catholic. Profession: Student optician. Parents' names: Frantsek and Maria nee BUJNAKOVA. Last domicile: Hamborek, district Sabinov; was arrested in Preschau on 22<sup>nd</sup> Dec 1944; On 6<sup>th</sup>/7<sup>th</sup> March from Concentration Camp Bergen-Belsen delivered to Concentration Camp Dachau, prisoner # 144125 transferred to Concentration Camp Dachau/Komando Landsberg (date not given) and as prisoner at Concentration Camp Dachau liberated by US Army.

Category or reason for incarceration "Sch" (= Schutzhaft) = protective imprisonment.

Documentation examined: Prisoner's personal sheet, office index card, and admittance book of Concentration Camp Dachau.

We remain,
Hochachtung
Excellent respect,
For A. de Cocatrix of ITS

# Shabbat with Lena

Kalman has gone away for his annual German-sponsored spa retreat, and I do not want to be alone on Shabbat. I buy two inexpensive candles. I have a tiny bottle of wine from the airplane. I invite Lena, Kalman's doctoral student, to have Shabbat dinner with me. We meet two hours before Shabbat at the Altneuschul, the oldest remaining synagogue that the Nazis left standing in Europe, with the pumps still regurgitating water from its belly. The rubble of damaged property from the flood has not been hauled away yet.

Lena wears a stunning black dress with a crocheted black yoke. Her lace black bra is visible from the sides. I note that women enjoy other women who are attractive. Her short black hair is cut in a French bob; she looks wonderful. I look tired and unkempt after a day out. I wish that I had gone back to my hotel to change, but it is a forty-five-minute tram ride in each direction.

Lena and I share Hebrew as our only common language, with her French/Czech accent and my American one. She is a little surprised by my candle-lighting request, but we sit in the glow of the simple candles as her office grows darker and darker. With me, if I don't light candles, an important shift in time has gone unrecognized; with her it is perhaps a superstitious ritual, and she is pleased that I do it in the privacy of her empty office. Later she disposes of the evidence.

"This is where I work, in an office in a monastery," says Lena. A vocal concert deep in the background adds to the atmosphere of stone archways.

"Virginia Woolfe wrote about women needing a stipend and a room of one's own; you must get a lot done here," I say covetously. As a married woman with three children, even an office wouldn't give me such space. Our marital status stands between us like the Vlatava River which graces Prague with its fairy-tale-like scenes. This, much more than the eight years difference in age, or the fact that she is an academic, separates us.

"I get nothing done here. I need to be completely alone to write. I can write only in Paris, although I carry out research in Prague and in Jerusalem." There are posters of Jerusalem above Lena's desk.

"So Paris is the place where you feel best?"

"No, well, no. I had a great trauma in schooling there. It had to do with anti-Semitism. I don't really want to talk about it." Lena looks sad.

"I have been like a magnet for anti-Semitic experiences. When Raphi was born, his babysitter discovered that he was Jewish and would not admit a Jewish baby into her house."

Lena's jaw drops open. She sits frozen, the dimming candlelight flickering shadows on her features.

I continue. "That was my reaction exactly. I was dumbfounded, couldn't answer back, couldn't argue."

"My experience was indefinable. Subtle. They could even deny that it happened, yet it damaged me... I am not... whole. I did the Baccalaureate," recalls Lena, in Hebrew interspersed with French. "Then my first degree. I was at a Catholic college. I worked very hard, I did well. They told me that I was haughty, immodest. I got good grades. They said that I was showing off. When I stopped trying due to my misery, depression, they said that I was lazy, wasting their time. They systematically tore me apart, piece by piece, until I was completely shattered."

"At least you had self-awareness of the double bind that they put you in," I suggest.

"No, not until much later, I was really a broken person when I arrived. And now Kalman gives me optimism."

There is a silence as we both digest this. The room is lit only by the candles. It has grown dark outside. Lena is all eyes. I understand without words what she is saying, but I want Lena to define it for both of us.

"How can a man who lost his mother, sisters, brothers, his nieces and brothers and sisters-in-law give you optimism? How can a man who was expelled from the work he loved by a Communist regime give you optimism?"

"Because he is so spiritual, because he has every reason not to believe in his fellow human beings, but he does."

# Belly Dancing

When my niece got married to an Israeli whose parents emigrated from Morocco, some of the tantalizing spice of being here in Israel was brought into our family, with the Moroccan engagement ceremony. I belly danced up to Grandpa visiting from England, and offered him some henna mud on his palm; being a terrifically good sport, he accepted the palmful of dyed goo and coated his hands with it. No echo of the formal tuxedoed affairs in English banqueting halls!

The groom's mother gave out gold-embroidered long gowns in hot pink, turquoise, dark blue and teal green to all the women, including English Grandma who is also a wonderfully good sport. Yossi, the groom's mother and her sisters sang traditional songs while everyone belly danced. Danny's brother Laurence made a special effort to come, as he does for all the joyful occasions. Laurence with his grey suit from England was belly dancing with Danny and with the other men. The bride was ushered into the small apartment, her hair dripping wet from the ritual bath used to celebrate her transition. The women had accompanied her there with tambourines and rhythmic singing. Henna mud, an earthy-smelling natural dye which stains the hands (it is also used in hair dye), is put on the bride's and groom's hands to protect them from the Evil Eye. Huge platters of homemade Moroccan sweets are waved above their heads while the women sing and ululate, "Lah-lah-lah-lah-leeah!" Scarves are waved, coins are tossed. The bride and groom receive kisses and blessings from each other's families. Avital got a gold chain. Yossi got a watch. We got ingathering of the exiles, and a visit from the folks back home.

# War Stories — 2002 and 1942

Raphi is guarding in Hebron. He is wearing a ceramic vest which makes it hard to sit down. He has a helmet on, and his gun and its ammunition weigh sixty pounds, a good third of his weight. It is the eve of Passover and an older Palestinian man comes up to the guarding station. "A good holiday to you," he says. "Sallam Alekem," Raphi replies.

He guards for ten hours and then will join a makeshift seder. The settlers in Hebron are making their homes ready, sweeping, washing, getting rid of any trace of leavened dough in their houses.

Two girls, who are no doubt supposed to be cleaning, lean out the window of their apartment above Raphi. They giggle and point and chatter. Soon a paper airplane glides and hits ground zero at his feet. He looks around and bends down to pick up the airplane, unfolding it slowly.

"Dear Soldier," it reads. Raphi looks up at the girls and winks. They are about ten years old.

"We are so sorry that you are bored and having to guard. It is our fault because we live here."

Raphi has a fifteen-minute break when Dudu comes to relieve him. He has a drink, stretches, and takes out his pen. He turns over the paper with its lines of triangle folds and writes on the back.

> Once upon a time there was an officer who made his soldiers guard day and night. They never got to celebrate their holidays or Sabbaths, and could never sit down or stretch. The conditions were appalling; there were rats in the kitchen that snuck in to steal bread.
>
> The officer yelled at his soldiers, so he grew whiskers.
>
> He didn't allow his soldiers to go home for Shabbat so he grew a tail.
>
> Grey fur appeared when he woke his soldiers up in the middle of the night for a patrol.
>
> Two little girls bothered the soldiers, and the officer yelled at them. He grew beady little eyes and went "squeak." And that was the end of the officer, who scurried away without even a piece of bread. Oh, I mean matzah for Passover.

Raphi folded the piece of paper, and sent it flying up to the open window. A flash of braid, a giggle — he knew that the eagle had landed.

This is all he tells me. There is an encyclopedia of war stories that he doesn't tell me, out of concern. Then when I ask him later, he says, "I am trying to forget." A fun-loving guy, he often runs the bar at the kibbutz where he lives. This is not like the blind beer parties at some pubs or universities; this is a bit like Mordecai's raising a glass of sweet wine every time I visit, *l'chaim*, to life!

War stories. By contrast, so different in their ending. Kalman's younger sisters, Esther and Liebe, were the first to go; they went with the first transports in March 1942. Their story ended differently. Kalman thinks that they were sent to Lublin, Poland. As young healthy girls they would not have been gassed immediately, but would have been shaved, starved and put to slave labor until they succumbed to cold or disease. This is why Raphi is now guarding.

# Mordecai's Odyssey — 1967

Mordecai also ached, but he never got the chance to welcome Rafi home. He traveled alone. When his son was killed, Mordecai set out on an odyssey to go to every important place where Rafi had served in the army. He made a lonely journey from El Arish on the border of Egypt to other sandy destinations. He was restless. He wasn't sure what he was looking for. Often he yelled at young officers who couldn't give him what he wanted.

"Is this where my son slept? What did he do here?"

"Right here. He played backgammon at the table over there."

Mordecai looked around at the dusty-looking soldiers wearing khaki uniforms, wearing the indifference of the young, smoking cigarettes. At the third camp he visited he saw what he was looking for: a soldier with light red hair and freckles like his lost son. But he was too tall, too husky, too stoop-shouldered.

Having never owned a car, Mordecai couldn't drive. He traveled to these far-flung camps on buses without air-conditioning in the burning Israeli summer of 1967. With little spare change for a bottle of grapefruit juice or a Coke.

On each bus he remembered something different about the children's upbringing. He stared out at the monotony of yellow sands, punctuated by brown bushes, dried and bare for the summer. The smell of perspiration on the buses made him queasy, but that suited his mood; he was disgusted with his memories too.

But the unbidden memories flowed. Rafi had had the belt from him more than any of his other children. However, Rafi took a certain glee in it. It didn't damage his spirit. Yes, he had stolen peaches from a neighbor's tree, but he had a great treat and had made a number of neighborhood children happy, so he wasn't worried about pain, and he avoided the humiliation of the beating by smiling a grimace and shrugging his shoulders. Homework was not first priority, but he helped everyone else with theirs. Rafi wasn't punctual or obedient, he was resourceful and fun. Mordecai chuckled.

Mordecai didn't have time or patience for fun. His sisters and brothers had died in the camps; he had to work so hard to scrape together a living. Life was not funny. His father had taken him to yeshiva when he was twelve years old. He was left to beg for his rent, and to eat at the houses of generous local Jews. This was a known practice and was called "eating days." A large family couldn't afford to have nine children at home, so the boys were sent off to fend for themselves and to get an education.

Lost in a reverie about his oldest son, Mordecai thought about how Yuval was an academic type, resourceful and extremely hard-working. No other son could live up to him. He was also generous and kind. He would go great distances to pick flowers and then would sell them for cash. (Rafi emulated Yuval, especially his business prowess.) When given a few *grush* to take a bus and buy chicken feed, Yuval would walk and save the bus fare, the only way he could ever have pocket money. He rarely got a beating, but once he took the money to go swimming in a pool instead of buying the feed. Only then he remembers catching it with a belt.

Mordecai thought painfully about the time that his daughter Ilana was send to a boarding school in Kfar Sava, miles away. She was disobedient at school and the principal advised the immigrant parents that it was best to send her away. They obeyed without listening to Ilana's pleas. She had nothing to wear to go away and was underweight. A package arrived from Aunt Sadie in America and she could go. She went off in a sailor suit, the height of fashion, in a time of deprivation and lack of basic food.

Rivka the baby, how similar she was to him. She could stand up to him, talk to him the way he talked to the others; she could make him laugh and wrap him around her little finger. He might try to discipline her, but it never ended up working out the way he had intended. Rivka brought disorder and…some joy, whatever he would allow in.

The children of immigrants, defiant, strong as can be, fun-loving, rebellious, capable, devoted, loving, good friends to neighbors, to each other, to those in need and to animals. Rafi tore around Ramat Gan on his motorbike, too fast, with his reddish hair blowing in the wind and his freckles in the sun.

The story is told that Rafi was very frustrated by not being part of the Six-Day War. His unit was not called up. On the fifth day they heard that Israeli soldiers had made it to the Western Wall. Rafi was moved and thrilled. He knew that his grandparents had died because they were Jews, and so had his aunts and uncles and cousins. Here were Jews defending their own country and reaching the historical sites in Jerusalem. There was talk of a mission to the Sinai Desert; it was considered dangerous. Rafi was not meant to go. However, a married soldier with a baby was slated to go, and Rafi insisted on taking his place. "I don't have my own wife and child waiting for me; I'll go."

He was stepping out of a helicopter when a sniper's bullet hit him in the neck. He arrived at the hospital alive, but bled to death before his family was notified. "We don't visit the graveyard too much, and we don't visit too little," Yuval once explained to me. "We go three times a year, for Remembrance Day, for his actual death day, and for his birthday." I only go on Remembrance Day; I never internalized the other two dates. But his family never miss any of them.

That was the day that Safta Sarah followed Rivka to school, with a terrible feeling in her stomach. She felt deep in her guts that something awful had taken place.

Mordecai and Sarah's remaining children sit around a table in northern Tel Aviv and recount the stories. Sarah's hearing aid isn't working today, and she is hard-pressed to be part of the reminiscences. We all eat my stuffed eggplant.

# Immigrant Ignorance and Innocence — 2001

Raphi went to the army two days ago. I ache. When he was born I took comfort in his little bent foot, thinking army boots would never fit his deformed feet. They straightened out. Like so many children of his generation Raphi could figure out computers by himself. I just assumed and took comfort in the fact that he would be in army intelligence in a computer unit. As the time approached these units interviewed him, but he decided that he wasn't interested. It was not for him. As part of a *garin* (youth movement), he had the option of going into the army with his group. This involves an extra twelve months of community service and then the regular army service, all together with his friends in the *garin*. When Raphi decided to do this, I was happy, even tickled, that he was going to a kibbutz where they milked cows, just like in Wisconsin.

It turned out that he worked in construction on the kibbutz. My son built a toilet in a pub which used to be a chicken coop! He worked hard, moving stones, roofing buildings, digging ditches, tiling, plastering walls. This was a wonderful balance to taking matriculation exams in high school. Also it facilitated being able to live without parents. He lived with his youth group friends in a row of small rooms, three to a room with a kitchenette for every six. They partied all night, smoking a nargileh and playing guitar, laughing, joking. Sometimes they drank way too much. Raphi didn't always know the limits of his joking, and he was known for his practical jokes and being wild. Some of the girls drove tractors, some picked dates, some harvested fish from the Red Sea, some took care of children, milked the cows; all had dining room duty.

Independence was a celebration.

Kibbutz Ketura in the far south of Israel, bordering on Jordan and not far from the Egyptian border, a splash of green palm trees and a flowery kibbutz with neat cowsheds and rows of houses on an expanse of desert between two sets of hills. Eilat with its coral and fish was a forty-minute drive, and Raphi and his friends went scuba diving on their rare days off. The fish look like Picassos painted by God in an extra creative mood.

Each young person was given a family to visit and to be part of. Raphi's family had six-year-old twin boys, and two camels as pets. One of the boys broke his leg, and the family asked Raphi to help with him. It was their birthday, and Raphi led a group of six-year-olds for a camel ride in the desert under the scenic hills that change color as the sun sets. Raphi's group, or *garin*, were saying Shabbat afternoon prayers. They looked out the window and saw the sight of Raphi leading a camel with a boy in a leg cast aloft, with a trail of six-year-olds bobbing along behind, and they rolled with laughter.

I stayed with my kibbutz delusions of milking cows, while Raphi tried out for a helicopter rescue unit, "so I can save people and help them." He made it through the grueling week of running with sandbags and climbing sheer walls, but was not accepted into the unit.

Now that he has been in the army for two days, I have learned just how active his unit is. They don't milk cows. I didn't know, I'm only an immigrant mother.

I am living my truth and great passion, living in Israel, working, part of a community, and because of that my son has to go to the army. And because he grew up in a youth movement, he is with them in the army, and he is not milking cows, nor leading camels through the desert under the pink and purple hills. His construction work waits for him, his studies wait, I wait.

The night before he went into the army, in the midst of parties and intense friendships and goodbyes, Raphi took his youngest sister bowling. He was too tired to drive, so I was a voyeur/driver. She is a natural at any game that involves a ball, and so she gave her older brother, twice her height, a run for his money. He treated her as a total equal, as he always has with his sisters. He used to talk to Shira as if she were sentient when she was one month old, explaining the truths of ducks and trees.

I watched and silently prayed, *let him be a father, he will be such a good one*. Immigrants only get extended families when they make them themselves.

# The Ends of the Earth — 2001

Perhaps if I run very fast and very far, I can keep Raphi's kite afloat. I run to Prague. I run to America. America? That's the hardest place of all, because it is where I did not choose to make my home.

In a Japanese kosher restaurant in Manhattan, I am introduced to a New York lawyer who works on Madison Avenue. The purpose of the meeting is business; Paul has volunteered to help me in my work in Israel. However, we subversively break the rules and click, relating on a personal basis, all thanks to him.

"My son is going to the army this year. He is eighteen."

"Oh, I have an eighteen-year-old son too. His name is Michael; he is going to Brandeis. And I have a sixteen-year-old daughter named Rebecca."

"Oh, I have a sixteen-year-old daughter named Shira, and her middle name is Rebecca!"

Paul smiles into my eyes; the ocean between our homes dries up to a puddle.

"My son will be visiting New York on his trip to America before the army."

"Oh, please tell him to call."

More than a sincere offer. The caring is evident; he understands in a piercing way that my son is guarding Israel. He interprets this as allowing his son the freedom to do what my son cannot. I am aware that his son is doing what my son might be if we had not emigrated from America.

Just before being inducted into the army, my son did turn up in New York with his best friend Nachshon. Paul wined and dined them both at the Second Avenue Deli. The mounds of meat were a treat, not just to the eyes of these eighteen-year-old boys. "Oh, and my sister is in town, Paul." Raphi said.

"Fine, bring her along too."

Another folding bed was unrolled, and Paul was late for the office as he accompanied her on the subway so that she wouldn't get lost in the underground maze. Annie, his wife, asked everyone about their lives in Israel with true interest and with humor.

Raphi and Nachshon were in Hebron. Paul and Annie ordered pizza online and it was delivered to their unit. E-mails arrived after every incident: "Everyone OK? How's the Mama doing?"

I met their son Michael in Prague where he learned Czech and wrote a dissertation, while Raphi guarded all night. He had trouble getting kosher meat, and I brought him dried kosher salami and took him out to a vegetarian Indian restaurant in Hradchanska.

Annie came to stay with us. She brought books and a mother's understanding. She also brought a mountain of blue over-the-counter sleeping pills, without which I wouldn't have slept the whole time Raphi was on guard duty. I stayed with my new friends every year when my work brought me to New York. Paul e-mailed every time there was a terrorist incident. They both read my constant e-mails. There was a listening ear, far away, outside the eye of the storm, that understood not only the fear, but the reason for a young eighteen-year-old boy to want to do what he was doing.

I ironed uniforms. Annie sent packages of sugarless gum. Paul threw in some reading material that made the entire battalion run to tear pages out of the magazines and pin them up on their tent flaps. Michael came to visit and spoke Hebrew.

When the Twin Towers collapse I frantically telephone New York. "Are you OK? Are your friends safe?" We stay up all night talking over e-mail about the terror in both our lives.

# The Fourth Floor — 2002

What's so good about living a long life and getting to be old, anyway? The night we have a little family get-together to send Raphi off to his induction into the army, Safta Sarah is taken to the hospital with palpitations. I just feel loss.

The day Raphi goes to the army, I decide that the best therapy would be to sit with Safta Sarah. I have been told that she is no longer in her private apartment on the sixth floor of the retirement home, but is on the ward for those who need more care on the fourth floor.

Yuval is there and explaining to her why she is now sharing a room. Her new roommate is delusional and has thrown Safta Sarah's bathrobe on the floor.

Sarah has a wild look in her eyes. "I will not stay with her, she is crazy and mean."

The other woman's hearing aid isn't working so she can't hear the long trail of insults that Safta Sarah hurls at her. This is perhaps the only time that I see Sarah unhinged.

We go to sit in the common room of the fourth floor. It is shabby and depressing, a marker of not having a real home, and Yuval has to sit on the seat of Sarah's walker. A woman with swollen feet and too much rouge shuffles past us to get to the bathroom.

A meal of yogurt, white bread and white cream of wheat is served. No color, no taste, no roughage. No aroma of food, either. Dinner is served at five o'clock; I guess bedtime must be at six or seven.

Yuval patiently explains again to Sarah where she is. "It's so that you won't be alone. So that they can look after you."

He explains to me that she had had two buttons to press, but when the palpitations started she had not pressed either of them. At the hospital, her hearing aid had stopped working. She didn't know where she was. A nurse told her to stay in bed, and dinner would be served. She didn't hear; she thought she had to get dressed and go down to the dining hall. The nurse thought that she was dangerous and was trying to escape. They bound her arms tightly and pinned them to her side, and tied her to the bed. It caused a bruise on her arm, and a deep wound of hurt.

"I have always been a good girl. Why are they punishing me?" she asked her children. They discovered that the hearing aid wasn't working.

"I still have something tied to me." I lean over and peek down the front of her dress. I tell Yuval, " She still has electrodes attached to her chest!"

He says he will get the nurse to take them off, but it is hard to find a nurse, even on the fourth floor.

Yuval says that older people lose their urge to drink. He goes to buy his mother some bottles of juice and water. As the elevator doors close on him, Sarah turns to me and becomes as lucid as can be. We live in the past together — that doesn't change. She gives me one blessing after another.

"I don't have to say how much I love you. If I love you, you just feel it, you know it. You can't lie about something like that."

"Your Raphi is like my Yuval. Devoted, kind. He will take care of you in your old age." These words soften the pain and dull it like novocaine; she has massaged the part that hurt. My Raphi will be like Yuval, who is now over sixty, not like Rafi, who will always be twenty years and three months old.

"I love your children as much as I love my own," she tells me. "I have two sisters in Canada. I will not see them again in this life. They never come here; I cannot go there." This sends me into a lonely reverie about not seeing my brothers; a deep pit of despair sets in.

An older woman bent over almost in half shuffles by. Sarah points to me, "This is my sister, my soul mate." This is not a delusional statement.

"I have been in Israel for sixty-one years. Yuval was born here and he is not a young man, so I have been here longer than that. This country saved me from Hitler, that bastard," Sarah continues. "All we need is peace here. We have everything else."

A woman as thin as an eight-year-old girl comes by with a frail-looking walker. She smiles with no teeth and says, "Are you new here?"

"No, I've been here since yesterday."

"I've been here three months. It has been good. Life is good, if you make it so. You have to be positive. Three months is a long time to be on the fourth floor. It was also good on the tenth floor; I was there for eleven years. What is your name?"

"Sarah."

"Sarah! I have a great-granddaughter named Sarah."

Sarah looks at her with a flirty, rascally look. "How many great-grandchildren do you have?" (Trick question: you can't have more than she does.)

"I have ten."

Singsongy. "I have thirteen." (Latest update, I think we're going on nineteen.)

"I knit. I made all my clothes. I am knitting for my great-granddaughter Sarah."

"Oh, I am a knitter. Come see my things."

"What room are you in?"

Sarah isn't sure. I say she is in room two. Dina is in room four. They offer each other friendship and shake hands. I look at Safta Sarah, impressed that she has found the one positive element of the fourth floor.

Sarah is called to eat her white meal. There is a great commotion over fixed seats. She sits in the wrong seat. I guess that's how they know if you're still alive — you show up for a meal.

I wander over to the television. Six civilians have been killed on a road in the north in a shooting. It is Linda's road. I call her husband. He says that she is trapped at work due to the shooting at the kibbutz where she is an art therapist with autistic children. I call Linda. The kids have been trying to escape and they have to keep them indoors. She can't talk.

Raphi in the army, Sarah on the fourth floor, and Linda trapped at work unable to get home. It really is a war. And where is Sarah when I need her most? Still with me, but on the fourth floor. Everything is tenuous.


# Remembrance Day — 2002


I didn't tell Raphi what to do, as a general rule, as he grew older. He was so responsible and took initiative. He wasn't spoiled, even though he had plenty of technological toys. Now, in the army, he has to get permission to urinate (during basic training, anyway). He is caught talking on his cellular phone during guard duty, and he is made to do laps. He is caught sleeping on guard duty; he loses a weekend home. His commanding officer threatens that he will not facilitate a day off on Remembrance Day. Raphi pleads that he has a grave to visit. He is sent to the kitchen to peel potatoes for eighty soldiers.

His friend Yonah is sent to simply stand with a newly bereaved family for the day, in the same cemetery that Raphi has to come to. It is a three-hour bus ride. Raphi peels potatoes and fumes about how Yonah will be where he wants to be.

Safta Sarah is too feeble to come this year. I am on my way to visit her — it seems this should now be part of the ritual — when I have a phone call from Raphi.

"Ema, I'm on the bus from Beersheva, and Rivka called to say that they're meeting early this year — at nine a.m., instead of at eleven."

"How did you get out?"

"I'll tell you when I get there."

"Gosh, I'm already in Tel Aviv, but I have to go back to Kfar Sava to get the girls." I think to myself that I won't have time now to visit Safta Sarah. "How long till your bus gets to Tel Aviv?"

"At least an hour, maybe more."

"How are you?"

"Fine, except there's a lot of traffic and I doubt that I'll make it in time. I have to get from downtown to the cemetery."

"Take a cab. Do you have money?"

"Yeah, I'm fine."

I turn the car around, and race back to where I set out from at dawn. I call Rivka and the girls on my cellular phone. Every year we come to sit by Rafi's grave, but this is the first year that Raphi is a soldier. He has been in the army about a month, and will arrive in uniform.

I hate to be late for anything. It is the "good girl" instinct. I can only like myself if I please everyone else. We park about two kilometers away from the cemetery and walk-run towards the grave. I have to stop at the bathroom as usual. There are soldiers with guns on the roof of the public toilets. Female soldiers give us stickers to put on our lapels that say "Remember." We arrive at

9:15, and rush towards Rivka, Jack and their married daughter Yael, who always stuns me — she is so tall and thin and striking. I am touched that Jack kisses me so tenderly. I hang onto Rivka. I need her more than she needs me today. Who has come to comfort whom? The smell of flowers is almost too sweet to bear; tens of thousands of bouquets are laid on graves, and there are flowering trees as well, as if we are in some exotic kind of garden.

"My friend Ella told me that this wave of terrorism is 'nothing' compared with previous wars. She was pregnant during the Six-Day War, and had a one year old. She didn't know where her husband was, and she spent her nights in bomb shelters. There were no telephones…

"I too was pregnant and ordered to have bed rest during the Yom Kippur War. I had my four-year-old taking care of me. I couldn't even get out of bed to pee. A four-year-old!" Rivka recounts.

"Didn't your parents help you?" I ask, thinking about Safta Sarah.

"Not really. It just wasn't done. They helped some, but it was each person for herself." She looks at me hard. Rivka became a grandmother at the age of forty-five, but I see signs of aging, like a mirror of myself. I am no longer the buoyant young mother that I was when I first came to Israel. I have a son in the army, and I feel my age.

"Yehuditkeleh," Rivka says kindly, reading my mind about aging, about stress and having a son in the army. "We have *never* known as scary times as this. Today you never know if your kids go out to have a good time if they are going to be blown up. You can't go shopping or hop a bus without wondering if you'll come back dead. In wars you can defend yourself. There is no defense against suicide bombers."

I feel that someone has heard me, someone has validated my fear. And then, "Yehuditkeleh," she says, "this is the hardest time to have a son in the army."

We chat about the family, talk about Safta Sarah's failing health. We talk about her clearer moments and that they are trying to reduce the number of drugs she takes for pain, to help her to stay awake and to focus.

I am aware that we have to wait ages for Raphi to show up. Yael and Shira have clicked. Yael is telling Shira about her law studies; she is disappointed in them and plans to get a master's degree in business studies.

It is ten o'clock. Rivka makes it clear that she is comfortable waiting until Raphi shows up. His little sister Ilana is the first to spot him. He is so tall, wearing a green khaki uniform (like so many hundreds of others). He is grinning shyly and loping towards us. Ilana has run to him, jumped up and he is carrying her, which doesn't slow him down at all. He also has a huge knapsack and a gun.

Hugs to everyone, he bends down low to squeeze Rivka. Sunburned and tanned at the same time, dusty, sweaty, hot-looking and very happy.

We all make a fuss.

"OK, I thought you were being punished, how did you get out?"

"All my friends peeled the potatoes with me when no one was looking."

Everyone questions him about his army experiences. Jack and Yael know just the right questions to ask. I never know the right questions to ask because it is beyond my experience. I'm an immigrant who never served in the army, which leaves me outside of the Israeli experience.

"How are the *chevre* (your gang)?"

"Great, they're my friends since second grade. In my tent there are eleven of us who grew up together."

"Are your officers taking you down a rank or two, telling you when to fart and when to sneeze?"

Laughter. "Yes, sir, you got it."

"Have you gone to the shooting range yet?"

"Yes, I even hit the target some of the time."

We are in a graveyard. The military is so…military. God. No innocence, no control, there is nothing I can do to protect him. Except maybe to go to peace rallies, which I do, but that only protects my psyche, and only for short bursts of time.

Rivka and Jack prepare to leave. "You will excuse us if we move on, we will not stay for the ceremony. We have about six other graves to visit." They can't take their eyes off Raphi. He bends down again and kisses each of them, gives them a squeeze. My eyes sting.

I am left with Raphi, Shira and Ilana. We move over to Rafi's grave. I have Ilana read out the inscription. I feel such love for my three children. They have come here for me. Or have they?

"Raphi, you are tired and hot. We also don't have to stay for the ceremony." My watch says 10:30; it will be another whole half hour.

"No, Ema, I came to be here for…for the ceremony. We will wait. We will…keep him company." The time passes quickly. Soldiers are giving out massive amounts of bottled water. I make sure that Raphi drinks.

At eleven o'clock exactly a siren is sounded throughout the country for two whole minutes. Everyone stands at attention. I steal glances at Raphi. He cannot take his eyes off the headstone; he is looking at the name.

# IV: Finding Eternity

## Content — 2003

Raphi has not met Kalman yet, he has been in the army while his two sisters have each traveled with me.

My third child, Ilana, has never been to a country that is covered in snow. We wear our winter coats about three times a year in Israel, except in Jerusalem which is high up on a mountain and actually sees winter.

It was an easy decision to take Ilana out of school twice, once to play in the snow in Jerusalem and to eat out at one of the only kosher Kentucky Fried Chickens in the world, and the second time to accompany me to Prague to meet Kalman, a "bat mitzvah trip." It is January, he is alone, and it is three years since my father died, since Ilana had an Edelman grandfather. We go to stay in a fancy hotel with a swimming pool. She is immediately rewarded with a foot of white snow, undisturbed in Kalman's neighborhood as there is little automobile traffic. Days later she asks why the snow in town is black.

Ilana brings kosher chickens packed in her suitcase among the jeans and sweatshirts and makes him her lemon-rosemary chicken as soon as we arrive. Then she meets his siblings in the photo album, the only place that they live.

In the way that only a child can, she poses two difficult questions to the professor of history. "How can one believe in God after the Holocaust, and what is the meaning of life?" I am delighted and amused, wondering how the professor will stand up to the pre-teenager.

Kalman says: "I must ponder these questions greatly. It will take time to come up with an appropriate answer for you." Several hours later, after dinner, he feels ready to address her questions with the seriousness that they deserve. They have bonded over her chicken, her questions, and his kindness.

> What is the meaning of life? Every people will answer you differently. Maybe to look for the answers is part of the answer. You were thrown into the world. When you were very young...

He gives her credit for being all of eleven years.

> ...it not depend on you. When the time comes that you begin to think, when you come of this questions. You must repeat over and over, all the time you give the same questions, but have a developing sense of the answers.
>
> When erudition is great, you discern meaning.
>
> When I was your age, I also looked for meaning.

He had already left home and was boarding with another family, studying and tutoring for his keep.

> Now at my age...

He laughs.

> ...I have other understanding.
>
> The second question depends a little with the first question. Religion. You can be a believer. Your parents can be either Orthodox Jews, Reform or anything else and educate you in this way. *Any* religion is a believer. Masaryk himself had dynamic belief and moved from being Catholic to Protestant, and then when he was older saw not all is good in the Church and became a Theist. He was not an atheist, his belief was not in the sense that he must adhere to the Church. One's personality and nature and character can also develop.

I marvel at Kalman's vocabulary.

> "Elohim": yes, there are all sorts of questions of existentialism.

Ilana is not used to being addressed on this level; she is very connected. She listens politely. Her mind is engaged, but also wanders. She politely brings it back. Kalman is aware of this and relates directly to her.

> When I was a young boy, I was educated Orthodox with all rituals. This was normal. There were only two Jewish families in my village, the rest, Catholics. All was clear for all of us, dictated, and defined. Then I begin to give questions. What religion of the Catholics, Jewish, which is better? I stayed with a family

in Brunn, I educated a little boy in Jewish studies, but the family did not keep God's commandments. I observed that God not punish me when not keep kosher. I rest safe and sound.

Kalman pauses and laughs with Ilana.

I became a Zionist. Conception of philosophy come later. Any person can connect with one hundred different points of view or concepts. One cannot find two philosophies which give the same answer. Elohim is the greatest question…

He gives her credit constantly for her question.

Nothing was for me sure, sacred. It is not so simple.

Exist in the world anti-Semitism and blood libels. Masaryk learned and studied with Jewish friends, and each was made aware of the meaninglessness of their prejudices through friendship. A little Palestinian girl can live near to you who can only read what is written and be fundamentalist. That same Palestinian child has her worldview and you have yours. Each people has wronged the other. Yet prejudices against each other are not right. Not all Jews are bad and vice versa. It will be a long and difficult process but it is possible to make peace. It is a question of meaning — possible to change the meaning as you grow. You have your convictions after experience, after you are older. You will not totally change, but you will evolve. Which way, which conviction? Your milieu is very important, which books you read, your parents, friends, school, character.

Content, content is what is important.

# Content II

Raphi's army unit, a group of friends — attached to kibbutzim — who go through the army with their own youth group, is doing a year of community service in Haifa. During this year, they don't carry weapons, but they do dress in uniforms. Eight young men and twelve young women, who have been in school, youth group and synagogue together almost all of their nineteen years, live in a communal house, cook together, and are supported by the Municipality of Haifa. In return they work with youth of the city who are either homeless, truant, parentless, directionless, or in need of attention. Social research has shown that young adults, especially in army uniforms, especially those from a strong social and educational background, can bring more order and meaning to the lives of these children than trained social workers.

Aryeh, whose mother has left Israel, works in a van that drives around at night offering rides to homeless children. During the day he accompanies truant children to school and supports them there. Who are these children? Children of parents who are destitute — some are new immigrants, some are Arabs, some are Jews, many have issues with drugs or parents in various kinds of trouble. Ganit befriends young girls who come to the day center which has a gym, a music room, a games room, a basketball court. Raphi plays basketball with children and helps them with their homework.

Many of the children do not have ambitions of going to school, getting a degree, finding a white-collar job. Raphi begins to visit work initiatives around the country. A sandwich business fits the bill in many ways; it can be short term or long term, marketing can start out small and become big, training is not intensive, it is easily learnable, and the results are immediate. The preparation of sandwiches could teach hygiene, keeping to a schedule, meeting the needs of the customer, money management. Raphi decides to go for it.

The sandwich business starts out with one child. Raphi together with his charge Sasha, who is under house arrest, takes twenty orders from an office building. Sasha's mother is a new immigrant from Russia, and has a baby as well. Fourteen, and stealing in order to support his mother, he may leave the house only in the company of an adult. Every day at five a.m., before the sun comes up over the Carmel Hills, Raphi takes a bus to pick him up. Watching the sea glisten as the bus descends the steep valley, they arrive at the day center at five thirty.

They go to the market and buy choice bread, lettuce, cheese, eggs, red peppers, onions of all kinds and tomatoes, keeping tabs on their costs. They buy plastic wrap, napkins, and condiments. A hawker yells to the two boys passing, "Buy your fresh pita bread here, freshly baked, two shekels a pack, right here!" Sasha, who once helped himself to everything that caught his eye in the market, smiles up at Raphi, the tall soldier.

Back at the center they scrupulously wash their hands. They fry omelettes and put them into baguettes with onion and herbs and mushrooms. They assemble various cheese sandwiches with fresh vegetables. They make tuna salad sandwiches. They wrap them neatly and put them into a basket. Raphi walks Sasha to the office building and waits at a distance while Sasha independently delivers the sandwiches. Elated after their first day, they count the money. It is one o'clock in the afternoon. Sasha wants to go out and get more orders for tomorrow. He covers a total of ten floors of office buildings while Raphi waits for him, to allow him independence. At seven thirty p.m. after doing the books and writing a shopping list for the next day, they have forty-five orders.

After a few weeks, they count their earnings. Raphi shows Sasha how much is profit, and how much covers costs. Raphi says, "We have made two thousand shekels. Come on, we're going shopping."

"But we shop for food at the market in the mornings, not now," says Sasha.

"I know someone who needs a new pair of shoes and some jeans," says Raphi with an impish grin.

This is the first pair of new shoes that Sasha has ever owned — Nike, no less. It is the first pair of new jeans that he has earned. "Next time we have a profit, we will buy you dress pants and warm shirts."

# Strong Women — 2002

The gap is a great one between my strength as a woman, and the vulnerability I offer to people, and to life events that throw me. Friends and even strangers can hurt me if they don't love me or don't express their love to my satisfaction.

Safta Sarah almost never asks me questions anymore. She has sunken into a more uncommunicative state.

I have decided to avoid getting hurt from relationships, and to focus on being a "strong and independent woman." I have never lived or coped on my own. A few hours on my own throws me into a panic. I look for people. This is very much on my mind as I make the huge effort in the summer heat to visit Safta Sarah on the fourth floor. I have to drive into the city, to park, to pass security checks.

Why am I willing to drive so far to visit someone who will not remember my visit? I am partly driven there by a feeling of how empty all of Tel Aviv, a metropolis, will be, when she is no longer there.

She is in the middle of eating lunch when I arrive, and the food actually looks and smells attractive. It has an aroma, unlike the white glop that is served at five o'clock before early bedtime. She is thrilled to see me, hugs and kisses, and gets attention for having a visitor during a meal when all are there to see.

She motions for me to wait for her outside the open-plan dining room, as it is for residents only.

Then she wheels over with her deluxe walker, which Yuval gave her, and we find a corner in the arts and crafts section of the fourth floor. This is a place where people come to live until they don't anymore.

"I am a strong woman," she says. I glare at her and cannot understand — how does she know what is on my mind? I think, "I don't pay you enough for psychotherapy!" In another age, she might have been a psychotherapist. Except that she usually talks instead of listens!

She pulls up her dress and shows a very thin leg all in ace bandages, several of them around all different parts of her foot, ankle, leg, calf. She fell yesterday. "I don't feel so good. I am a strong woman, I never think about my woes, and would you believe that I didn't get out of bed yesterday? I slept and slept."

Is she depressed?

"Rivka is so good to me. She takes care of me as if I am her daughter and she is my mother. She came here with Amit, who lost my needlepoint needle…she was so cute. All my children are so good to me. Ilana was here on Shabbat. Yuval is coming tonight. I have had trouble with my hearing aid while he has been away in England.

"The problem is that I don't have any work now. I am a strong woman, I have always kept busy."

There is a very pleasant woman sitting nearby. Overweight, big smile, and she clearly has her senses about her, unlike most of the skeletal figures on the fourth floor. "Who is she (pointing at me) to you, Sarahleh?"

We get to do our thing, our act. Sarah giggles. "Oh, if you only knew." We tease this woman and don't tell her immediately.

I exaggerate when I yell out, "She is my soul mate, my love, my best friend."

"Yes," Sarah agrees. "She is also related to me, she is the Kind (child, as in Kindergarten) of my late husband's cousin." I am proud of how lucid she is. "I always adopted the new immigrants in my family. First my husband's brother and his wife — I took them in to live with me after the D.P. camps. Then Yehudit, she came much later. *I always took in the immigrants in my family.*"

What a resume. To be able to say that when you get to the Accounting Desk at the end of your life. Then she remembers that her sister-in-law Sarenka, the one who gave her a lingerie set, has died recently. She turns to me: "She was so young, just a pitskelach, were you aware that she died? They all die now. There aren't many left."

I nod. "Kalman is alive," I say. "I am going to see him in two weeks." She gets very excited. I tell her that I am going to Prague with Shira, in order for her to meet Kalman. She turns to me in a very unusual way and asks, "But what is it that you are going to do *exactly* in Prague?" She has never asked me a question like that before. How does she know?

"I am going to take a whole week to myself and to write, *about you.*"

She squeals and turns to the overweight, kind woman in the plastic chairs near us and tells her in Yiddish that I am writing a book about her. The woman clicks her tongue and shakes her head in awe.

Sarah says, "And when you come back it will be finished and I can hold it in my hand? Oooh, I feel much better. I am no longer ill. I am strong again. *You will do my work for me* during this time."

Just on a whim, I ask her, "Have you heard of Thomas Masaryk?" She squeals again. "He is my father. That is, I don't know him really, but I love him, he saved the Jewish people, the president of Czechoslavokia."

"Kalman has been engaged with reseach on him for the last fifteen years, you know."

"I know," she says. "Not many people know this, but it is because of Kalman that I married Mordecai."

I understand this and yet I don't.

"He came to visit us in Hachshara, what a sweet young man. What a gentle person. So full of life. He treated me so well. And he saw that we were a couple. I cooked for him and spoke with him. Mordecai was as…as…as he was. But after that I knew that I would marry Mordecai, that if Kalman was going to be my brother-in-law, that I married into a good family."

Sarah — cooking, nourishing. "Sarah, do you know that Kalman cooked me a beautiful chicken meal? He was eighty-three years old and he koshered a chicken, and he cooked it for me."

"I didn't know, but, of course, they were religious. Then Mordecai strayed from the religious path, in Hachshara. He was no longer religious, but we thought of him as the yeshiva *bochur*, such white skin, not tanned from hard work, such a learner, not a worker, but a very smart man.

"Your father and Mordecai, they were the same thing. Cut from the same cloth. They both had heart problems and they both were very smart. All those Edelman boys were very smart."

I think of Kalman, who is still researching and lecturing and writing at age eighty-four.

When I go home I telephone him to make plans for Prague. We have written very warm letters. An e-mail is waiting for me from his student to convey how worried he is about the violence in Israel.

"I love you very much," he says on the phone. I think to myself, I can be a very strong woman indeed. I can't wait to go to Prague to see this loving and vital man whose mind and body are so active. I reassure him that we are well and tell him what time we will be arriving and at which hotel.

A white-haired hunched-over woman is wheeled to the park in a wheelchair, with a crown of flowers in her hair. Sarah is ninety-two. She waves regally through the fog, at her children and children's children's children. Nir, who quite improbably is a father of two, considering that yesterday he was a boy of ten showing me the fruit trees in his parents' garden, says, "I can't understand why in America parents give birth to children and then the children move to another state and they don't share lives anymore. I don't get it. It's only a biological function?" Nir lives on the same street as his brother and two sisters, a short drive from their parents and grandparents, in the clan model. This is content for those with families and those without.

# A New Reality — 2001

Nachshon, Raphi's best friend, kills a bird. He is shooting at the target, something that might save his life one day soon, and the bullet collides mid-air with a bird. The boys wait till the all-clear signal is given, and then they run forward and stare at the dead bird. Of course, they slap Nachshon on the back, and tease him about being an amazing shot, but they are horrified that a life has been taken. He is made a sharpshooter soon after this event.

# Back from Prague — 2002

Safta Sarah is very old now. She has a growth in her ear. I don't understand it. How is it that a person works so hard and survives so many losses and changes, and then gets rewarded with crumbling bones, shooting and constant pains, and a growth in her ear? Is it the C-word? She is not afraid of death, but she is not done living either. She has great-grandchildren numbers fifteen and sixteen to wait for. She always giggles when she speaks about the number; she has more than anyone else at her home for the aged.

Sarah understood that I was going to Prague to see Kalman and to write. She had asked, "Could I hold your book in my hands when you get back?" She was not frustrated in the least that she cannot *read* it in English. Although, I realize that I must go read it to her — spend an entire day or two, and sit by her side and read her life story to her!!

But this is what I do: I make a beeline for Safta Sarah's home when I get back from Prague. It is still scorching desert hot in Israel. There is no air-conditioning in her home; the residents wouldn't be used to it. When I arrive on the ward, I see the residents gathered around one of the workers, who is reading the news into a microphone from a newspaper. She is paraphrasing it. "The army has withdrawn from Jenin. You know where that is? It is in the north of the country." She uses the microphone as an extra aid to people's hearing aids; there are about fourteen of them gathered around her in chairs, with their walkers pushed off to the side.

It is informal, but organized, so I do not just approach Safta Sarah. I wait.

The worker, with a puffy hairdo and a large bosom, turns and smiles at me. I say, "I am a relative of Sarah Edelman; may I speak into the microphone?"

"Of course!" she enthuses, glad to have something that might break the monotony.

I greet Sarah, hug and kiss her, and then go to the microphone. "I am Sarah Edelman's husband's cousin's daughter. We are very close. I named my son after her son, Rafi, who fell in the Six-Day War." Exclamations of surprise — people didn't know that Sarah had a son who died in the war. The workers didn't know. Puffy Hair says so.

"I am writing a book about Sarah's life, her aliyah. She has had a very interesting life, and I have been to Prague to see her husband's brother. I wrote a lot when I was there. She asked me to put the book in her hands when I got back. She wants to feel its thickness and to hold her life in her hands. I am going to do that now."

Everyone perks up. Puffy Hair puts a hand on her huge bosom. There is an expression of compassion on the usually blank faces of the residents — I want to say "inmates."

I ceremoniously pick my way among the walkers, and approach Safta Sarah. I hold out the book. She holds out her hands. I put the book in her hands. She feels it. She weighs it, and makes a face as if to say, "This weighs a lot, it is quite a stack of paper."

"It is your story, Sarah."

"You did a good job, it feels wonderful," she says, delighted with the fuss. Some of the residents are asking her questions about her son. Or telling her about their losses. All have had losses. We hug and kiss and hug and kiss and celebrate the thick stack of paper.

I tell the worker that sometime I will come to tell the residents the story written on the pages.

Sarah is truly happy. She knows how to celebrate and praise. I give her the box of chocolates from Kalman. She is thrilled. She inquires about his health. I am in a quandary as to whether or not to tell her that his prostate cancer is progressing. Each one does not want me to worry the other one. Yet, they have no means of communication at this stage. Sarah doesn't write, and can't hear well enough to talk on the phone.

I have a brief flash of facilitating my father's last conversation with his twin brother before Dad died. He was disoriented, did not know what room he was in, or what that "thing" (his oxygen mask) was doing on his face. Yet, one evening when I dialed and handed him the receiver, he put on a strong voice, became jovial and strong, joked, kidded and chatted for twenty whole minutes, and sounded twenty years younger than he was.

"Sarah, why do older folks who have worked hard all their lives, and have struggled and suffered, why do they get sick in their later years? Is that fair?"

"Yehuditkeleh, my bones hurt. They say I have a growth in my ear. I have had a terrible infection and have been in the hospital. But if I didn't get old and crumble, then I wouldn't be here to see Yuval, Ilana and Rivka's children have babies and put them in my arms."

# Sending Packages — 1945 and 2002

Kalman's living room in Prague belies the poverty in which he lived, as a boy in the hamlet of Hamborek, Austria-Hungary, as a refugee during WWII, in concentration camps, on death marches, and when he was out of work during the Communist rule. He has known hunger.

I am most moved by his books. They cover an entire wall of his living room, in glass-covered simple wooden shelves. The overall effect is elegant. There is another bookshelf on an adjacent wall. Slowly, it becomes apparent just how many of the books were written by Kalman himself.

Clean modern rugs in a light green pattern cover the floor. A path is laid out on them by throw rugs, which look like they are from the Arab market in Jerusalem. There are two understated Czech crystal chandeliers. The furniture is very simple: an extremely well-kept three-seater upright sofa with no padding. The artwork is eclectic but leans toward the modern. There is a Dali poster of a naked woman with alluring breasts. She is either being stalked or sniffed by tigers. There is a modern cloth wall-hanging with nature and butterfly motifs.

Photos of Alena and Kalman in their last years together are propped up between the books and the glass sliding doors. A black-and-white headshot of Alena adorned only by her youth is framed on the wall.

The apartment has a minimalist appeal, which is intensified by its tiny adjoining kitchen and bathroom. The thigh-high refrigerator looks circa 1950. The kitchen makes me feel as though I have been reincarnated; maybe I cooked here before I was born.

The letters that Kalman keeps in his precious family photo album are from my Grandma Sadie. Kalman was exceptionally ill after the war, and Grandma Sadie commented on this in her letter. Uncle Milt is the only one who came to visit, but Sadie sent packages.

She sent him a coat, a blanket, a tie, a button-down dress shirt (she had to guess his size, never having met her nephew, her husband's brother's son). She sent several packages of cigarettes for Kalman to barter for food. She sent powdered eggs, popular during WWII, and other packaged food.

I feel a kinship with Sadie, assembling her packages, doing what she could to care for her young relatives from across the ocean.

With true mother's guilt, I feel bad about leaving Raphi in the army, while we are living it up in Europe. He is finishing basic training; here I am in Europe, being wined and dined, and my son is eating battle rations in the field. My father called them "SOS," or "shit-on-shingles." Take twelve hungry young men, who have been running in the sun for five and a half hours and smell like it. No one bothers to wash his hands, nor is there any way to do so. There are no plastic utensils. In groups of twelve, crouched above the sandy ground, they receive a package of rations. Each group receives a large can of "loof" (a bastardization of the word *loaf*, as in meat loaf) in a can, but it looks about as appetizing as dog food. Our cat won't touch it. There is a can of tuna fish too, no mayonnaise or lemon to make it palatable. There is mustard and ketchup. There is overly sweet grape juice to drink, which has never been anywhere near a grape, and it makes you more thirsty. There are peanuts and raisins, and two bread rolls per person. That's lunch.

As an immigrant mother I was not aware that my new occupation in lieu of worrying 24/7 would be sending food parcels to my soldier son. My last one was a work of art (guilt of leaving him behind while I travel?). I have moved from the craft of sending select junk food to nutritious, filling food for a whole tent of boys. Apparently, these parcels last between twenty seconds and five minutes.

1 variety pack of mixed Kellogg's cereal

a carton of long-life milk

cups to be used as bowls

coffee and sugar

2 cans of stuffed vine leaves (I was proud of this idea: nutritious, delicious, different)

2 cans pineapple

1 package dried hotdogs

2 packages Pringles potato chips

chocolate chip cookies

1 package squashed Doritos

There is also a love note with small change in it for the kiosk or Coke machines on the base.

I discovered after I left for Prague that Raphi had told his friends on the base to go ahead and open the package without him. He was at home recovering from bacterial dysentery, diarrhea and vomiting. He was sent home the day before I left, after I had sent the package. I got to hug him tight before I left, to take care of him and make him chicken soup. He slipped a note in my hand luggage that said, "I am so glad that I got dysentery so that I could see you before you left. Love, Raphi."

He missed the package but he got the love that was in it.

Mordecai used to pour a *l'chaim* and tell me again and again how my Grandma Sadie's packages in the 1940s were a godsend when everything in Israel was rationed. She sent his Ilana a sailor suit and a ballerina dress and a coat. These were Ilana's delight as a young girl. Later she was sent well-tailored clothes to take away to boarding school. I don't know how Sadie knew the size.

Ilana calls me up a month after I get back from Prague. "Did he get the package?"

"What package?"

"Didn't Raphi say anything?"

"No, we don't get to speak with him on the phone very much. About once a week. What did you send?"

"Oh, I made a project of it with my grandchildren. Each child put something in the box for him. They drew pictures. I told them exactly to whom it was going, and we were very excited. We sent a backgammon game, and cookies and chocolates and crunchy things. It was a huge box, and it was a family cross-generational effort. I sent it to the base."

"Oh, how wonderful. I think he has moved addresses, he is no longer in basic training in the desert."

"Where is he? Oh, I hope my package didn't get lost! What is he doing now?"

"He is guarding the northern border. Yes, he has a new address. I will check with him about the package."

It takes another three weeks, but Raphi demands that the army transfer the package from his base in the south up to the base in the north. He is delighted with the children's drawings. He calls Ilana to thank her.

His great-grandmother Sadie is making hats in the next world, and as she sews and watches her offspring, she is smiling to herself about poetic justice. "They are still making packages; perhaps they learned from me."

# Spirituality

Recipe: Go find a very old person. Look for wrinkles, health problems, graying and thinning of hair, age spots, and dental problems. Look for vigor of attitude if not of energy. Look for smile lines, and the laughter that made them. Find a very old person who has had many tragic losses, sharp changes in life situation, forced emigration. Find people whose parents and siblings were taken from them, whose destiny was beyond their control. And then talk to them about your life, about politics and suffering, and you will find activists and open-minded people, the most positive sources of hope and understanding of the human condition that there are.

# How Kalman Was Captured — 1944

"At the very end of the war, I was only caught for six months, but was the guest of six concentration camps: Saxenhausen, Bergen-Belsen, Landsburg, Neuengamme, Kaufering, Alach (Dachau). Afterwards I was on two death marches."

"How were you captured?"

"I managed not to be caught for a very long time. I did not wear the yellow tag which labeled Jews as 'Juden' as expected from March 1939 in Bohemia." One could be shot for disobeying the law to do so and Jews often were. This was just a few days before Sarah and Mordecai sailed for Palestine.

"I considered myself a Slovak, my physiognomy was not Jewish, and maybe this was an omen." I look at Kalman. It is true, he looks like an Irish nobleman, with elfish features and an impish grin. His nose is small, his cheekbones pronounced. Yet, he also looks like Mordecai's brother, and Mordecai had more typically Jewish features.

The first transports to Theresienstadt were in September or October 1941. All of Czech Jewry was transported there. Kalman received his invitation in March of 1942, when Sarah and Mordecai were already settled in Israel and had a child. "But I was just decide not to go to the transfer."

Kalman studied in a Jewish high school connected with the Reform Movement in Brunn from 1933 to 1940. While at the Jewish school he had a bar mitzvah with no family members in attendance. Sandor, his father, sent him ten crowns. Kalman was called up to the Torah on a Saturday morning in November, with his teachers and youth group *madrichim* cheering him on.

He matriculated and went to study optometry. He lived with a family, the Fleishers, who dealt in travel. The firm had connections with the Germans. All the family members were arrested at the end of 1940. As an elderly man, Kalman's photo album has many more photos of the Fleishers than of his own family. They were wealthy; they bought him a bicycle and took him on skiing holidays. He had enough to eat and nice clothes. In return he gave lessons to Karlheinz, their young son. Kalman tutored him in all subjects; together they studied Schiller, Guther. Kalman the poor son with nine siblings became the company and companion as Karlheinz was an only child, in some ways a poor little rich boy. Through the Fleishers, he met many influential and important people. Like Helga who was the great love of Peter Kien after WWII. Kien, who married someone else, wrote a famous love story about Helga. There are pictures in the album of Kalman and Helga.

He shared his new wealth and fortune with his family. He took the bicycle on the train to his sisters and held it while they wobbled around the farm, and laughed with them when they fell. Liebe, the youngest, especially loved these visits from Kalman; she adored her older brother.

Kalman was also arrested and put in prison. "It was very bad in prison. Men killed." Kalman was in solitary confinement and knocked on the walls. They were made of stone and were closing in on him. He was yanked out and shoved down a dank corridor for interrogations for three days. He was asked again and again if he was an accomplice to the Fleisher family.

On the second day of interrogation the Gestapo officer proclaimed, "You are a Zionist, you educate the young man in the family." Kalman denied this and said that he was merely a student. Nothing would make him utter his young student's name.

On the third day of interrogation the Gestapo officer was in a good mood. He told Kalman that he had been married that very morning. "You are Slovak Jew, leave, go."

Kalman left but did not return to Slovakia. He now, in defiance of the Gestapo's accusations, became an active Zionist. He went to a kibbutz training farm, just as his brother had many years before. In March 1942, he was forced to go underground with his group of friends. The name in his passport was Kalman Edelmann, later to be replaced by false papers and a false name.

A friend from the youth movement Hashomer Hatzair was also in the underground. The two of them had lost contact with their group while fighting as partisans against the Nazis. They made contact with a group that was transmitting Jews to Poland and Slovakia. They provided the money for bribes and came to the border where the Czech Republic met Slovakia. One man showed them the road to the mountains. The weather was overcast with purple and black threatening clouds. It was exceptionally muddy and lightning struck the mountain path. Kalman, who was no longer a practicing Jew, but more one who believed in a national solution for the Jewish people who had nowhere to go, said the blessing for thunder and lightning which he learned from his father. He said it silently, "Blessed are You, Lord, our God,

Ruler of the universe, Who has filled the universe with His power and his glory."

"Amen," Kalman's friend said out loud with a teasing grin. He had seen Kalman's lips moving.

"I meet two guards who are womens. I have only a little sack. My friend is wearing torn clothes. Good morning I said them and they are surprised. And they let me go."

Kalman and his friend walked through the rain which had now broken free from the clouds and went to the railroad station. "This not too far from Yasina where Sarah was from."

They managed to buy tickets and to travel to Preshov where Rachel, his oldest sister, lived. Kalman worked in an office as a correspondent. There was comfort in being near family but they all could just vanish, fall into a pit, be enclosed by a stone wall. He could cling to his older sister, to her little girls for a while, to feel some kind of normalcy. He could not save them nor protect them. Kalman watched as they were taken away and deported in the dismal autumn of 1942 when most of Europe's Jews died.

Kalman found work in an office as a bookkeeper and correspondent. The boss was a Slovak and not a fascist sympathizer. She knew that Kalman was a Jew, and she controlled her uneasy feelings about harboring a Jew.

One day Jan Gajan came to the office. He flirted with two girls who worked there, complimenting them on their cleavage and slim waists. He reeked of beer. Kalman did not know when he looked up from his paperwork that he was looking at his future name, his false passport, his safe haven. He merely saw a drunken man leering at the office workers.

The office sold fabric and wood, often to the Gestapo themselves. Kalman worked at this office from March 1943 to October 1944, a time when the world knew of gas chambers in Europe. The Edelmann family had already disappeared.

The war was ending in Slovakia. Preshov had just been liberated. Kalman spoke German and had contact with Germans through his work. Once he was chatting with a colonel in the German military, who offered him a cup of brewed coffee. When the colonel went into the small kitchenette to prepare it, Kalman opened the top drawer of the desk. The colonel, whose bald head and broad shoulders could be seen taking control of the kitchenette, was close enough that Kalman could smell his aftershave and his body odor.

In the front drawer of the desk Kalman saw an official rubber stamp; he thought of his friend who did not have papers. Kalman opened a lower drawer in the desk; there was official letterhead, nearly stacked. The meticulous nature of the Germans in storing everything so neatly and accessibly caused him to smile to himself. The German officer was laboring over the coffee in an equally meticulous way, although Kalman knew that he only had a moment. He took the rubber stamp and a tin case with black ink. Just as the colonel approached with the coffee, he stamped the letterhead and put it to dry on his knees under the desk. It was like a joke between them that Kalman was sitting at the desk and the colonel was serving him. The colonel graciously motioned to Kalman not to get up.

Kalman answered the officer's chatty questions, and quietly folded the paper and put it in his coat pocket, slightly obscured by the desk.

The colonel smiled at Kalman, "Pretend that you are not a Jew." Under the circumstances, this was the kindest thing that he could say.

"This ended well, but was dangerous. Yet in the end, I was captured on twentieth December, 1944, and was arrested. I was walking towards the furniture factory, and was ordered to stand still." Two Gestapo had reported on Kalman and his friends. These were the last Gestapo left in Preshov; the withdrawal had begun, and the town had been destroyed.

Kalman and his friend began to run. The soldiers shot in their direction as Kalman twisted, jumped and turned. The soldiers overtook both Kalman and his boss and held on to them. They were immediately put under the custody of the Gestapo.

There weren't enough prisons to incarcerate all the Jews who were rounded up. Russian soldiers had also been arrested. An elementary school in Preshov had been made into a prison. There Kalman was kept until January 13, 1945.

As they sat at desks made for children, next to black chalkboards with irrelevant white scribblings, Kalman and the Russian soldiers discussed how to escape. The Russians told Kalman that while millions of Jews were murdered by the Nazis, nearly twenty million Russians were killed on the front. Kalman lost contact with them just after the first internment in the concentration camp Sachsenhaus where he was transferred next.

Everywhere that Kalman went he forged relationships with his fellow prisoners of all nationalities. He was kind to them and they were kind to him; they spoke about things that mattered and shared food.

> Sachsenhaus was outside Berlin and it was possible to exist for only two to three weeks there. Bergen-Belsen was horrible and other camps were HELL. At night we were squashed together. I cannot sleep. Nor to turn over. The youngest men, I among them, were transported to Lowenger. This was a town in which Hitler had headquarters on one time. There were twenty-three French prisoners, they became a conspiracy group. They saw I from Czecho-slovakia and were very kind to me in the evening. I spoke not good French then, to tank friends.

Kalman's eyes well with tears as he is telling this and I cannot follow him into his memories or across the language barrier. Yet I understand that his survival techniques were fighting back and befriending people of all nationalities, and hiding under a false identity.

> They came to me help.

He wipes his nose.

> They gave food so I not perish. I survived to be sent to more camps.

Kalman was sent from Landsburg to Kaufering, and from there to Dachau. He was liberated on April 13 after being sent on two death marches. American troops liberated him between April 13 and May 1, during which time he starved and wandered, slept in Nazi barracks in the camps with nothing to eat and nothing to wear. He then went about the business of finding out which of his relatives had survived. He had one brother left in Palestine: Mordecai. One brother survived in Europe: Tuvye. He was a partisan — a freedom fighter, fleeing in the woods, fighting the Germans and Poles whenever he could, but mostly just trying to survive.

Prague had not yet been liberated from troops. On May 5, 1945, there was an insurrection.

> We returned to Czechoslovakia, twenty-fifth May, 1945. In Bohemia, still very difficult to travel to Slovakia, Preshov. I knew my family...come back not. Mother, sisters, brothers.
>
> Yaakov Moshe and Simon went with mother not to let her go alone. As an older woman, about aged sixty, I assume she was gassed right away. All sisters

went to camps. A half-Jewish family, Elsa Mann in Preshov, kept the photographs and a few things.

I have asked Kalman to will me the photograph albums to have after he is no longer with me. He has written my name on them in Czech. Kalman has no children to pass them on to. He is worried that his family will be forgotten and that their deaths will mean nothing.

# Couples — 1950 and 2004

When we arrive at his apartment, Kalman gives Shira an amber ring that belonged to his wife. He holds it out, looks at me teasingly and says, "This is for Shira." It suits her hand and makes it into a hand that has known culture, history, and has been loved. Deeply, by a man who values love. Later when she thanks him again and again, he says, "If Alena were alive, she would give it to you yourself."

Kalman married Alena Nejemnesha in 1950. About six relatives of Alena's were present. No one was present to stand up for the groom. Hitler had taken care of that. His two living siblings were in Israel. He was bareheaded and it was a secular affair carried out by a town official. Both the bride and the groom wore dark suits; hers was a skirt and a jacket. The one remnant of romantic tradition was the white bouquet that Alena carried.

They met at the Faculty of History at Charles University. Alena received her PhD soon after they were married. She was a strong and determined woman; Kalman was the warm and supportive one. Intellectual research was her life. A historian, she wrote the screenplay for the film "Documentary on a List of 2000 Czech Notables." Her mother, called "Babushka," and her brother Karl constituted a close family who embraced Kalman, an orphan, as their own. Babushka said after the ceremony, "Now I have three children."

"But she liked me the best of her children," says Kalman conspiratorially.

Kalman has been frequented by two recurring nightmares in his life. Thirteen years after his wife's death left him orphaned from the comfort of a couple, the dream still visits him. Before Alena died she slowly lost her sight. Kalman and Alena walk arm in arm as they did throughout their life together. Suddenly, Alena trips and falls, and then vanishes. Kalman calls out to her but she is gone. He wakes up calling her name.

This reminds him of another nightmare, right after the war. He dreams that he is in the middle of a stone circle. The circle is very high. He cannot get out. Then the circle gets tighter and tighter. He is hungry and tired and he cannot climb or dig.

Tragedy struck Alena's family. Karl's daughter, the one who made everyone laugh, and the light of all family gatherings, was hit by a car and killed in her twelfth year.

Both Kalman and Alena had lost nieces tragically. They went walking together in nature and held on to each other. Every step depended on the other. At the beautiful cliffs at Sarka not far from their apartment they hiked together. They sauntered to the ice-cold swimming area, where the natural spring water gathered. It was too cold to stay in the water for very long. They had to take a brisk walk under the hills and in the forest trails to warm up. Or on very warm days, to lie next to each other in the sun around the pool. Then gathering up their towels and picnic baskets, step in step, Kalman held on.

When the Communists came to power Kalman was expelled from the university, where he had had close ties and many successful publications. However, Alena was more radical and more belligerent against the Russian regime's hold in Czechoslovakia than Kalman was. He was a survivor, he was warm and kind. In light of his popularity, he was given a position several grades lower than professor, to teach French and German language.

Alena was given no such work and was out of work from 1970 until her death nearly twenty years later. It was dangerous to stay in Prague; they had to leave. Later this decree was cancelled. They moved to a poorer neighborhood and lived at subsistence level for twenty years. My father and Milt sent checks.

They were allowed to travel only to Eastern bloc countries. Kalman was invited to Bonn in February 1968. He used the opportunity of being out of Prague to visit his brothers in Israel. He had not seen Mordecai and Sarah since 1939, and had not seen Tuvye and Sarah since just after the war. He had received photographs of the children, but had never met them. He was one year too late to meet his nephew Rafi.

"Alena was so engaged here all day must do work. But she wrote me and all Israelis often."

There is a photo of the united brothers. Mordecai and Sarah took Kalman to the Dead Sea, to Eilat in the far south. Tuvye and Sarah took Kalman to Tel Dan, the Banyas in the far north. He stayed half the time with each brother.

Each brother complained about the other to him. The wives tried to make peace. All the nephews and nieces were warm and loving. They spoke to their Uncle Kalman in German or in English. They knew it was an important visit. Brothers are important. Ilana and Rivka missed Rafi, as did Yuval who was living in Canada.

Kalman hoped for democracy in Czechoslovakia. He hoped for peace in Israel. When he arrived back home, Alena was ill.

"It was undefined, but later I discover it was Alzheimer's. When she had forgotten all identifying features, and on her last days, she always knew my name." Kalman keeps her ashes to be buried together with him. She was not Jewish. They will share a grave. When he walks with her again, then his steps will be steady and sure.

Couples. Danny is English. That means while I run around taping up windows during the Gulf War, he makes himself a cup of tea and practices his art of indifference. It means that when I start my guard duty of worry at four a.m. for three and a half years of Raphi's army service, and eat every chocolate chip cookie in town, he snores loudly next to me. He remains trim and slim, ages well, swims three times a week. He never tells me, "I'm scared." I think that would have helped the most. After years in the Middle East, I am not so gentle and kind anymore. I am more and more difficult. He is the only person who can tell me who I was when I was nice, before I became a displaced person, an army mother looking for some anchor in the turbulent sea.

# Revolution

There is a photo of Kalman wearing an SS uniform after the war in 1945. "They told us to help ourselves from the wardrobe of the camp." Kalman looks like an Aryan. You can hardly tell that he is sick and starving in the photograph, but there is no hint of humor or joy in his face.

After the Velvet Revolution of 1989 Kalman was reinstated at the university. It was a bloodless revolution which successfully expelled Communist rule from the Czech Republic. There are photos of Kalman wearing ceremonial robes, a velvet hat, a chain of honor as one of the regents of the university, conferring PhDs on his students. There is a photo of a small class under Kalman's tutelage. The female students are all holding bouquets.

"He become a famous professor, she do important work, she become a famous professor," and so on, tells Kalman with his modest pride about his little group.

Revolution runs in the family. I once attended a lecture on revolution given by my father, Murray Edelman, a professor of political science. He came by the topic honestly.

# Another Soldier

I speak to Raphi about my work situation. He says: "You are not in the army, you are a free person. Release yourself from their authority if they are limiting you so much." I am in awe of my mature and thinking son. I also feel sad that the army is making all his decisions for him and limiting his freedom. Raphi says to me that his greatest wish is to come home more. He loves being home. I cook him schnitzel and give him Danny's rendition of Safta Sarah's stuffed cabbage.

I am so afraid. I want to help Raphi when he is in Hebron, by being loving and pleasant to be with. By continuing to send packages and cheer in a potentially disastrous situation.

My mother is learning mindfulness and meditation. This is ironic because I think we could rent her out to find The Problem in any given situation. She could run the official National Worrying Bureau. She is not sure she can get to her mindfulness workshop because her pain is bad before eight thirty a.m., but she can use ski poles to get through the ice and snow to the garage, providing that her pain medicine hasn't made her sleep through the alarm. She will be so tense by the time she gets to the workshop that any amount of mindfulness will probably be wasted.

I have started saying the morning blessings every morning. I am grateful for the light, for being able to see, for being a free person… I am grateful for Danny whose never-ending patience is a wall to lean on. I am grateful for Shira's leadership and creativity. For health. For Ilana's physical fitness. For Raphi's sense of humor. For having two paying jobs and income in this time of unemployment.

I call my brother to speak to his little daughter. "Emily! I'm calling from across the world, can you hear me?"

Giggles. "You are invited to my big people's birthday party and also to the kids' party. To everything."

"What do you want for your birthday?" Now I'm in trouble.

"A bicycle."

"Oooh, how about something bigger. An elephant? A giraffe."

"No, I already have some of those."

When we finish our banter and flirting and giggling, I speak to my brother again. He has two little children, is a well-thought-of lawyer. He has many in-laws and lives in a world of birthdays and Christmas, Easter bunnies, Halloween costumes. His extended family knows how to celebrate life, how to indulge and raise children, in a tribe of extended family. I have enjoyed spending two consecutive Thanksgivings with them in America. My brother's extended clan by marriage, none of whom are Jewish, ask me good questions about Israel. They can't quite understand why we endanger ourselves, when we could live in urban or rural Wisconsin. It is such a good life there. Candidly, they admit that there are in fact certain dangers even in rural Wisconsin.

So when I confide in my brother, who does not approve of Raphi's being in the army, I am taking a big risk, of ridicule, of blame. Of responsibility for his safety. What kind of a mother am I, anyway? We have joked about how we will allow our children to drive just as soon as they are forty-five years old.

"Sam, I don't know if you want to know this or not, but Raphi is being sent this week to a place…that is not good."

"I would rather know than not know."

"He is going to be in Hebron. That is in the West Bank. There have been some troubles there. Some bad ones. It is really my worst nightmare."

"Oh, that is just the hardest thing I can think of. I always have a baseline of worry, but now it is going shooting up." He lets me know that I can tell him, and that he loves us.

"Yes," I say. I am so grateful. He has not reassured me, nor has he made it worse. In fact, he has reacted the best possible way that he can. He is there for me and is not judging me.

Faded in a drawer I have an aerogram — I still remember the blue folded paper — saying that *he* is not responsible if something happens to Raphi in the army. He is right, he is not responsible. He is absolved.

*And me?* Am I? I made aliyah, I *chose* to come to Israel. Raphi would not be here if I weren't here. He would be drinking beer on some university campus in England or America, and thinking about meeting young women and studying or not studying for his next test. He would live near his grandparents and enjoy the cross-generational support that parents and their offspring cannot give to each other during teenage years. This is the worst pressure on me: am I responsible for putting Raphi in a life-threatening situation?

There was a movement in psychology in the 1960s that said that the mothers (all the more so immigrant mothers) were responsible for autistic children, for children with developmental disabilities, for depressed children, for those with behavioral disabilities. They were also responsible for the sexual preferences of their children. Later this was debunked and seen as chauvinistic — to blame mothers for everything.

Am I an all-powerful god who can make him happy? Can I keep him safe anywhere? From traffic accidents, AIDS, natural disasters, terrorist attacks? He and Shira visited the Twin Towers one month before they collapsed, on their travels that all Israelis do before the army.

A spurious motherly fear visits me. Raphi is very tall. It is my pride. To hug him and to rest my head on his chest, I have to stand on tiptoe. He towers over the tall men whose height I have always delighted in. So I am worried that he stands out of a crowd and that the sniper will be able to see him first, from a distance, above all others.

The point is that I have no control. No way of protecting him. So am I responsible? Did I do this? Is it my fault, even though my brother was very kind? Can I be responsible and unable to control fate at the same time?

I remember the summer he was six. I think a lot about his childhood now. We stayed in Wisconsin for a month, and Raphi went to a Jewish summer camp. Camp Shalom — Camp Peace. The brakes on the bus were cut in an anti-Semitic act. In Wisconsin. Where it is safe.

I think about a cartoon that was in the newspaper. There is a Holocaust victim in his striped concentration camp uniform floating on a cloud, and looking down on an Israeli soldier in full battle gear; the victim is saluting the soldier. Like a mirror or an echo, there is a color photo of soldiers standing at attention as the siren for Holocaust memorial is sounded. The Holocaust victims and the soldiers, each honoring the other.

Was it Safta Sarah's mother's responsibility that some of her children remained in Europe and died in the Holocaust? Sarah came to Israel against her mother's wishes. Sarah's mother couldn't control the fate of her children. But that sent her out on a ledge with a piece of rope. Those whom she protected were slaughtered, and those who left her protective wings were saved. None of this was her fault.

I thought I could offer my children a better life. Today, this day, it is not better. Raphi is in Hebron. In full combat gear.

# Telegrams — 1967

Sarah, Yuval's wife, is pregnant with her first child. This will be Safta Sarah and Mordecai's first grandchild. Yuval is in Canada getting his master's degree in engineering. Sarah misses her mother, but loves the financial ease of life in Canada. Ilana and her husband Zvika are living in Tivon, with a view of the Carmel Hills. Rafi is in the army, and Rivka is in her last year of high school.

Lital Ednat is born in May 1967. Yuval and Sarah are thrilled. Yuval knows that this first grandchild will make his mother's and father's hearts leap. Yuval had no grandparents. His mother was an immigrant mother.

There was not a bevy of aunts and uncles to help bring him up. The only way to build the family is this way. He is a scientist, and a thinking young man, but when it comes to writing this telegram at the post office, his hands shake. He asks the post office clerk for a new form and tries again.

"Mazel tov, you have a granddaughter! Lital, six pounds, healthy, beautiful. Love, Yuval and Sarah."

Sarah and Mordecai leave this telegram on the dining room table so that everyone who enters the house will see it first thing. They tell all the neighbors.

Four days later the Six-Day War breaks out. Yuval sleeps at the airport in Toronto trying to get a flight to join his unit. There are no flights. Rafi is waiting for his unit to be sent to Sinai. He hears that Jerusalem has been reunited and the Western Wall of the Temple is again in Jewish hands. There is euphoria among the Jewish people.

When Rafi's family hears of his death, someone finds a piece of paper on the table and scribbles the details of his death on the back of it. The next day Mordecai, who keeps important mementos of his family's history, is horrified to find out that someone has defaced the birth announcement of his first grandchild. It is defiled. On one side is the joy of Lital's birth, the happiest event in Mordecai's life so far; on the other side, the details of the death of his son, the saddest event in his scarred life.

# Ilana

Some of the best food that I make, food that wows my guests, is made at the holy altar of my cousin Ilana's kitchen. She is as good a cook as her mother.

### Ilana's Eggplant

Take a plump, large, shiny purple eggplant. Cut it in cubes and salt them, drain until the brown juice flows out. Meanwhile take a large red pepper, and a medium green pepper, and cube them. It doesn't matter if a few of the seeds stay with them, it adds to the mix. Mince a large onion or two smaller onions. Cut up four cloves of garlic.

Heat olive oil in a large frying pan. Use either a cast iron pan or a Teflon pan. Fry the eggplant cubes and onions first. After seven minutes, add the peppers and garlic. Stir and fry until all vegetables are nicely browned.

Flavor with a tablespoon of brown sugar, or artificial sweetener if you are diet conscious. Add a few grinds of black pepper, a little salt. Add half a cup of tomato paste, and enough water to cover half the vegetables. Stir and cover, simmer for fifteen minutes.

The eggplant turns out sweet and tangy, spicy and soft and juicy, like Ilana. Serve hot if you wish, but it is great when it cools.

### Ilana's Rosh Hashanah Honey Cake

This is the only honey cake I would ever make. No one else in my house eats it. I eat the whole thing myself. Ilana warns us not to worry that it looks runny before it is baked.

Mix all the following ingredients in a food processor until mixed and fluffy.
1 cup sugar
1 cup honey
½ cup oil
4 whole eggs
1 cup strong coffee
2½ cups self-rising flour
cinnamon, a generous amount, around two teaspoons

Sprinkle blanched almond halves on top.
Bake at 350 degrees F until it is done in the center.

### Ilana's Frosting

Once Ilana produced a cake with about two inches of chocolatey pudding on top. The guests stuck their fingers in the cake and licked their fingers. Zvika and Ilana just laughed.

Make a regular sponge cake. Then make the following for frosting:

150 grams cooking chocolate
¼ cup milk or water
3 tablespoons sugar
100 grams butter

3 egg yolks
3 egg whites, beaten until stiff

> Melt the chocolate with the water. After it cooks add the yolks and sugar, fold in egg whites, put on cake, cool.

Ilana is colorful, and she laughs a lot, especially when Zvika is around to flirt with her. He knows the best swear words in English and uses them good and proper. She is Middle Eastern. She will tell you exactly what is on her mind, give advice freely, size up a person and say so, for good or for bad. She is both pepper and garlic, but she is sweet, and sustaining, something special.

When I first met Ilana she was the young mother of four children. She enjoyed them, and they were well brought up. I was amazed when they kissed her cheek and said, "Thank you, Ema, for the good food." How many children thank their mother after every meal? The joke in the house was that Zvika did a fair amount of the cooking, but he insisted that they still kissed their mother's cheek and thanked her for the good food.

Ilana, a hairdresser and cosmetician, and a stunningly beautiful woman, always noticed people's looks. She thought her daughter Shirley, age two, was beautiful, whereas Ronit, age four, was "charming," with her reddish hair and freckles. Ilana scrutinized her hippie cousin from 1960s America. "You don't shave your legs? You don't pluck your eyebrows?" I must say my ideals did not survive twenty years in Israel. My style now bears more than a passing resemblance to Ilana's.

Ilana told me that Zvika was so happy to have a daughter finally after two sons that he gave up smoking when Ronit was born. She also told me that when Zvika is away on business trips she sleeps downstairs with the children — too many stunning memories upstairs in their shared room. That painted as exciting a picture as the view of "Little Switzerland" from their patio.

And they did always seem like a close couple. We had a picnic in the Safed countryside at an adventure playground for the children. I joined in with the children going down a rope swing, sliding down long slides and climbing up chain ropes. Ilana and Zvika lolled on a blanket in the shade and hugged and kissed. I took a picture and Ilana was horrified. Then we all went swimming in the sea of Galilee.

We drove around the Galilee, to give me a sense of Israel. We passed Arab and Druze and Jewish towns, olive trees groves, picturesque mountains and hills. The children sang songs about Israel. "My Israel is beautiful and flowering, and I built a house, planted a tree, paved a road, built a bridge and wrote a song, in my beautiful land of Israel." I used that song for years when I was teaching Hebrew school back in America.

Nir, who was eight, showed me the pomegranate trees in the garden which he tended together with Zvika's father. He was so proud of them. The American cousin: "They grow on TREES? I thought they grew in supermarkets." Today Nir is the father of two. In fact all of Ilana and Zvika's children are the parents of two children, and all of them have attended the kindergarten in Ilana's backyard. They have all their grandchildren at their house every day, and thereby save their children the expense and worry of sending their children to nursery school.

Ilana has had some hard blows in her life. She lost her brother. She had to learn to live with her in-laws, who were wonderful and loving, but there were inevitable tensions. Like when Nir would yell at the top of his lungs, "Safta, my parents are abusing me," and Ilana had to tell her mother-in-law she couldn't come to interfere even when he yelled for her. Her father was abusive to her and she never learned to stand up to him.

Dror and Nir were little boys digging in the garden. They uprooted the carrots and replanted them upside down. There was the smell of fresh upturned earth, carrots outside, and Sarah's stuffed eggplants wafting from the porch. Ilana was a stuffed eggplant herself, eight months pregnant with Ronit. Her father discovered the boys at play in his garden, and turned around and smacked Ilana on the face, on the arm, and then in the belly. "You don't know how to bring up children; they are little hoodlums uprooting my carrots!" She faced his wrath many times and could not understand how Rivka could stand up to him when no one else did.

There was no money the first ten years of her marriage. When I came to visit, we went shopping together in Nazareth, at the Arab market. I bought a long Arab dress which I wore for years, and she bought a more feminine dress, very cheap, and said it was the first dress that she had bought in four years.

Ilana's voice is always hoarse from being a kindergarten teacher. She knows how to enliven any party with songs, special foods, surprises.

Her generosity knows no bounds. She has taken each of her grandchildren to Europe. She babysits after kindergarten hours. She and Zvika helped to buy each of her children a first house, a car, a dishwasher, to make their lives easier than hers was. She bought my Raphi his first tricycle when we could not, and sends him packages. She gives and gives and gets great pleasure from it. Now her health has made it harder for her to cook and entertain, but the last time I was there, she served me the most amazing sweet and sour bean soup.

"It's very easy," she says. "Fry an onion in a soup pan. Add half a can of tomato paste (the other half from making her eggplants). Add a teaspoon of hot chili oil, half a cup of vinegar, and a bag of yellow frozen beans. Cover with water."

Ilana always has homemade pickles and olives in her kitchen, and a jar of homemade coleslaw. She keeps her freezer packed so that she can produce a delicious meal in little time for her grandchildren or any wandering guest. Ilana is the grandmother of nine and keeps her family very close to her.

She is sensuous and full of flavor, she is delicious and sweet and sour, she is imaginative and she chooses life.

# Sarah's Hands

Sarah's hands helped to picked the vegetables. Sarah's hands helped to knead the dough. They petted the calves, and squeezed the udders of the matronly soft cows.

They braided her sisters' hair. They laid out the Shabbat cloth. They set the table. They carried the water bucket, up the slippery hill and down its treacherous icy slide in the winter.

Sarah's hands held her friends' hands in the Israeli dancing circles at the youth movement that she went to illicitly, against her parents' rules. They banged on the door to let her in when her parents locked her out.

They embroidered monograms on sheets and pillowcases for marrying sisters.

They held her sister's hands in childbirth. They held the new baby.

They packed a bag to go to Hachshara. They sliced onions and chickens, carrots and turnips, and pulled the ends off beans in the kitchen at the train-ing farm. They decorated chocolates in the chocolate factory with a Gestapo officer watching.

They hugged her mother and father goodbye. They touched her nieces' braids for the last time.

They held Mordecai's hands and a handkerchief on the train, dripping with tears.

They held the railing on the boat. Sarah's hands swam in the Mediterra-nean Sea to get to shore. They stroked the sands on arrival.

They fed chickens on the kibbutz. They dusted the house of the rich American woman who was bedridden.

They groped for Mordecai's body in the dark in the kibbutz while they were waiting for their turn to get married.

Sarah held out her finger for a golden ring and felt Mordecai's familiar hands put it on her index finger.

Sarah's hands held her first son, cupped her milk-filled breast. Then a daughter. Then another son, then another daughter. Her hands were wet with bleach from four in the morning, with laundry scrubbed up and down on the washboard. They changed, washed and folded the diapers.

They scattered feed for the turkeys, the geese, the hens; they picked up the eggs, weeded the garden, planted the seeds.

They stirred the chicken soup, cut another salad, whipped the batter for the cake by hand, cut homemade noodles on the wooden board. They scoured the house. They knitted vests and dresses and sweaters and caps and trousers for the children.

They put some coins in a secret place so that the children could have popsicles. They made jam from the apricots that Rafi picked. They washed the floor.

They brushed the girls' hair, and laundered the army uniforms.

They played cards. They waved in the air during the dancing at the weddings.

They worked harder than ever after Rafi was killed.

They held the first granddaughter. Then the first grandson. They gave the grandchildren a bottle.

They made meals for three married children and nine grandchildren.

They pushed the baby carriages of the grandchildren put in her care.

Sarah's hands made sugar cookies, gefilte fish and schnitzel for her guest from the States.

Sarah's hands did needlepoint. Sarah's hands visited the sick.

Sarah's hands put on a wig when her hair fell out.

Sarah's hands taught grandchildren how to knit and cook.

Sarah's hands touched Mordecai's arm, and felt that it was cold. Her hands patted his smooth gravestone.

They held a cane at the weddings of all nine grandchildren. They wrote checks to give each grandchild comfort in the new life. They reached out to hold on to each one, to bring them near for a kiss and a hug; her hands could not easily raise her from the chair.

Sarah's hands held the rail in the elevator at the retirement home.

Sarah's hands held the letter every year from the Ministry of Defense thanking her for her sacrifice.

Sarah's hands held the reparation check from Germany.

Sarah's hands cradled her first great-grandchild. And her second. And Amir her seventeenth. Her hands held mine. Her hands held mine.

# Rivka Remembers

My mother always said, "One hand washes the other, one hand shakes the other." It takes two hands and teamwork to cope in a strange new land.

# Weaving of Stories

"What were Sarah's beliefs?" I ask Rivka as we meet at a designer coffee shop in North Tel Aviv, her grandson baby Harel climbing on her daughter Yael's torso as she reaches across to cut her granddaughter Amit's pie. They are all such good cooks, I cannot imagine that restaurant food will excite any of us. However, Rivka seems thrilled with her spinach and onion pie. Yael has dried tomatoes, basil and feta cheese, and I have a salad artfully constructed of pears in red wine with Roquefort cheese and walnuts.

Rivka gives Amit a pen to draw with, takes a sip of her coffee. It is a treat for all of us to be together. We don't live a clan-like existence together. I bring my American individualism; Rivka and her gang bring their Israeli kibbutz-like collectivism. But it feels like family.

Rivka quotes Sarah:

> My mother always said, let things take their natural course; she was referring to the ways of romance and love. She treated absolutely everyone equally; everyone was equally wonderful in her eyes. The important thing was to be a peacemaker, to get along with everyone, to compromise whenever necessary — that is how you gain, because harmony is more important than winning.
>
> She loved people; she gave with no end in sight. When Rafi and I got into fistfights, she was the peacemaker.
>
> She believed that if you give, you receive in return, but the giving itself held its own reward for her.
>
> She worked hard and believed in the healing and cleansing power of work. She had time for absolutely everyone."

I go into a reverie as I skewer a wine-marinated pear and a blue-veined piece of Roquefort. When my co-workers phone me they often apologize for cutting into my time. My colleagues are the people for whom I should have the most time. Safta Sarah had no modern technology to help; she washed her clothes by hand and baked her own bread. But she always had time for everyone. How did she do it?

Her house was an open house. There were cookies baked and ready at all times, not to mention the sumptuous four-course meal that would appear within minutes. None of this American inviting people to come over in three days' time for a cup of coffee. Every visit, perhaps especially a spontaneous one, was rewarded with a royal reception and feast.

Jack, who came from an Iraqi background, loved Safta Sarah's cheese-filled strudel. Rivka loved the poppy seed cookies. Fresh baked goods, hot apple turnovers, juicy apple strudel were always on hand, ready for neighbors young and old who were drawn to the house by its smells. Sarah made falafel from scratch; noodles from scratch; bread, cakes and cookies from scratch.

Rivka laughs:

> I was upset that the carp arrived home alive and swam around the tiny bathtub. Pleading for its life and for justice, I screamed as the carp was conked over the head with a rolling pin and sliced. They were female carp full of eggs. My mother served fresh fish caviar, never from a can, but from the bathtub carp.

Her mother looked at everything in a positive light. I think about all the years of being drawn from my busy immigrant-mother struggle into the magic of her kitchen. I had the never-ending cycle of work and children, yet there was time out of time in her kitchen sipping her soup.

When Rivka got her first period, she could talk about it openly with her mother. Everything was a subject for discussion. But her father took her shopping for her first bra. He was a modern father, finding his way in the new world. Perhaps as a reaction to Sarah's fight against her parents' religious restrictions, Rivka was allowed to go out without a curfew and to do as she pleased. Sarah was not allowed to go to Hashomer Hatzair, the secularist youth group, or to Noar HaOved, the socialist youth group. So in contrast, no one objected to Rivka's learning ballroom dancing, to having dates with boys.

Rivka's granddaughter Amit knows how Rafi died. She senses that I am a keeper of family lore and she, at five, knows some. "Safta (Rivka) was seventeen. She went to the store on the way home from school. She threw her knapsack and ran. How did you get your knapsack back, Safta?"

Rivka's fork stops halfway to her mouth. She looks at Amit with the respect that she gives to all people.

> Yes, that is what happened. I stopped at the store to carry home my mother's shopping. She usually left it for me to carry. Everyone in the store was staring at me. I sensed something was seriously wrong. The shopkeeper said, "Rivka, you'd better go straight home." I dropped my school bag on the floor and ran, feeling terror and knowing what it was. The Six-Day War had just finished. Rafi was in the war, he hadn't come home. I knew what had to have happened to make everyone in the store stare at me.

Amit looks at Rivka. "But how did you get the school bag back?"

> They brought it to me.

Who told you that Rafi was killed, did they break it to you…gently? How?

> No one told me.

What?

No one told me. I arrived home. The house was filling up with people. There was an awful silence. No one knew what to say.

I was the one to tell Ilana. No one wanted me to go. Ilana was worried sick about her husband Zvika who was in the war. She was pregnant. My father tried to hold me back, but I took the bus all the way to Tivon in the North. It was a longer trip in those days. When I got there, Zvika's father was pacing up and down the street. He thought he might lose his son. Although he was a very stoic and unemotional man, he was panicked. He saw me, and he fainted in the street. Dead away. I was in a rush to get to Ilana.

Ilana was halfway up the steps to her mother-in-law's house. When she saw me, she sat down hard and almost fainted as well. She knew the minute she saw me that her brother had died, and with all the tension of waiting for her husband, she was a mess. It had never occurred to her that her little brother might be killed.

My mother didn't talk about Rafi. I didn't ever see her cry. Can you believe it? She lost quite a bit of her hearing after the news of his death came. She simply became deaf. Perhaps it was so that she'd never have to hear bad news again. She became apathetic. I was seventeen, and I became the adult in the house. The functional one. Yuval was in Canada, Ilana was in Tivon, and I was the one at home. The only one left.

Rivka's daughter Yael continues the story. "Safta Sarah never spoke about Rafi to me until I was pregnant with Harel. She never asked any of her children or grandchildren to name someone after him. But about one year ago when I was pregnant she asked me with some urgency to name him Rafi. I couldn't say the name on a daily basis. It is too sad. Only after I'd named Harel, which means Mountain of God, did I realize that Rafael — which means God Heals — and Harel rhyme and share four letters!"

This leads to a discussion about religion. Rivka and her children are secular Israelis. "My parents who grew up Orthodox took comfort in a Reform synagogue in Ramat Gan. They went to intellectual discussions about the weekly Torah portion." Sarah and Mordecai were active members of their synagogue for thirty years.

"We went with our grandparents," says Yael, holding Harel, who has bedroom eyes and bedroom lips.

Amit doesn't want the portion of food that she ordered. Yael remembers,

"There were always four courses of food. If you ate three and a half of them, Safta Sarah would say you didn't eat anything."

Rivka looks at her grandchildren. She seems to see the past in them. She says, "My father didn't suffer fools tolerantly. My mother received everyone equally; everyone was special, pampered, wanted." She goes on:

> My mother's belief was centered around hard work. It wasn't so much avoidance, as it was the focus that gave her life meaning. Busy hands, usually with the goal of giving to other people. But before the morning sun had risen, she had her laundry hand washed and hanging on the line. She had a good-girl instinct. Do it right, do well, do all of it. She had time for everyone, an open house. That might have been the goal of the work. She prepared a lot of presents for people. These came in the form of cakes, cookies, knitted sweaters, dresses, shawls, embroidery and tapestries.
>
> Her greatest gifts were food made completely from scratch. She made falafel from scratch, starting with soaking the beans. She made noodles from scratch. Her stuffed vegetables were a masterpiece, as was her chicken soup and her strudel.
>
> She had a sense of fun. Until Rafi was killed, Sarah got dressed up for Purim. She would parade the neighborhood with baskets of baked goods with a clown face, or wearing a man's suit or Mordecai's baker hat from the factory. She would make huge picnics on Israel Independence Day, truly a meaningful day for someone whose family died in the Holocaust. After Rafi died, we never celebrated Israel Independence Day. It was the day following Remembrance Day, too close, too sad.

Soon we ask for the bill. We kiss, we hug. I drive back to Kfar Sava. They drive the other direction to North Tel Aviv.

# Prague — 2003

Danny and I ask Kalman if we can celebrate Shabbat together. At first he is hesitant. He hasn't made Shabbat in such a long time. Many years. The last time with an Edelman family member? Perhaps in 1965 when he visited Israel, perhaps not even then, perhaps before WWII.

Simon, Kalman's oldest brother, with a very handsome face, and good nature, was the first to leave religion. Most of the others followed.

Kalman decides to celebrate the Sabbath together with Danny and me. He gets out candlesticks. There are no appropriate candles in stock so he uses Hanukah candles instead. He also brings out a memorial candle and places it solemnly in front of the Sabbath candles. In my ignorance, I ask, whose Yahrzeit, whose day of memorial is it? "For everyone," he replies slowly, "for them all."

I feel humbled. He lives with their deaths every day. It never gets better; in fact with old age it probably gets worse.

Danny and I boil chicken with onions, carrots, celery, and squash. We use a kosher chicken cube as well as salt and pepper. The aroma fills the entire apartment. When the broth is rich, I add chopped parsley and thin noodles. Kalman sets the table with his best dishes — he and Alena acquired them years ago, and they are truly beautiful. He puts out crystal wine glasses which Prague is known for. It is time to light candles.

Kalman often thinks of Dafni, Yuval and Sarah's daughter who died in an automobile accident. She looked like Rachel, Kalman's older sister who bought him papers. I look at the photo and am shocked, like a knife of understanding slicing through me. Family is holding the same memories, the same sadnesses. Ilana and Rachel and Dafni are from three different generations and from three different branches of the family, yet they all have an uncannily similar rich European beauty.

Kalman lights the memorial candle with dignity. Danny and I wipe away tears for our relatives who died in the Holocaust, who at that moment feel like brothers and sisters. Kalman illuminates them for us as I kindle the Sabbath candles and Kalman stands next to me and weeps quietly. Then, wanting to mark our closeness, I ask for the blessing of the Cohanim. Kalman is a Cohen, like the other men in my father's family. Priests of the Temple. While I feel that the class system is outmoded, I love the family connection of Kalman giving me the Priestly blessing. He says that he doesn't remember it. My prayer book is too small to see. I say it for him, but we are too charged with emotion to get all the way through it because he has just been given a daughter, and I am standing next to my father. Then I ask him if he would do the blessing for the wine. He says he would be happy if I did it.

When Kalman was growing up, it was always the men who said the blessing over wine, and all public prayers. I know he has lived all his life in equality with women, but he has never heard a woman say Kiddush over wine. As I say the words, they come back to him across time, and he mouths them with me.

"You are a *balabusta*, a great homemaker, Yehudit. A modern one who works hard and says the Kiddush. But it was of great enormous value to be a *balabusta* when I was growing up, when Sarah was growing up. If you were rich it was easy, there were servants, store-bought cookies and cakes. But if you were poor — and my mother and sisters and Sarah were all poor — it was a gesture of overcoming impossible circumstances, an impressive feat."

I jump. My father often used that phrase: "an impressive feat…"

# The Photo Album

I lived for twenty years in America without ever knowing of my cousins in Israel or in Europe. My aunt Hazel wrote an elaborate family tree which I treasured. In fact, I knew in theory — in words — that there was a brother named Kalman, even though I didn't know his fate.

I am forty-five years old before I meet my cousin Simon, who steps out of the pages of the photo album and surprises me. Mordecai had told me that their oldest brother Simon had chosen to go the extermination camps with his mother so that she would not be alone. That sentence was the extent of him. Yet, Kalman's photo album insists that Simon had a life before he lost his life. He was more than just the oldest son.

Hamborek was so small that there was no post office. Yet Simon loved the village. He had a woman in the village that he loved, Elsa. She loved him back. Simon was in his last semesters of medical school in Prague, at Charles University, when he was deported. He wore suits and waistcoats and had a pocket watch with a chain and a dapper hat with a brim. However, he had no financial help to attend university and it was a struggle. He was unable to finish but he served as a doctor, even without a certificate. He sent a letter from Lublin to the family, telling them of his medical work.

He didn't look Jewish and was the first to leave religion. My very favorite story of Simon was that when he put on prayer phylacteries to please his father, he sang Brecht under his breath while his father thought he was saying the blessing. He smiled, he whistled, he wound the tefillin around his arm, seemingly with great joy, but he was concentrating on his Brecht.

Once he had a pernicious fight with Mordecai because he arrived home on Shabbat clearly having taken a trolley car part of the way. All hell broke loose.

Mordecai yelled, "I cannot fathom that a brother of mine, who grew up in this house, would desecrate the Sabbath!"

Simon smiled and adjusted his hat to a jauntier angle. "Maybe God will strike me dead."

Mordecai was getting very worked up. "You are breaking Jewish law, the sacred day of rest. How can you spend money, buy a ticket. You're a material-ist, you have no spiritual side."

"But I don't degrade my brother at least. Your ways are outmoded."

Mordecai said, "You are doing Hitler's work for him if you don't treasure Jewish life. The Sabbath preserves the Jews, but the Jews have to preserve the Sabbath."

Simon bowed to Mordecai as if he were praying. Mordecai raised his fists. Simon walked out of the room, purposefully jingling the loose change in his pocket, something that is also forbidden on the Sabbath.

It was Simon who pointed Kalman gently in the direction of his life, suggesting that he go to a school that was Reform, not Orthodox. Simon did see value in the traditions of his family, but not in the strict form of the law; he could see living in the modern times and taking some of the practices with him, but not the restrictive ones.

Rachel struggled with the very limits of Jewish life. She was the eldest daughter and she developed an illicit love connection. Their aunt, their mother's sister, was ill. She lived in Circe not far from Hamborek. Rachel was dispatched to take care of her. Every day Rachel walked to the market to buy small food items for the aunt. She cooked for her, cleaned for her and ran the household of five girls.

A man named Bohosh, a financial official, was brought into the home by the uncle. Bohosh saw Rachel's ability in the kitchen, her wit, her ability to make the home pleasant, and he started to visit more frequently. A very great love developed between them. He was enchanted by this beautiful Jewish girl. Rachel blossomed under the attention of his daily visits; his air of confidence reminded her of Simon. She began to brush her curls in new ways. New feelings grew in her, bubbling up like air bubbles. She had never met a man who earned a regular salary. He bared his thoughts to her after her visits to the market. He came to sit in the kitchen. They both made the most of Rachel's aunt's illness; she couldn't chaperone them.

They were young and the war had not started in earnest. Soon they were meeting in the kitchen, stealing long embraces, deep sensuous kisses that made Rachel ready to leave her family behind. Bohosh massaged the small of Rachel's back. He breathed his excitement heavily into her ear. He felt her soft curly hair with his lips. The aunt limped into the kitchen for a drink of water just as Bohosh had his hand on Rachel's breast under her dress.

There was a Hasidic wonder rabbi in Circe, who could cure the sick, change financial fortunes, create matches, and give spiritual healing. He visited the aunt, but seemingly nothing was going to cure her. She had a kind of cancer caused by a psychic premonition about the war. She was killing herself before she would have to see her five daughters shorn and butchered.

The wonder rabbi was told about Rachel, and about her non-Jewish suitor, the flames between them. He spoke to the uncle and said that there was no cure for it but to send Rochi home. Bohosh said that he would give his life to Rachel if she would stay, if she would choose him over her family and her religion. But no one really asked Rachel. She felt shamed, heartbroken, and returned home. Within two months she was married to a Jew; she felt that she had no choice.

When Jews married non-Jews, Nazis pressed for divorce. In March 1945 those with mixed marriages were sent to Terezin Concentration Camp.

"I wonder if she had married Bohosh if it would have saved her," Kalman pondered to me about his sister. She married a very kind widower with two lovely girls. They ran a *mikvah* together and Rachel had a wonderful connection with the women that she served. But her passion had been Bohosh.

Liebe was about the age of Anne Frank when she died. She had just developed a woman's figure, to judge by the pictures, but still had long braids. Kalman narrates to me with his special way of speaking English. "She was the youngest. Here is a picture of her in our garden, holding potatoes. From our garden. Not big. All vegetables, fruit trees, from a Jewish landowner and on this place all year, potatoes gratis. We were poor, but enough rich. Potatoes gratis."

Kalman grins to himself and looks away. "In the beginning my father had animals. One cow," he chuckles, "one goat. Only chickens give eggs. The kosher butcher was in Brestwice. Boys took the chicken or goods or *hahn* to the butcher. We had goose fat all year.

"Here's a picture of our barn. Pessy, Rachel, Liebe, and Esther, my four sisters, not long before they were transported. In this one I am wearing a sweater made by my mother. I think all clothes were made by my mother."

Pessy, Rachel, Liebe and Esther help me get through Raphi's army service by reminding me about why I have to live in Israel. They guard over Raphi and are kind and warm to me.

# Alzheimer's — 2003

I have learned from my immigrant lessons that whenever we leave anything that is dear to us, anything that has defined us and that we cherish, we go through a kind of crisis. We swim in a sea that is too large for us. The waves are too big, and we cannot find our footing. There is no sense of self in the endless vast saltiness…where you could die, where no one would find you. And if they did, they might not understand your language. You might be expressing love and enthusiasm, and the natives might look at you and see naiveté and innocence, no contact with real life, denseness, someone who made the wrong choice, who wears the wrong clothes, who has a funny hairdo and who will never lose her accent. Your customs and ways of celebrating confuse and offend them.

Every time you leave something that has defined you — a lover, a stage of life, a marriage, a country — you are an immigrant, learning immigrant lessons the hard way.

Rivka and I go to visit Safta Sarah on the same afternoon.

"So, darling, how's your mother?" Sarah asks Rivka.

"You are sitting so close to her, why don't you ask her yourself," Rivka says ironically.

"Where, where is she?"

"Ask yourself. You are my mother. I am your daughter."

"You are Nelly. You are my sister." Sarah laughs uncertainly. "You are laughing at me, it isn't nice."

When I go to visit, she seems so happy to see me and seems to know me. An Israeli scout troop is singing with the old folks at the home. Sarah sings along with the crowd. She seems more involved with them than with my visit. "This is a nice kibbutz where I am staying. There is a good dining hall. Would you like to stay for lunch? Then we will leave and go home," she says to me. She is in a home for the aged where she has lived for eleven years, but she makes it into a kibbutz, much more romantic and appealing. Perhaps Sarah and I are close because we both see the gold in a manure pile.

Every time I go to see her, she greets me with the same exclamation. "How did you know where to find me?!"

I answer, "I would find you anywhere you are. Besides, I've been here before." She laughs and is thrilled that I am so devoted to her to find her anywhere.

She is past the stage of wanting to eat. I go to visit during mealtimes and see that she asks for a smaller portion, then hides the food in the waste bowl on the table put there for used napkins, banana skins, yogurt tops, and olive pits. She eats and drinks almost nothing, but is always a good girl about taking her pills.

I tell her stories about her food. How her stuffed eggplant is the juiciest and spiciest dish that there is.

I go home and put a pot of eggplant to boil on the stove. It is bubbling away and smells wonderful. Are smells remembered through the fog of Alzheimer's?

Just as I am leaving one day a woman with dentures that don't fit and with shockingly blue eyes is being transferred from her wheelchair to the table. Yet she can speak. "What relationship is this young woman to you?" she says to Sarah nodding towards me.

Sarah smiles, unsure of the intricate details of our relationship, hesitating about the words and the puzzle of it all. The mysterious joke that we have always cultivated about our relationship has become real for her.

She smiles very secretively. "She is my relative. She is a brand new immigrant to this country. I took her in to live with me." This captures the essence of the truth, although I have been in the country twenty-one years at this point, and I never lived with Sarah in the physical sense.

I add, "My father and her husband were cousins."

Blue Eyes says, "Hitler took all our families. Families are very important. Therefore all family is close family. It is important to adopt family as you have done."

And she is in the Alzheimer ward.

Kalman writes:

> You are, my Judith, strong, that you went to see Sarah; but I was a unhappy and a little surprise as for her Alzheimer Disease. I know what this signify — my Alena suffered also with this insidious illness. She also not recognize, in the last months the human people — only my person she identify till the last minutes.

Kalman reports that his heart is going boom boom in his ears. He says if I want to see him again I must come soon. I say that I will come in the autumn. He agrees that he will wait for me until then. He is attending conferences on Masaryk and anti-Semitism. He is filling in his last months with meaning. I speak to him every week or two by phone and we have a bond of letters. Letters are a lost art in the modern world. Friendships with people whose lives have spanned the last century give me something that is lost in our technological world. Home visits. Unhurried time. A home-cooked meal. Face-to-face talking and listening. Family. These friendships have given me family, across generations. People who can fill in all sorts of gaps.


# Ideology and Safety


I love living in Israel. There is no other way to put it. It is so hard, and so meaningful. My Ilana is playing basketball, an all-star team to mark the end of the season. A big celebration. There are girls on the combined team from an Arab village. One of the girls is wearing shorts, a basketball tank top, and then incongruously, a white head scarf covering her head and neck, tied under her chin. I ask the family sitting in front of me if girls' basketball is really acceptable to them as traditional Muslims. They say, yes, until age fifteen, then she will have to stop and have an arranged marriage.

I don't know why I love living in Israel when Shira is on guard duty in the territories. It is just too awful. We shouldn't be there, there should be peace, and Shira should be making movies and going to college, not wielding a gun and tramping over rocky sunburned hills in big army boots. She is reading left-wing political novels on guard duty. This is her latest rebellion against the army.

I bump into an old friend whose eldest son is being inducted into the army in a few months. "How do I cope with his going in? I have tried to get him exempted from active combat by telling them that my husband lost his brother."

"You can take a survey of women — I have, mothers throughout the country — and none of them will have an answer for you."

She turns to leave.

"But I have found an answer for me," I say tentatively, unsure of myself.

I continue: "We have no control over our children's safety and this is unbearable. So take control over the one thing you have to control. Just pour love onto him."

She looks at me skeptically. She is a rational, intelligent person and I am telling her, just love him. I am not telling her that no one will harm him.

"How?" she says with anger facing inward and outward.

"I sent Raphi great big packages, filled with all sorts of things to spoil him. I drove huge long distances to pick him up at every opportunity. We are very close. He now really knows he can count on me for anything. I entered the territories in order to visit him, even though I am ideologically opposed to doing so. For him, I would risk ideology and safety."

I am in Israel for my children. I had to leave my parents to give Israel to my children. My children give Israel to me.

# The Urge to Have Children — 1940

Sarah and Mordecai lie huddled in his tiny kibbutz room, Sarah will have to go back to her job in the city in the morning. It is rumored that there might be concentration camps back in Europe.

Concentration camps. Sarah has not heard a word from her mother, father, sisters or brothers since her aliyah. It seems that her dream of the bones is coming true. Her mother will turn to bones. Sarah has seen her first bulldozer and tractors in Israel.

Does this mean death for the Jews? Suddenly she feels an urgent, irrepressible need. She needs to hold Mordecai as close to her as she can; she needs to crawl inside him and be protected from Evil, she needs to hide, to give and get comfort, to merge with Mordecai, to forge a child, she needs a baby sucking at her breast. She holds his head between her breasts, voluptuous through her nightgown, and wraps her legs around him and begins moving.

He understands, he grasps her tight, and outlines her breasts, hugs them, kisses them, comforts her, strokes her till she is at peace but it only makes her feel more urgency to merge, to merge and create. They become one, and crawl inside each other's mouths, and hands and legs move with the flow of juices of excitement, and there is comfort, and then oblivion.

"Be fruitful and multiply and fill the Land."

And the Lord visited Sarah as he had said, and the Lord did to Sarah as he had spoken. For Sarah conceived, and bore Avraham a son in his old age, at the set time of which God had spoken to him. And Avraham called the name of his son that was born to him which Sarah bore to him, Y. And Avraham circumcised his son Y being eight days old, as God had commanded him. And Avraham was a hundred years old, when his son Y was born to him. And Sarah said, God has made laughter for me, so that all who hear will laugh with me. And she said, who would have said to Avraham, that Sarah should give children suck?

And Yuval laughed.
And Ilana laughed.
And Rafael laughed.
And Rivka laughed.

But the seed of Avraham created Yishmael too, his firstborn, and his first-born struggled with Y, and Y struggled with Yishmael until today, and the children who were to bring laughter after the Holocaust were to fight in uniforms with the children of Yishmael. And Rafael fell to the sword of Yishmael, and no laughter was heard in the house for a very long time. Avraham was glad that his younger son could defend himself against his older son. But he lost his son Rafael, who never had a son.

And Yehudit came to Israel and was mightily afraid for her Raphael, who brought baby laughter back to Sarah's house, to bear arms against the children of Yishmael.

# Siblings Get the Least Help

We go to the graveside of Dafni who has been dead for ten years now. She is Yuval's middle daughter, and was killed in a car accident, driving home from attending the birth of triplets, a part of her internship. She was twenty-five years old and just married. She wanted to bring children into the world; she loved children so much that she had almost completed her studies as an obstetrician. Her family was changed from being a carefree clan to moving forward with a broken heart. Safta Sarah almost didn't react; perhaps it was one tragedy too many.

We all go back to Yuval and Sarah's apartment to hear a psychologist speak about how siblings get the least help after the death of a family member. After the talk by the psychologist, Rivka speaks to me.

> I was just seventeen when Rafi died and my life changed forever. And here was a spoiled, pampered, irresponsible child. But from the moment that I was told that my brother Rafi was killed, I took care of my parents. No one ever helped me.
>
> I took responsibility immediately. I was the only child at home. My parents were out of commission to say the least. They could not function, they could not even go through the acts of mourning at first. Someone had to tell

Ilana. I did not want a stranger to tell her, and I did not want her told on the phone.

From that day forward, I made decisions for my parents, looked out for them. It was not coincidental that when you met us, I lived a block away from my parents and they did my childcare. We remained one unit after that.

My husband Jack came into the family three months after Rafi was killed. He drove us down to Kibbutz Be'eri, where the war dead from Sinai were buried for a year until they could be reinterred near their parents' homes. He took my parents on together with me. I broke up with a wonderful boyfriend who was with me until Rafi's death. I told him that I was not good enough for him. He is married now. He was heartbroken, but I was just not the same person afterwards; I didn't need someone to pamper and spoil me, but someone to share my mission of taking care of my parents. Hollywood love is not what really endures and makes life softer.

Every time my father went to the hospital, Jack took him. My father helped buy the car when Jack became a private driving instructor. When my father died, Jack wouldn't let the ambulance driver and helper lift my father's body; he put him on the stretcher and wheeled him to the ambulance.

We called Yuval who was abroad in Germany to tell him of our father's death. We told him that we wouldn't make any funeral arrangements until he came back. He insisted that Jack make the funeral arrangements, saying that he would abide by anything Jack set up, as Jack had always been so good to my father.

# Seven Days in America, Seven More Days in Israel — 2001

I try to tell my children that it is OK for an old man to die at the end of his life. It is part of life. It is not a tragic death. Besides, I am bargaining: old people can die, young people can't.

When my father dies, it is an earthquake in our lives, as it has been a threat hanging over us for three decades because of his heart troubles. He was a medical miracle and he had hospitalizations and operations for thirty years.

His loss leaves a bigger hole than his shrunken body could have made, he who was never more than five feet short.

My brother calls very sensitively and tells me, "This is IT, Judith." It has been IT so very many times. I say stupidly, "How do you know?" He says gently but firmly, a good parent, "This is IT." I ask to speak to my father. I hear a rasping, rattling kind of breath. "I love you, Daddy, I love you, Daddy" I say. Danny listens too. He tells me that this is the "death rattle." I hope that he'll hang on till I get there.

Two hours after the phone call the two of us are on the plane. My travel agent meets us on the highway to the airport at ten thirty at night having ordered the tickets from her home, rushing out in her bathrobe. That's Israel. The human component is very strong, especially at times of disaster. I am leaving home to say goodbye to my father, and to my home, where it will never be home again.

Transferring planes in Canada, we cannot get through to my mother by phone, and therefore do not know if my father is still alive. We arrive in Chicago still three hours from home. Danny calls my mother's house. My brother tells him that my father died early in the morning. It has finally come. I cry at my shock and the knowledge that it is final. No going back now, and I have missed the actual moment of death.

That Friday my brothers and my mother gather at home. My mother is looking for her checkbook. She has some urgent business. When will the funeral be? Tuesday, it seems, four days away. It can't be over the weekend and the cremation takes a while to order. We will need time to invite people. I am used to Jewish customs, Israeli customs, and people being buried the same day. My dad will not be buried at all. I can't quite deal with that but I know how explosive fights would be at this time and carefully steer around them.

On Shabbat I can't pray. I can walk. We have jet lag. The four a.m. January dawn brings temperatures of twenty below zero Fahrenheit, with a windchill factor of minus forty. Danny has never walked in the snow at dawn, nor experienced American winter. I tell him that two layers on every part of the body are a necessity, but he says, "I'll warm up from walking." After the first block, we have to retreat and put on some more layers. But after that we walk across Lake Wingra; we crunch through the snow to the Arboretum where we stand on a frozen pier looking out at frozen bulrushes on a frozen lake. We hike in the dark from the Union along Lake Mendota and watch the sunrise from

Picnic Point, a penninsula with bare trees reaching far into the large snowy lake. Ice fisherman drill holes on the lake and drive their small trucks onto it. We walk on the frozen prairie of the lake reflecting the vast empty expanse of the loss of my father, who sailed on this lake even when he was ill.

In the whole mess my older brother and I are in perfect harmony about the funeral. He wants the whole service in Hebrew so he won't understand it, objecting to religion. I want the whole thing in Hebrew so that I will understand it. The rabbi laughs. What a traditional service, he jokes, all in Hebrew. That is what my father wanted. My younger brother isn't available for the meeting with the rabbi; he has taken his children to a theater production. Jewish customs of sitting at home and not engaging in worldly life are not known or practiced. He struggles with wondering if my father would want a Jewish service when he was not religious.

All three of my father's offspring write separate eulogies for my dad. A wise friend comments, it was such a tribute to your father: one spoke like a lawyer, one spoke like an academician and one spoke like a novelist.

It is a funeral flowing with tears and laughter. Laughter? Dad's twin brother Milt reads our recollection of my dad's Shlemiel and Shlemazel stories, about two Yiddish ne'er-do-wells. Dad is dead, but his twin brother, who shared the same womb eighty-two years previously, is alive. There is a similar timbre of voice, the same eyebrows, the same smile and comic/tragic face. Watching Milt is a gift for me, and yet for him it is painful to eulogize the brother who shared a womb with him

Milt reads out our remembrances of a classic story of my father's, a child's bedtime story in a singsongy voice which reflects my father's.

> The Worrying Business
>
> Once upon a time Shlemiel and Shlemazel decided to start a new business. It was the Worrying Business. They would rent themselves out to worry, so that other people could go about their own routines, worry free. Mrs. Cohen baked pies, and was very worried that someone might come to eat them while they cooled on her window ledge. With certain doubts and suspicions, she hired Shlemiel and Shlemazel to worry for her.

Milt chuckles and the whole crowd chuckles with him.

> Mrs. Cohen was freed to bake her blueberry pies. She left a batch of them cooling on the window ledge. Shlemiel and Shlemazel paraded up and down

in front of the window, making a great show about how worried they were. This activity made them hot and tired, and very hungry.

Milt chuckles again. Some people blow their noses, laugh and cry.

They were so hungry that they consoled themselves with one of the pies. Mrs. Cohen caught them blue-mouthed and chased them out of town with a broom.

Years later, missing my father, I go to visit Milt, after a stroke, in the hospital. "Who read to you, when you were boys?" I ask, searching for my father. His face cracks into a hysterical smile. "Murray did; after all, he was twenty minutes older than me."

My sister-in-law, who was exceptionally good to my father, goes to pick him up at the crematorium. She straps the can with my dad's ashes in the baby seat and plays classical music to the can of ashes, even though Sally prefers good folk or jazz.

When we sprinkle him by the rose bushes in a beautiful spot in town, I am surprised by the fact that it seems right to me that my father was not buried. He will be part of the wind and the roses and the earth. He will not be rooted in time, space or place.

My older brother combs the finances and labels them for my mother, muttering, "If I ever meet another woman who doesn't know her assets…" I would never tell him, but I decide just as soon as I get home, I am going to make a sheet on the computer called Assets, however short…as I don't have a clue! My younger brother does all the legal paperwork and gives succinct advice to my mother.

I want to help too, to do something tangible. I decide to take care of Dad's personal belongings. Soon I will be far away; to wait for a polite cooling-off period, when my mom is ready to go through his belongings, is not possible.

I discuss it with my brothers. They wisely suggest that we donate his clothes to the homeless who might need good suits for job interviews. I make a few phone calls. Then I load my father's diminuitive clothes into boxes. His good suit jackets, his white button-down shirts, his casual corduroys, his ties, handsome sweaters, some hand knit, some from travels around the world. It seems to me that he has only a modest amount of clothes for a university professor.

Danny and I drive through the snow to the Salvation Army across town, to the poorer section. There is a Jewish folktale that every beggar could be the prophet Elijah, so one would be wise to greet each beggar kindly; he may be here to bring good to the world.

We tentatively get out of the car and look around for the office to unload the four meager boxes of clothes. A man with a white beard and black skin approaches me. "Hey, lady, you got a coat for me?" He is wearing a thin shirt and a frazzled rag of a jacket, in the snow. He is wearing slippers. He is small of stature, but a presence; he stands straight and looks deeply into my eyes.

"Yes, I do, I have a good one for you." I open the station wagon door and rummage through a box. I hand him a wool checkered coat which will cover most of his body, like a warm blanket.

"Lady, you got any size eleven shoes?"

"Size eleven? Well, I…I do, take your pick, whatever you want." I open a box with several good pairs of shoes, size 11. I am aware that Jewish tradition holds that it is better to give anonymously. I do not want to embarrass this man for having to beg. I search my mind for a way to make us more equal. I feel the mourning coming up big, choking me.

I decide to share my story with Elijah the prophet. "My father died this week. He would be so very gratified that he could pass on his good coat and shoes to you. Do you need any belts or shirts? Help yourself."

"Why, bless you, daughter. And bless your father, may he rest well," the man says. He hugs me warmly and holds on as I release the tears that are ready on tap that week.

After seven days of a shivah more or less by myself in America, I board the plane for home and leave home. I have e-mailed my friends Susie and Jeri in Israel: "There is no receiving line of mourners at the funeral, there is no one to make a minyan to say Kaddish, and there is no one to sit shivah with because it is just not a custom that they know." Yet I wouldn't have missed that week with my family.

When we reach our apartment in Israel at nearly ten o'clock at night, there are ten friends waiting there to receive me as a mourner in a traditional way, in two straight lines. As I pass through the lines they say, "May you be comforted among the mourners of Zion and Jerusalem." Susie has organized them to be there for me to say the Mourner's Kaddish and evening prayers, every day for seven more days, so that I will experience a shivah. Jeri has arranged for close friends to bring food every day for seven days, something that I myself have organized many times. Linda does not leave my side for most of the shivah. "Do you need anything?" she keeps saying. But mostly she just sits by my side so that I will never feel alone. It works. I remember how she has stood in for our lack of a grandma at the kindergarden Chanukah parties.

The first Kaddish is almost impossible for me to say. Now that there is a community of friends to say "Amen," to acknowledge my loss, I cannot pronounce the words. The first night I whisper them inaudibly, and my friends, straining to hear in between sobs, say, "Amen." They show up every day for seven days. I have lost my father forever. I am beginning to know where home is. Now he will never be an ocean away at the Passover Seder. He will be just as much with me as he is anywhere.

At thirty days after my father's death, which marks the end of the initial heavy mourning when it is hard to function in the world, I hold a memorial evening for my father. I am missing my mother and brothers very much. As friends with great depth of academic and social understanding, Yocheved and Byron explain my father's work to the crowd. I scan the sixty friends and see Yuval and Sarah, Rivka and Jack, Zvika and Ilana sitting among them. I cry hard to see them — there are other Edelmans here.

Just before my taxi comes to take me to the airport at the end of my visit to Prague, Kalman says sadly: "A man is born alone and a man dies alone. Of all my great family, from tomorrow I will be alone to die." I silently note to myself, I hope I can time it right to be there to hold his hand when the time comes. I vow to myself to visit twice a year. That way, I will be with him when he is alive, if not when he dies.

# Inventory — 1996 and 1941

Raphi is thirteen years old and I have invited the family from America to come to his bar mitzvah. My Aunt Esther and Uncle Milt, my father's twin, fly over. They bring generous presents; they help arrange flowers and are moved by Raphi's donation of prayer books in memory of his great-grandparents, Milt's parents. They are present for the family photograph. That way in photographs no one knows that no one from my immediate family came for the bar mitzvah.

At first my parents came to Israel yearly when they were healthy, but now my father is not, and my mother won't leave him. My brothers cannot understand what the fuss is about, the price is prohibitive, and there is terrorism just a bus ride away. My parents feel that I am making too big a deal about a bar mitzvah; they were not at Raphi's *brit* (circumcision), either. Perhaps they feel I am making too big a deal about Judaism and that somehow it is a value judgment about them, that it is more secondary in their lives.

There is a part in the ceremony when the entire extended family all stand up to recite a blessing thanking God for allowing us to be present at this occasion. "Blessed are You, Lord, our God, Ruler of the universe, Who has kept us alive, helped us to prosper and to arrive at this moment." It is a moment when friends in the congregation get to see how much family is there, and who they are. Sometimes three generations stand up; sometimes there are lots of aunts and uncles, sometimes lots of cousins, usually around ten people at least. For immigrant friends there are always relatives from abroad, and this is the time to parade them out.

I am tense. Doing inventory silently. Feeling alone. No mother, that's minus one, no father, that's minus two, no brothers or sister-in-law, that's minus three more. Five down. Good — the English on Danny's side of the family are here, but my sister-in-law and brother-in-law from England are out in the lobby — they won't be counted and tension mounts, but they return just in time with their two sons. However, upon request, even though no one from Safta Sarah's side is a synagogue-goer, all children, spouses, their children and one or two of the first great-grandchildren are present. Everyone gasps when Safta Sarah, her three children, their spouses, their eight children and spouses, and three great-grandchildren stand up together with my aunt and uncle, and Danny's entire family from England. Nearly forty people stand up, all across the hall; this was not part of my inventory.

A warm dance circle of devoted friends forms. We have all danced at each other's celebrations throughout the years, attended each other's seven days of mourning for first-degree relatives, have watched babies be named and adopted, welcomed new members, driven each other to the doctor, are there together. I am happy to see that I have blood relatives as well as friends. I do have them, and they join the circle and dance a colorful and inclusive dance.

There is a snapshot moment in the bar mitzvah that cannot be photographed because of the Sabbath observance. It happens that Raphi's Torah reading includes the Ten Commandments. Seven groups of people are given the honor of being called up to say the blessings before and after the Torah. Raphi's English grandparents are called up and they hold Danny's and my hands as we go up together. Raphi reads, "Honor your mother and father." Several good friends who have been more family than family over our time in Kfar Sava are called up. And then Yuval, Ilana and Rivka, my second cousins — but who's counting — are called up. They stand up, and I notice that these three siblings are standing next to Raphi, named for their brother Rafi, as if the four of them are reunited by this moment.

Sarah is sitting in the front row. She is smiling. Although she walks with a walker, she has symbolically passed the Torah down to Milt, to me and Danny, to Raphi. Her children have all been called up to the Torah. She knows that she is there as the Mother of the event.

At Sarah's first son's *brit*, neighbors baked sugar cookies, and Mordecai bought some schnapps. No parents were alive to admire this blonde infant. No aunts, no uncles. No siblings in Israel. Mordecai sent a telegram to Europe.

Yuval's bar mitzvah. Mordecai's brother Tuvye was in Israel. No parents, no aunts, all long dead. None of Safta Sarah's family ever attended any of her life-cycle events.

Just before Ilana was married Sarah dreamed of her mother sewing a trousseau for her daughter. How her mother would have loved to see this bride. This girl who was marrying such a kind, happy man.

At Rafi's funeral, her father would have known which prayers to say. He would have known what to do at the seven days of mourning. He was a religious man. There were so many customs. Sarah and Mordecai did not keep separate dishes for milk and meat. Should they now cover the mirrors, stop shaving, sit on low stools? What did one do? How Sarah longed for her father when Rafi died.

Mostly she did not think of them. But she did feel terribly guilty when she thought of her mother. "Take me with you." On youth aliyah? How could she have taken her with the youth group? She couldn't take anyone. Her mother was too old, her little niece Feigele too young.

*This was a nice celebration. We are here with Yehuditkeleh. She is not alone like I was.*

# Into the Heart of Terror

Someone said that everyone is separated in Israel only by two degrees. I know so many people who have been touched by terror. We all fear for our children, our partners, our colleagues. Fears.

I have had a fear of death all my life. I was trained in it, as my father was "dying" for thirty years, and there was a lot of worry over his heart condition. Death seemed beyond what I could cope with.

I have left home to come home and at home there is more terror. I am terrified, the country is terrified, and yet I have learned all my coping mechanisms here. Do I cling to Safta Sarah because she is a survivor of terror?

My first meeting with my family was at the graveside of Rafi. They have given me only life since then, only positivity, only coping, only support. There is nothing they haven't given me. A place to sleep, approval over my children, even money at times, baby gifts, more approval, sharing all generations, accepting, knowing who I am, seeing beyond my accent, never switching to English, sharing their mother, sharing their stories.

One friend here lost her great-nephew. One friend lost his sister-in-law and her mother. One friend lost her son. A man at our synagogue was blown up on our local bus. A friend's daughter got a nail in her face during a suicide bombing. Raphi has lost friends in the army. One was approached by an Arab dressed as a religious Jew. He was carrying something under his tallit. It was a gun. Raphi's friend was killed. Shira lost a comrade who was a Bedouin, a fellow soldier on her small base. Terror. Too close.

# Pace of Life

Still, I found the tempo of American life a bit strange. I need enough space around everything I do to let me think it through properly. Our workers may not have the American get-up-and-go, but they do a good, accurate job of things. We place quality above quantity.

— *Talks with Thomas Masaryk, Karol Capek*

Kalman, without ever having learned about Buddhism, brushes his teeth mindfully. He takes his time. He bathes, shaves very pedantically, first with a razor, then with an electric shaver. He dresses in neat clothes and looks like a gentleman. His clothes are elegant and simple at the same time. Clean. Like his house. When he takes his pills, he takes each pill one at a time, checking that it is the right one, swallowing each one carefully and slowly. He does not have a pill organizer, but I am sure that he doesn't need one. I think it might cramp his style to have one, because then he might not need to be so mindful. He washes the dishes between dinner and dessert.

When he is in town in Prague, he is mentally present and cognizant. He notices each gargoyle, historically places each fresco, understands each statue, points out paintings on the outsides of buildings. He is where he is. He is a good listener, and a fantastic speaker. He always has something to say, yet he can ponder questions silently.

He asks questions that matter. He is present. He does one thing at a time with one person at a time.

# Family

Family is what is taken away from an immigrant and family is what Sarah brought me. My own family. Just ask at the old folks' home how we are related. We may do our routine for you. I was terribly afraid to live like my friend Susie. Susie lost her daughter in a hit-and-run bicycle accident, and then she defied death by living. I never believed that there could be family after immigration, nor joy of living after loss. Perhaps that was what glued me to Safta Sarah, like the rice expanded inside the eggplant, made part of it with the heat of the cooking.

After immigration, and after loss, there is stuffed eggplant, there are knitted sweaters, there are birthdays, and visits, and smiles and shared moments at the graveyard.

Immigration is like reincarnation.

# Crowns — 2004

On my Dad's seventieth birthday an article was written in the local Madison paper about him as a retiring professor, a local icon. About his progeny it is written that all the children are graduates of UW, listing my brothers' professions as professor and lawyer, "...*and Judith lives in Israel*." This always stung me. Judith lives in Israel. Doesn't my father know my profession? Or is "Jewish educator" too alien or too undefined to print? Too bad I didn't get a rabbinical degree. There is a certain ring to it, my progeny, the Professor, the Lawyer and the Rabbi. It would have excellent boasting and humor value. It almost sounds like a rabbi joke.

This Yom Kippur I fidget in my synagogue. The memorial prayers always bring my father's loss so close. It is as if he died five minutes ago and the shock of hearing the words has not yet worn off. At most memorial services, his approving and loving face smiles large before my eyes. This year his image is foggier.

I have always been so terrified of death. It is a trial to try to come to terms with the death of an older man who lived until the end of his life and died peacefully, surrounded by people who loved him. This is supposed to be easier than tragic deaths. At least it is the correct order of the world. I was not at his bedside when he died; I was back home in Israel after visiting him three weeks before. I missed his send-off and this compounded the loss, a result of living far away.

I say the prayer for a deceased father in the prayer book, then it is time for Kaddish. An image appears above my head and I close my eyes to the written page. My dad is in the next world, surrounded by his parents, grandparents, relatives, his dead friends and mine. As I say the words *shemay rabba* (His great Name), a crown appears on my father's head. There is a gasp and giggle of delight on his part and exclamations of admiration by his gathered family.

"Murray, how wonderful. Oh, how beautiful." My father's twin brother must also be uttering Kaddish across the world because my grandparents, Sadie and Kalman, and Seymour, my father's older brother, are also wearing crowns. I quickly add a Kaddish for Nanny, my father's grandmother, a very pious woman who lived to be 101. A crown pops up on her head, perched on her delicate, thin body. My dad is lauded even more by his family. European cousins crowd in behind my father and his throng. There is Yaakov Moshe holding a kite, and Liebe pushing a bike, and Pessy with her embroidery and Esther with a ladle and Rachel with false papers for Kalman and Simon dressed like a university student. I say Kaddish for them and my father proudly nods his crown and they reply with a bow of their crowns.

"I know what Judith does now," says my father, turning his beaming face to his gaggle of family, "she says Kaddish for me. She is my daughter who says Kaddish." He bends down and cups his hand by his mouth directing it towards Earth. He speaks in Yiddish. "She will say Kaddish for you too, Kalman, one day, she will be your daughter for Kaddish."

# New Jewish Cemetery, Prague — 2004

I have seen Kalman cry numerous times, when lighting a memorial candle for his brothers or sisters, or when telling me about his nephew who was killed in a motorcycle accident. He lived in the next-door apartment and was like a son to them, the son they never had.

Kalman also cried when he intimated that he would like to take me to Alena's grave.

Every day we have a long luxurious lunch and he shares his meals on wheels from the Jewish community. A magic meal, modest, but divided in two with the addition of instant soup, it is enough for two healthy portions. With Kalman's interesting table conversation, he provides me with even more nutrition.

On this particular afternoon he wakes me up from my nap in a fluster. "The gates of the cemetery close at three." He is taking me to Alena. I dress quickly to please Kalman. I forget to have a drink of water and my head throbs as we racewalk to the bus. I am a water addict, but I don't want to slow things up and shock Kalman by paying so much (in his view) for a bottle of water. Somehow we make it to the cemetery across town by three fifteen; it is open until four. As it is we get locked in.

The New Jewish Cemetery, off the tourist path, is adjacent to the bus station where I sent Shira off to Germany two years before. A huge wrought-iron gate bears the reminder FROM DUST YOU CAME TO DUST YOU WILL RETURN. I somehow find that thought comforting, as if troubles are somehow temporary. It reduces life to whom you love and who will mourn you.

We walk arm in arm along the wide path with large, majestic gravestones on both sides. There is a smell of damp leaves after a heavy rain. A sign catches my eye, indicating Franz Kafka's grave. The smell reminds me of "home," this time meaning America in the autumn rain or something even more ancient. It is like a walk in the woods, except that instead of looking at the eternal and enduring beauty of nature, and the nature of beauty, we are looking at the truth. This truth is that rich, famous, poor, learned, kind, wife-beaters, are all here together, whatever one's resume. Some have a marker and someone to visit.

Alena's grave is very modern and beautiful. I hadn't realized that her last name would be Gajanova. Women in the Czech Republic take their father's or husband's names and add an -ova — I would have been Edelmanova. Her PhD is proudly etched on the marble. I am touched by the Hebrew letters at the bottom wishing her a peaceful rest. Kalman explains to me that recently, Gentiles can be buried in a Jewish cemetery. He busies himself with brushing the wet autumn leaves off the grave. He is working so hard. I do not interfere as I feel he needs to tend to her.

Suddenly Kalman sobs. "She was a better Jew than I was. She gave me Judaism back after the war. I thought I would survive one month after she died, but I have lasted ten years." I hold him. I cry with him for his lost wife. So often I remain distant when other people are angry or sad. He haltingly adds, "I hope you will visit me when I rest here."

I pause and then speak what is so hard to say. "I will say Kaddish for you every day; I want you to know that."

He composes himself very quickly. Ten years later you are not allowed to mourn too heavily. We make our way to Kafka's grave. The cold is beginning to penetrate my fleece coat and fleece hat. A film crew is filming Kafka's grave. The three names on the gravestone — Kafka, his mother and his father — are etched in Hebrew! I smile as I think of a man metamorphosing into a helpless cockroach, a symbol of the helplessness of our own fate. Leaning against Kafka's stone is a marker for his three sisters who have no grave; they all died in the camps. Had Kafka not died of tuberculosis in 1927, he might not have lived beyond 1942. The film crew films me placing a rock on his grave, as if immortalizing my appreciation for a great and sad storyteller, whom I love to read best while in Prague.

Darkness is falling and as we head towards the exit, Kalman points out memorial plaques on the wall of the cemetery facing Kafka's grave. They are commemorative plaques for artists, writers, actors and musicians who died in the camps. We walk arm in arm in the freezing drizzle. We find that we are locked in the cemetery, but we are released moments later when the gates are opened for the film crew.

# The Greatest Victory — 1938 and 2004

The ox was the stupidest animal that Kalman had ever encountered. He was in the Hachshara training farm, learning how to be a farmer, which he never actually put into practice, unless university faculty can be likened to farmyard animals. The huge ox drooled and its nose ran. It ate and it eliminated. Kalman had to put a yoke on the ox, which did not want to stand still.

Carrying a load of straw to spread on the upper pasture, he had to drive the ox. The beast would not move, let alone climb. The farmer laughed and refused to give driving instructions. When Kalman yelled "left" and cracked the whip by the ox's right ear the ox bolted forward lurching to the right. Kalman spent hours of frustration and failure with no hope of getting either the straw or the ox to the upper pasture.

Shira's *garin nahal*, her youth group/army group, spends six months on kibbutz before basic training and then active duty. No one wants to sit next to Barak who works in the cowshed; he has cow dung all over his plastic boots and his overalls. He is good-natured about it, and sits at the end of the table. "Shira cleans the toilets in the guest houses and you let her sit next to you," he says.

In his youth, Kalman was a counselor at camp. The nights were spent by the glow of the campfire playing the guitar under the stars and listening to rousing speeches about creating our own home in a Jewish homeland. When the Nazis came into power, Kalman and others from the camp escaped to the forest and served as a force of resistance without any formal training or weapons, let alone food and shelter.

Shira and her friends have all been counselors at summer camp, and at camp there were fires, guitar evenings under the stars and rousing speeches about how Jewish partisans had hidden in the forests and saved many Jews from the Nazis, and had planned illegal immigration to Israel. Now Shira and her comrades protect the people of Israel, until soldiers aren't needed anymore.

# Free at Last

The reasons that brought me here are not necessarily the reasons that I am here. Raphi strides into the sidewalk café where I am breakfasting with my friend Zamira. A few days' growth of beard, dark skin, a huge smile, civilian clothes, Raphi is carrying two bursting knapsacks with laundry and bedding. He is done with his mandatory service!

I laugh, my throat closed. I feel his solid height in my arms and we rock back and forth. I keep the moment light, although I am heavy with all the goodbyes we've said to each other during his three-year army service. "I am going home to shower." He greeted me first. First town, then mother, then home. I know he will never come home again to stay, yet, he is at home within himself.

Raphi has a habit of bringing home newcomers to Israel every Shabbat when he comes home. Two are young Americans who have come to volunteer in the Israeli army. They speak Hebrew, study Middle Eastern Studies, and have an apartment in Tel Aviv. Raphi is devoted to them and sees them most of the pressured weekends that he is home. A third is a young woman, a returning Israeli. Raphi helps them by giving them a home and speaking only Hebrew to them. It is not foreign to him to hear accented or halting Hebrew; he has heard it from his parents all his life.

When Raphi got his induction envelope from the army, it was an earthquake of fear inside me. Three long years later, Shira, his baby sister, is a curly-headed nineteen-year-old drill sergeant training new recruits in the army. She walks her trainees through how to put on uniforms and how to make their beds, run, and answer their officers. My joy cascades like a waterfall at watching her go off to be a teacher, a nurturer, an educator, a personal example of strength. At that time I needed to hear the content of the same message that she is teaching to her young recruits, which is that they too "can be strong and able." I wish Shira had been my drill sergeant twenty years ago when I made aliyah. That was the lesson that I needed to learn. What strong women she and her friends are. Some of the new immigrants are a little shocked to see a female giving the orders, and tell her that. She will set them straight, I am sure.

I delight in Shira's army service, not because she is safer as a girl, but because she is a girl and can be a leader and can cope. So can I. I tell Safta Sarah that Shira is in a mixed unit of boys and girls. Out of her dementia she quips, "Then they don't fall asleep at night, huh!" Shira assures me that there is no attraction to sweaty, tired people in green.

One of the girls in her unit is a new immigrant from the former Soviet Union. Before the army she lived in poverty, with no parents to support her, but rather has to support her grandparents. Without parents, no bed to sleep on, she and her Russian-speaking grandparents have no food to eat. Shira takes a day off her busy schedule in the army and takes this new immigrant to various offices, pays her depts, and arranges for the army kitchens to be open to her to take food home to her grandparents every weekend.

Shira and her unit are sworn in at the Western Wall. There is a comic and moving moment when the girls are sworn in, their higher-pitched voices contrasting with their male comrades' "I swear" in the feminine verb form. We all attend a ceremony in Latrun when Shira has completed the course as a drill sergeant. I have gotten acclimatized to the ceremonies in the army; to see my curly-haired daughter among them is a source of joy.

While our daughter is training to protect Israel from terror and war, Danny is waging peace. He attends a meeting of parents who have lost children, both Palestinians and Israelis. We have all fronts covered.

# More Alzheimer's — 2004

"Yehudit, how do you know Rivka?" Sarah asks me when I go to bring her another box of chocolates from Kalman.

"I am her cousin," I say.

"You are similar," she says, "but how long are you visiting Israel for?"

"Yes, I have an accent, but I *live* here. I am like you, a pioneer. I have lived here for twenty years. I have two children in the army."

Raphi has actually finished the army; he is now on the kibbutz cleaning the dining hall. How is it that my kids are professional cleaners everywhere but at home?

I tell Rivka that I have found a description of Sarah and Mordecai's immigrant ship documented in a history book, including the exact date and place. It turns out that Rivka knew the entire group of twenty, just one of the youth groups on the ship that came with her parents to the land of Israel. She gives all the names. All the women were called Rachel, or Hannah. The part about the live cow on board is documented! Sarah gets foggier and foggier, and her story unfolds more clearly when she is in the Alzheimer's ward, from her daughters and son.

Sarah is particularly foggy today. I turn to her and ask her why she fell in love with Mordecai. Her answer surprises me. It has none of the romance of younger years, only the clear-cut vision of the elderly years. "Because he was an egoist and I liked that."

A picture of Sarah at her ninety-second birthday party shakes in her hand. It is a photo of herself with a crown of flowers on her head, in a wheelchair in the park. "This is my mother," she says staccato, starting and restarting to see if she got it right. "No, it must be my grandmother. My mother didn't live to be that old; she jumped when she saw the Nazis marching into the village. Yes, it is my grandmother."

# Song — 2004

We are having lunch at Kalman's house. He wants everything to be right for me. He pours me some liquor, he puts a basket of bread on the table, and he puts some cantorial music on the new CD player that his student Lena bought for him. They both like cantorial music from France.

"You can hear the sorrow of the Diaspora in this music," Kalman pronounces.

I named Shira "song," because it was melodies, in the Diaspora, that brought me closer to Judaism. It was music that gave me an intimate knowing of Israel. I named my daughter song.

# Why I Made Aliyah

There are some people who are complete in their soul where they are. And there are some people who are missing the answer to the missing pieces in their souls. They cannot find it in the place that they are most familiar with. They long for union with the Promised Land within themselves. The illusive place where they are loved, where they love themselves, where their work is meaningful, their relationships are a balm for their troubled souls, and where their actions are kind and meaningful. It is promised and it is far away. So when you make aliyah, you don't know why particularly or you don't really come for the reasons that you think you come.

Sarah had Hitler chasing her, it is true. But she might have come anyway. I had everything, and I had nothing. I had a husband and a baby and a job and house and a garden and a cat. I had a group of friends, a community who cared and enough to eat. We went walking in the country through the green hills of the English countryside. We had family there. I had proved myself in two challenging jobs, one supervising criminals in community work, and one supervising youth in creative programming in large projects.

I think I always experienced anti-Semitism as a personal comment on me. I was not good enough; I was not acceptable, wanted, liked. Even though, as a youth worker, I was doing something to fight ignorance in the school system and in the universities, still, I could not abide where I was not wanted. I was in a place where I did not want myself. I made aliyah because of hate; I stayed because of love.

I did not know why I came here to Israel, even though I had a catechism of *reasons*. As I was missing parts of myself, I could only become myself when I went to the dry, colorless desert of Israel. I worked and lived with other people who were missing parts of themselves, but who were colorful as a scarlet sunset over a purple desert hill.

I organized and orchestrated bar and bat mitzvah coming-of-age ceremonies for children who were usually disenfranchised from communal life. These were children with Down syndrome, cerebral palsy, autism, developmental disabilities, behavioral issues. Together we celebrated that which I did not know I had come to Israel for…and that which I did not knowingly seek. Each child took a place of honor in the synagogue. These human beings showed me that people who are not whole can reach the greatest heights. Safta Sarah was bent, wrinkled, disabled, and later had dementia. She was full of understanding and quiet truths about survival. Kalman was a displaced person; he was put in prison camps just for being born into a Jewish family. And he is the freest person that I ever met. He did not live in Israel, but he lived in his own promised land of freedom.

I am American, and English and Israeli. In the Israeli fight for existence, among the lonely people in Israel, alienated from the rest of the world, I found that I am a full person from having had such a rich tapestry of a life. Perhaps there are some Czech threads in there too, inherited ones, and adopted ones.

So much of the best of identity is adopted and not innate. Then it becomes so innate that it is unshedable.

And I do not have to feel envy of Safta Sarah's brood. They are indeed my family even if our lives are not intertwined. And they are mine and I am theirs. We can all belly dance to Morrocan music together on special occasions.

My mother had an eightieth birthday orchestrated by my brothers and me, thanks to e-mail. E-mail must have been created on the sixth day; it is a Divine invention. I sit in the sunny living room in which I was a teenager in America. The grand piano is gone, and so is my cello. My father's favorite chair will remain empty. Danny and the older children couldn't get away. Shira is still in the army, Raphi is taking college entrance exams. Ilana and I make Safta Sarah's stuffed eggplant for the party. I am overwhelmed with a deep feeling of love towards my mother, who has aged so well, still making pots, still singing. She and her gentleman friend sing a duet, I accompany them on guitar. It is good to be home. Home is transitory; this home is concrete.

It touches me very deeply that our coming together is that of a clan. All three of my mother's children are here, and four of her six grandchildren, and this is for her. E-mails tie us every day, phone calls, and these visits. My mother's eyes and mine are full of love, as well as distance and longing. I have learned to value this clan by being adopted into another clan.

I came to a desert. It was barren. Twenty year later, it has sprouted lavender almond blossoms, the crimson crowns of pomegranate blossoms, purple irises growing out of the sand dunes of Netanya, silver and green flickering olive trees gnarled out of the rocky ground, sunlight oranges set in their dark green leaves, because I am blossoming in the barren soil. With my sandaled feet in the gravely desert sands, I can smile with my face towards the home of my childhood.

# The Shit in the Basement — 2004

A friend of mine is visited in his basement by a flood of sewage that barges in late one night. It is a shock to see the toys and books, an old computer floating in brown water that smells like sixty drunks have been sick together in his basement. A cleaning crew is hired to come in, but they want to charge him highway robbery.

Within a few days the old carpet has been thrown out, all the old furniture, books, toys, and junk in the basement totally cleaned out. There is a pristine basement that smells exactly like a public toilet, left to go rancid. Every once in a while, I ask him if it's getting any better yet. He says that it still smells like a public toilet.

Israel is a truly beautiful country, whatever ecosystem you choose — seaside, desert, mountain, lake, forest. Of course in Israel generally there is only one of each of those because the country is so small, although there is the Mediterranean Sea, the salty Dead Sea and the Red Sea. Perhaps that is why everyone is always fighting over it. Because it is so very beautiful. No wonder Abraham walked from the waters of Babylon to the shores of the Mediterranean. It was worth it. Abraham never stopped walking, like all of us, looking for what we can't find.

However, there is a lot of Shit in the Basement here. The immigrants of modern Israel were poor remnants of people, some who were spat out of the camps and gas chambers, or who lost relatives in the camps. Or they were Jews from Arab lands who were lucky to escape with their lives. Wars come at regular intervals, punctuating each decade or so. There is terror, suicide bombers, rioting, and shootings. Children are raised in idealism and then have to become soldiers and eat dust at the very least for two or three years. Today there is a guard posted at the entrance to the post office, the entrance to every mall, to every building, every school and kindergarten. Bags are checked by guards at supermarkets, and cars are stopped and searched in public parking lots.

I always thought that my problems were those of an immigrant. If I had been born here, I was erroneously convinced, my children going to the army wouldn't eat my guts out in the way that it does. Because I choose it for them. I choose it *for them*. I *choose* it.

I go to a conference on National Trauma, Jews and Palestinians. There are speakers who convey the trauma of Palestinian children living under occupation. Speakers from across the political spectrum, including even the religious right wing, and a theater troupe does improvisations on people's national traumas. Each player, mostly people in their twenties, wearing black, steps forward with an introduction.

One actor speaks:

> I was checked by a security guard several months ago at a restaurant. Restaurants have to check people, because so many coffee bars have blown up. The guard obviously couldn't tell if I had an accent by what I answered him, so he asked me a second question, and then let me pass. Then I became a security guard — that is an easy way to find work these days, as every public business and building needs one. A man came by; he was dark and swarthy-looking. I couldn't tell if he had an accent or not by the first question. When it turned out that he didn't have an accent, my whole body relaxed. What have we come to?

Another player:

> And I saw a death notice of my upstairs neighbor on the notice board outside our apartment building. She was fifty-three years old when she got on the bus to go shopping.

Members of the audience are called up to the stage to share a story of "national trauma"; the players will take on roles and act it out. When they are looking for the first volunteer three hundred people feel uncomfortable and put on the spot. I expect to hear from people who have been on buses that have blown up under their feet, but a woman comes up who is a social worker for a family that lost a mother and a father. The interviewer points out that the volunteer has a Russian accent. I am enraged on her behalf — why are we always pointed out as immigrants? This woman works with a family of immigrants and the children and grandparents have a cultural gap. The actors take on the roles of the orphaned children, the bereft grandparents, the volunteers and the confused social worker trying to bring everyone together. They are creative and expressive.

Yet, I wish that someone would speak in first person. For the second round I see my hand volunteer itself. I look at it in horror, thinking, my story is the story of an immigrant — it is not about a bus bombing, only about fear, and no one will relate to it. My hand is chosen and I have to follow the offensive limb onto the stage.

I tell my story simply and succinctly.

> I have an accent too, that is the point. I am an immigrant and my "national" trauma happened before I came here. My cousin Rafi was killed in the Six-Day War. A cousin I never knew.
>
> I came to know and love his parents, especially his mother Sarah. When my first son was born, I called her from England and asked her if I could name my son Raphi. She understood that I was trying to fill in a hole in her life.
>
> Then with great hope and idealism, I came to live in Israel.
>
> Now my Raphi is himself a soldier in uniform, as is his younger sister. I don't sleep at nights. I am very torn.

The theater mediator asks me to pick someone to play me. I look for the thinnest and most beautiful actress, as a private joke to myself, because I have a weight problem. Then she says, "Now pick someone else to play you." I pick someone with dark honey blonde hair like me, but with a terrific figure. "Now pick someone else to play you." Surprised that there are three me's, I pick a robust brunette bursting with life and beauty. So far, this is fun.

The thin, beautiful actress takes a red scarf and makes it float and fly in a curve.

> Idealism, dreams, hopes — it will be good here. I will make it a better place. Red, red! RED!

It sounds like Genesis, like Esau and his red, red stew. Red is the color of this place. Then she wraps the red scarf about her shoulders and takes its ends in her hands and tries to wash them out.

> Red, red, it won't wash out, it has stained me, followed him.

She stares at the red scarf, bereft.

Silence.

The dark honey blonde kneels on the stage, no props. She thrusts her hands out and says:

> Raphael. I have named him Raphael out of love. Kindness. Hope. Helping. A

beautiful name, the name of an angel of God. He protects children when they sleep at night. But not the mothers. Oh, what have I done? Have I set his fate? Is this name a curse? Rafael, Raphael. I had such hope. It is so scary.

Rinah, as I later find out her name to be, then cries real tears. She sobs and repeats the name.

The robust brunette bursting with life and beauty sings a sad song about the day after war. It is a heart-wrenching song. Two men in the background play organ and drum. Beat. I begin to shake, to cry.

The theater mediator asks me what I want to say to the actresses. I say that I saw my soul dance, cry and sing on stage. Rinah is looking at me with pronounced empathy on her face. I do not yet know that she will magically appear in my life again one day, unexpectedly, during the seven mourning days for Safta Sarah.

Then the most unexpected part of all takes place. During lunch, an older native Israeli man, wearing jeans and a casual shirt, holds onto my hand for five minutes speaking about how I expressed his fear and anguish. I say, "But I am just an immigrant; it was in immigrant's story." He says, but I was idealistic too, and now I am scared. A woman with an elegant black dress and a neck scarf in pinks cries to me that her son was in the army and that he was saved from being a combat soldier by the fact that she almost died from an incident of medical malpractice. I don't know whether to envy her or pity her, because I have survived three years of Raphi being a combat soldier and we are both survivors. I have been strengthened by coping with the level of love demanded of me. I have been strengthened by overcoming my aversion to all things military and by ironing Raphi's uniform, and sewing the stripes on Shira's. I have been strengthened by seeing how strong my children are, how they help other soldiers and other civilians, how they do not complain, not of the sleeplessness, not of the hard work.

Apparently, as an immigrant I can talk about the fear that the native Israelis also feel but *cannot express*. A young religious woman with curly, long locks and a long jeans skirt to the floor says that she is very moved because she is so afraid of her brothers' service, but that in her family, third-generation Israeli, one cannot admit to fear. I learn that my story is not that of an immigrant, but of an *Israeli*. At that moment I am at home, with all the fear, with all the sleeplessness, I am at home!

I am an Israeli, with a past, like squares of a quilt which have been sewn together: some are mine, some are Sarah's memories, some are Kalman's, some are my father's. I am home!

I am no longer an immigrant because I am so much at home. I dream in Hebrew. I think like an Israeli. I prefer Israeli informality and humor to other cultures. That is the last of immigrant lessons.

# Joie de Vivre

I never know when the last time I see Safta Sarah will be. She is way past her due. Whole systems in her body have shut down. The last time I go to see her in the retirement home, she is not in her bed. I panic. She is not in the cafeteria, not playing cards with her afternoon caretaker under the wooden trellis.

I run swiftly back to her locked ward. I stop a nurse. "Where is Sarah Edelman?" I fear the response.

"I really don't know," she says. But this is a closed Alzheimer's unit — how can she not keep track? She looks at her watch, somewhat blasé. "This *is* the time of day that her private caretaker takes her out. Look outside."

Both Sarah and her caregiver look excited at having someone run over to them to break the routine. As I approach, I see Sarah laugh, her white, wispy hair blowing rapidly, like a leaf caught in a whirlwind. "How exciting," she says, "who is this?" "Oh, it's you (not knowing my name). How wonderful that you came to find me."

"I always find you, Sarah." And to the *metapelet*, I say, "Why are you traipsing about like this?"

"It was a nice day. We play cards all the time; today we are just getting some fresh air. She sits too much."

I kiss Sarah and hug her and make a fuss of her.

"Let me push," I offer. "And who will push when you are not here?" asks the caregiver. "I manage fine."

"I like people who are completely open," Sarah says suddenly, "I don't like gossip." She makes a face of total disdain. "You can tell when people are real. All we really need is peace, also inside here." She points to her chest.

The *metapelet* adds, "And health is important."

"You can't expect good health at my age," Sarah laughs.

We park on a bench and the caregiver moves aside to talk to one of her colleagues. Sarah and I steal a few moments alone together.

"I lived with different people, Ashkenazim, Sephardim, in the neighborhood, we were like one family. I never met a bad person all my life."

She is lucid on and off today, so much so that I decide to bring my issues to her. "And Sarah, were you never afraid?"

"Oh, yes, I was afraid a lot. I worried about my children, I worried about the country. I still do," she says, and then adds, "She needs peace."

"Sarah, did you find what you wanted in the Promised Land?"

"Yes, I did. Did you, Yehuditkeleh?"

"Did I find what I wanted? I don't know, but I am so much stronger for the looking."

"If you come back to visit me," Sarah says slyly, "you won't find me dancing up a storm, you know..." This at nearly ninety-two with Alzheimer's.

I did come back and visit. Twenty years of visiting, first in her kitchen and dining room, and then in various facilities for the elderly, sitting on her bed. I came back again and again. Giving to and learning from other immigrant mothers, like Safta Sarah, sharing in their joie de vivre, in their secret immigrant lessons that come from sharing lives deeply, is what helped me to find the positive in life.


# Rafi


I am still with Safta Sarah. "My Raphi has finished the army now." She looks delighted. She is generous-spirited enough that she takes joy in my joy, one she did not have with her second son. Just then, I turn and see a pale figure. I recognize him from the photos, even though I have never seen him in person. He beckons to me. "Come over here."

I stand up and we leave Sarah with her caregiver who has come back to her and wonders where I have vanished to.

"But I didn't say goodbye to Sarah, your mother…"

"It's OK," my cousin says to me. "Come." I see that he is on a motorcycle, and I hop aboard and put my hands on his thin waist. I want to hug him, but I don't really know him very well. We whiz off and are on a cliff overlooking the Mediterranean Sea. We are very close to the edge, and the wind makes my eyes tear. The ground is a blur, but the sea far below is clear and it is so vast. I murmur the blessing for seeing the sea. I am not a brave person. This is so reckless, so wild. I might as well dance up a storm while I still can.

Rafi guns the motor, sways near the precipice and then kills the engine, and we dismount. "Weren't you afraid?" he asks. I am fascinated by being able to see into his eyes for the first time. They are blue and very kind. With laugh lines. He is younger than my Raphi, and smaller. He is a boy, and I am a woman, even though he was born over ten years before I was.

I laugh very hard. "Afraid? Yes, I was afraid. I have always been so afraid that I could barely live. I was afraid of partings, afraid of death. No, I was not afraid of your motorcycle and riding on the cliff, or of meeting you."

"I suppose I should say thank you to you for being a daughter to my mother. But Israelis don't say thank you very easily."

"No need, Rafi. I suppose I should say thank you for watching out for my Raphi. I have no trouble saying thank you."

"How *did* you make a new life here?"

"Really, death has become so familiar, so constant; it keeps coming at a more and more rapid pace. At first it kept me from living. But now, I see that death has given me life. It has given me life in this land of contradictions. And as your mother says…"

"I like people who are completely open too," Rafi says.

"You were eavesdropping." I shake my finger at him. He throws back his red hair and laughs.

\*   \*   \*   \*

Rafi walks away from the helicopter, stepping over his limp and bleeding body. It will not stop breathing for two days. He walks over the stony desert.

He is desperate for a cigarette. "If only I had a cigarette and my motorcycle, I could go and see Egypt, just across the Suez Canal."

There is something for him to do in the desert. He is not sure what it is.

The sun is glaring, reflecting off the uniforms of Egyptian troops engaged in fire with the Israeli troops. They have their backs to him. He keeps walking. He has covered a lot of ground which peels away beneath his boots.

He finds himself in Egypt, in a dusty city, and there are American troops. They are wearing uniforms from twenty years ago, in WWII.

He sees a tall soldier who looks just like his father. It is his father's cousin Milt, the twin brother of Murray, father of Judith. How he wishes he had his motorcycle so that he could impress him again.

No one can see him, but Milt, who looks young, about age thirty, can.

"Rafi, look, you are probably still getting used to your new…uh…transition."

"Yes, I just walked away from the helicopter right now. I had to walk all the way here. Do you remember…"

"Your motorcycle? Yes. How you accompanied us out of town. Yes. But you will not be going back. I just wanted to tell you that. Rafi, you are dead, but we will remember you."

"Milt, why do soldiers die in wars? Why do they die in peacetime? Did you die, Milt?"

"No, I lived my whole life, to be an old man. Your mother lived to be an old woman."

"I know, I saw her a week ago. I hate to think what it will do to her; she lost all her family already…"

"And how did she survive her family after WWII?"

"She lived. She cooked, she worked hard. She had babies. Me. She will not want to lose me. I am the naughty one!" Rafi ponders something and looks searchingly at Milt. He wants something but it is hard to form the words.

"She was plagued by a dream when she was young. Now I am shot and bleeding to death. Soon she will be notified. Isn't this worse than her dream of skeletons? Her younger son…"

Milt and Rafi both have red hair. They both have freckles. They are both wearing army uniforms. Milt, Rafi's father's cousin, looks at the boy who is becoming paler and paler. "War! No one ever wins. But maybe the fact that you were involved so that there will be no more Holocausts of helpless victims…at least not here…"

"And will there be peace?"

"You are a soldier, Rafi. There is a lot of peace in the graveyard where you will lie. But in those who come visit it?" He looks wistful.

As the sun sets in the west, they see a silver plane streak across the sky. The clatter of gunfire fades out. And they shake hands, part forever.

# Epilogue

I desparately wanted to leave Safta Sarah alive as I wrote this book while Raphi was in the army. I wanted to leave Raphi alive, Sarah alive. To end it with her in life. I did. They did. Yet her death was as magical to me as her life; her death kept writing its own story.

Where does it start? With her pneumonia? With her hospitalization, when she almost died in my arms, but I called for the nurse? Regret visited me that I hadn't just let her go. The final two months were not a gift.

Every few days my friend Sunita and I would arrive at the retirement home with Sunita's harp. Sarah was propped up in her wheelchair, looking most uncomfortable, having trouble breathing, but it was never clear to me how she would make the transition from breathing to a cessation of breathing.

It was the tears in Sunita's eyes that reflected how I felt. I stroked Sarah's hair; I had more physical closeness with her at the end than I had while she was mobile and active, cooking in her kitchen. Then it was the smells and tastes that entered our bodies. Rose-smelling hand cream on her face and shoulders, so tired, rising and lifting with a shudder. Sometimes I would cross the tiny hospital-like room and bring back the dusty photographs of Mordecai and Rafi.

"Oh, what a good-looking soldier," she said to Rafi's smiling face. She stroked Mordecai's picture.

"Rafi, come and take your Ema's hand," I said out loud. "Sarah, Mordecai and Rafi are waiting for you. I am holding your hand on this side; they will hold your hand on the other side. It is not a big distance."

Come, Rafi, come and get Ema, I prayed and prayed. He seemed so far away. Sometimes out of her stupor, she would talk to the photos on the wall. Sunita was sure that angels came into the room when she played.

The staff got used to the harp being carried in, in its enormous case. Unpacked. Rivka, Ilana and Yuval cried when they heard the celestial music. I cried. Sunita played "The Eucalyptus Grove." "When Ema came here young and beautiful, Abba built her a house on a hill; half a century has passed and the curls have turned to gray." At the New Year the holy tones of the prayers that Sarah knew so well sang out. "Our Father, our King, come and bring us home."

Come, Rafi, come and take Ema's hand. Now?

One day I was at classes in Jerusalem. I have finally, at my ripe old age, started to study what I have always been in my soul, a rabbi. I got to tell Safta Sarah that I was studying for the *rabbanut* and she said, "That is good, then you will always do something meaningful and give to other people with love; you will learn and you will teach." That, with Alzheimer's. I got a phone call that the end might be near, that Sarah was on morphine. I had nine hours of classes that day, then I had promised to make a blessing for orphans of Kfar Sava who were having their bar or bat mitzvah.

Danny is so tired in the evenings after an eight-hour clinic, yet he suggested that the moment the celebrations were done, he drive me to the retirement home. Rivka reassured me that there was no need after such a long day. They had already gone home after a long vigil; it could wait till morning.

I blessed the orphans under a prayer shawl. I told them how loved they were. I felt that I was becoming an orphan at that moment; I was joining them. My Safta Sarah was leaving me.

Danny picked me up late in the evening and drove me to the next town. It was dark on the Alzheimer's ward. Ghostly quiet. The patients had been put to bed and were sleeping a drugged sleep.

Sarah looked quiet, small, white with an oxygen mask on. It expanded and relaxed. I petted her head and wondered how one could tell if she was alive or not. The nurse, whom I knew well from the local swimming pool, entered the room after Danny and myself. She said in Hebrew, "Oh, look, she has stopped breathing." I didn't know what this meant. She added kindly in English, "She is dead."

Dead. I have always been afraid of death. I bent down and kissed Sarah's forehead. I held her. "Bless you on your way, Sarah. You are with your mother and father, with Mordecai and Rafi. Rafi, come take Ema's hand."

Sarah, as always, held my hand and led me gently across the threshold of seeing a dead shell of a body for the first time. It was peaceful and gentle.

We called her children; they came to part from her.

When we put her in the ground the next day, which is very visual and visceral in Israel because there is no coffin, I felt that she was in the earth of the land of Israel that she loved so much. I shoveled the dirt myself with a shovel and with my hands. So did her granddaughters, wrapped in her hand-made shawls. So did her daughters and son. I ripped my shirt and sat shivah and observed mourning rites by sitting together with the family for a week, recounting tales of her life. I read parts of my book out loud. We watched a video tape from eight years before, before dementia, and I was struck by the deep love between Sarah and myself. I had lost a relative, a dear friend, the most positive person and influence in my life.

Several magical moments took place. Sarah's eighteenth great-grandchild was born twenty-four hours after her death: Ronit had her third child, a boy, Doron. This means "gift," and the first syllable (*dor*) means "generation." A gift from generation to generation. Also the number eighteen (*chai*) signifies life in Hebrew.

Another magical connection was when the actress who had played me with tears of pain on stage appeared at the shivah. She was Rivka's upstairs neighbor.

The great-grandchildren had a party together and bonded and laughed and sang. They drew me pictures, as Smadi had done years before. Many of them had not been together for a long time.

Thirty days later, marking the end of the heavy mourning period, we gathered at the newly remade joint gravestone. Black marble reflected four generations standing around the joint eternal bed of Mordecai and Sarah. The children had added a pillow of marble with Rafi's name resting in between, like a child who sleeps with his parents.

I called on my cell phone on the way to the memorial service.

"Rivka, do you have a rabbi for the event?"

She paused, and said, "Yes, the only rabbi we need or want...you."

I had been in rabbinical school for about a month. Sarah had already ordained me.

I looked at Jack, a secular Jew from Iraq — he was talking on his cell phone and I wanted to begin the service; at Rivka, a secular Jew born in Ramat Gan; at their children and grandchildren, who could only relate to Judaism if the rabbi not only didn't have a beard, but was female, a relative and loved their mother. I was very nervous, standing in front of them with a bright embroidered yalmulke on my head. How could I make Judaism, mine and Sarah's, relevant to them? How could I comfort them? It would have been a challenge for a much more seasoned rabbi.

"In the beautiful stone that you have rebuilt for your mother together with your father, I see my name, EDELMAN, shining in the marble. I am the only one of you who still goes by that name, yet we are all family. I want to thank you all, that there has never been a whisper of jealousy of my relationship with Sarah, that you shared her with me; she was my mother too. I was with her when she died, and you were all so relieved and happy that she was not alone." I looked at the children. "Your love for your great-grandmother is on the stone: it says, for our mother, grandmother and great-grandmother. That's you. And your history is here. Sarah's sisters and brothers and parents are mentioned here, and none of them have gravestones."

I read a poem by Yehuda Amichai, "My mother is the prophetess of small things." What was Sarah a prophetess of?

Everyone laughed, and then contributed.

Jack: "What is true, is true, she used to say."

Rivka: "Thank God that I have the use of my hands and feet."

Ilana: "All people are really good."

Yuval: "She saw the good in everyone."

I handed Smadi the prayer book; she read Woman of Valor. The part about working all night while her house slept was so real.

I sang El Malei Rachamim (God full of mercy) with tears in my voice.

At the house Iraqi kubbeh with beets was served. When we had all eaten, Yuval made a short speech. "Ema did not leave a lot of precious jewelry behind. Both of her daughters have a ring. She had one gold necklace. Someone mentioned jealousy today; no, Yehudit, no one has ever been jealous of your love for our mother. So much so, that you can prevent jealousy. We will all be happy if you will inherit this gold necklace that our mother always wore."

And the magic keeps going after Sarah's death. I took my student who is deaf and has developmental disabilities and ADD to give out flowers at the Alzheimer's ward before Shabbat. A lot of the staff remembered me, and some of the patients too. A holiday atmosphere took over the dismal dining room, with festive flowers and a young girl's hand touching withered hands.

The nurses handed me a plastic bag with Sarah's clothes that she had worn the day she died. In it was one more shawl, and Lital, who didn't get a shawl, and wanted one, will now have one.

This summer, I arrived at my uncle Milt's bedside one hour before he died. He greeted me heartily, but had a rasping rattle in his throat. I had heard that sound only once before. The death rattle. Milt lost consciousness. I remained calm. Holding his hand, I asked him to send fresh regards to my father. I told Milt that I loved him, and what a good uncle he had been to me, making sure that I always had family at my children's bar and bat mitzvahs. Then I said the prayers that are said just before death. We were joined by my Aunt Esther and Milt and Esther's daughter Laney, who gave me my connection with Sarah and Mordecai. Laney said Shema Yisrael, and her father left this earth.

Laney performed the funeral and shivah services; as my "twin" cousin, she is also interested in rabbinical work. Every night Esther sang with her amazing voice, and I played guitar while my cousins sang. There was both humor and tears, just like with my father's death. I wonder if my father arranged for me to be with Milt at the end as I could not be with him.

I am editing the final draft of this book in Prague.

Kalman is still with me. He has phlebitis of the leg and has had salmonella for a few weeks. He forgets. But he remembered to buy me a necklace of white gold, remembered to ask about the children, remembered that I love to walk around nature spots in Prague. Kalman was present at Kol Nidre when I gave a sermon at the Pinchas Synagogue. Just as we entered he pointed out that he had "visited" four of the many concentration camps etched on the walls there. There are the names of seventy thousand Jews who were deported from Prague on every wall of the synagogue. I heard them harmonize as I helped to lead the services. Kalman and I discussed the recent war in Israel. "The Jewish people need a state," he said, "history has proven that, but we also need visionaries who can bring peace."

There is a hot threat of terrorism in Prague while I am visiting. Do fear and death follow us everywhere to make sure that we choose life?

It occurs to me that Sarah first appears in this book by kissing the sandy ground of Israel. When she was lost in the fog of Alzheimer's her kissing and embracing were alive. She sanctified life with love. She had a wisdom that was not taught in a school room. Sarah was a kiss on my sore immigrant's heart. She now sleeps in her beloved sand. But her immigrant lessons are still with us. If you are a new immigrant or a displaced person, new to a place or a relationship or a situation, struggling with the unfamiliar, Sarah is in the kitchen cooking up some schnitzel, and she wants to invite you into her kitchen for some stories and some hot soup with freshly cut noodles; or would you rather walk around the garden first?

# Acknowledgments

Thanks to my different kinds of readers, who really are part of this book, in the order in which they were given the book: Dr. Paul Ruskin, Prof. Murray Edelman, Dr. Bernie Green, Linda Gollub-Berger, Martha Rabin, Frank Widman, Rabbi Jonathan Perlman, Jeri Hahn-Markowitz, Yocheved Welber, Dr. Eric Moss, Carol Novis, Nurit Novis-Deutsch, Prof. Kalman Gajan, Dr. Jeremy Rose, Susie Dvoskin, David Lerman, Rabbi Gail Shuster-Boskila, Rabbi Dov Edelstein, Dr. Yuval and Sarah Ednat, Lital Ednat-Goldstein, Ronit Hadada, and Yael Natan. A magical garden to Rinah Sheleff and Rabbi Helaine Ettinger, who both got me going on this project in creative ways. Beautiful fabric and evening walks to Rabbi Lee and Jackie Diamond who introduced me to Gefen Publishing. To ALL of you, your heart and wisdom fill my life.

Special thanks to Kezia Raffel Pride, who proves that there is a benevolent God, or at least a benevolent editor. Kezia is an immigrant mother, and while rushing to get a draft to me before this current Prague trip had to miss a few days' work because her baby was rushed to the hospital with a twisted bowel. Kezia, thank you for understanding in mind, in body and in spirit, and may it take you less than ten years to find your balance on the sandy shore.

Safta Sarah, Judith Edelman-Green, Rivka and Amir — one of Sarah's
great-grandchildren.